LONG ISLAND

"Long Island's Enterprises" by Leila Zogby
Produced in cooperation with
The Long Island Association

Windsor Publications, Inc.
Chatsworth, California

LONG ISLAND
Shores of Plenty

An Economic Celebration

Diane E. Ketcham

R
974.721
K
c.2 (s)

Windsor Publications, Inc.—History Books Division
Managing Editor: Karen Story
Design Director: Alexander D'Anca

Staff for *Long Island: Shores of Plenty*
Associate Editor: Jeffrey Reeves
Photo Editor: Loren Prostano
Assistant Director, Corporate Profiles: Phyllis Gray
Editor, Corporate Profiles: Brenda Berryhill
Production Editor, Corporate Profiles: Una FitzSimons
Editorial Assistants: Kim Kievman, Michael Nugwynne, Kathy B. Peyser, Pat Pittman, Theresa Solis
Publisher's Representative, Corporate Profiles: Sherry Wasala, Karen Singleton

Layout Artist, Corporate Profiles: Mari Catherine Preimesberger
Layout Artists, Editorial: Michael Burg, Ellen Ifrah
Designer: Christina L. Rosepapa

Library of Congress Cataloging-in-Publication Data
Ketcham, Diane E. Long Island, shores of plenty/Diane E. Ketcham.—1st ed. p. cm.
Bibliography: p.235 Includes index.
ISBN: 0-89781-264-6
1. Long Island (N.Y.)—History. 2. Long Island (N.Y.)—Economic conditions. 3. Long Island (N.Y.)—Description and travel—Views. 4. Long Island (N.Y.)—Industries. I. Title.
F127.L8K47 1988   88-20668   974.7'21—dc19 CIP

©1988 Windsor Publications, Inc.
All rights reserved
Published 1988
Printed in the United States of America
First Edition

Windsor Publications, Inc.
Elliot Martin, Chairman of the Board
James L. Fish III, Chief Operating Officer
Michele Sylvestro, Vice President Sales/Marketing

Previous spread: Solitude on the Sound: a Port Jefferson fisherman enjoys the day's end. Photo by Ken Spencer

The early morning fog rolls into East Hampton. Photo by Ken Spencer

Contents

ACKNOWLEDGMENTS • 11
FOREWARD • 12

PART 1
LI, NY: NOW AND THEN • 14

I
MODERN TIMES • 16
Long Island's mild climate and beautiful setting make it a wonderful place to live and work. Eighty percent of the Island's diverse work force now stay on the Island to work in the wealthiest region of the country.

II
WIGWAMS TO LEVITTOWN • 26
Occupations by the Indians, the Dutch, and the English, through the era of whaling and farming to the rise of Gold Coast mansions and suburbia, have given Long Island a rich and enduring history.

III
NORTH SHORE/SOUTH SHORE • 40
From North Shore/South Shore to North Fork/South Fork, Long Island is a region of regions, and Long Islanders are proud of their local communities.

IV
AT YOUR SERVICE • 52
A broad range of services make service Long Island's number one industry, with tourism and related industries leading the way.

V
MAKING IT • 64
Educational institutions and research facilities, combined with the availability of venture capital, put Long Island among the country's high-tech leaders.

VI
FARMING THE LAND AND SEA • 76
Diversification into new areas such as vineyards, horse farms, nursery stock, and mariculture has kept Long Island's agricultural and seafood industries strong.

VII
ON THE MOVE • 88
While the automobile and the Long Island Expressway remain the Island's primary mode of transportation, other options such as the Long Island Rail Road and MacArthur Airport are making travel easier.

VIII
A SEPARATE IDENTITY • 98

As Long Island becomes a thriving region in its own right, the Island's media have acted as the most influential identity-makers.

IX
ISLAND AT PLAY • 108

Surrounded by water and enjoying a mild climate, Long Island is a recreational paradise that also offers championship professional sports teams and numerous entertainment facilities.

X
CULTURALLY SPEAKING • 122

Long Island has formed its own cultural traditions, preserving its rich historical legacy while promoting growth in the arts.

XI
SHORES OF CHALLENGE • 132

As Long Islander's prepare for the twenty-first century, they are taking stock of their past as they carefully plan for their future.

PART 2
LONG ISLAND'S ENTERPRISES • 138

XII
NETWORKS • 140

Long Island's energy, communication, and transportation providers keep products, information, and power circulating inside and outside the area. The Long Island Lighting Company, 142; AT&T, 146; The Long Island Rail Road, 147

XIII
MANUFACTURING • 148

Producing goods for individuals and industry, manufacturing firms provide employment for many Long Island area residents. Lumex, Inc., 150; Sedco, A Raytheon Company, 152; Quantronix Corporation, 154; Pall Corporation, 156; Altana Inc., 158; Grumman Corporation, 160

XIV
BUSINESS • 164

Building on the past while planning for the future, Long Island's business community moves into the forefront of technological innovation and financial leadership. Long Island Association, Inc., 166; Halbro Control Industries, Inc., 167;

Florence Building Materials, 168; Dale Carnegie & Associates, Inc., 170; Allstate Insurance Company, 172; Fairfield Properties, 174

XV
PROFESSIONS • 176

Long Island's professional community brings a wealth of service, ability, and insight to the area. Henderson and Bodwell, 178; TSI, 180; The Law Offices of Andrew D. Presberg, 182; Marine Midland Bank, N.A., 183; The Bank of New York, 184; National Westminster Bank USA, 186; Chase Manhattan Bank, N.A., Long Island Region, 188; EAB, 190; Citibank, N.A., 192; Farrell, Fritz, Caemmerer, Cleary, Barnosky & Armentano, P.C., 194; Meltzer, Lippe, Goldstein & Wolf, P.C., 196; Cushman & Wakefield of Long Island, Inc., 198

XVI
QUALITY OF LIFE • 200

Medical and educational institutions, along with recreational activities, contribute to the quality of life and entertainment of Long Island area residents. United Presbyterian Home at Syosset, Inc., 202; St. Joseph's College, 204; Healthplex, Inc., 206; C.W. Post Campus of Long Island University, 209; Board of Cooperative Educational Services, 210; Central General Hospital, 212; State University College at Old Westbury, 213; The State University of New York at Stony Brook, 214; Molloy College, 216; Southside Hospital, 218; Polytechnic University, Long Island Campus, 220; New York Institute of Technology, 222; New York Islanders, 224

BIBLIOGRAPHY • 227
INDEX • 228

Grazing deer are a common sight in the many woodlands and meadows of Long Island. Photo by George Michell

In memory of my father, Arthur Campbell Shields, whose love of journalism is with me always.

The sun sets over Orient Beach State Park. Photo by Ken Spencer

Acknowledgments

When people wondered what my book was about, I'd say, "Long Island." "Well, what about Long Island?" they would ask, and I'd respond, "Everything."

Writing "everything" about a region as large and diverse as Long Island ensures you will leave someone or something out. To the Long Island companies, organizations, and individuals who may not be mentioned in this book but have helped to make the Island the extraordinary place it is, a special thank you and a request for understanding that not all could be included.

To my editors, Jerry Mosher, who selected me for the project, and all the Windsor editors who assisted me through the final product, thank you for your support and your encouragement. My thanks to Patchogue-Medford Library Director Selma Kelson and the always helpful staff of that library's Long Island/local history room. Their diligent clipping of newspaper articles makes that facility one of the finest resources for present-day Long Island statistics. Thanks also to the Connetquot Public Libary.

To Jim Larocca, Valerie Scibilia, and the entire staff of the Long Island Association, thanks for always being willing to at least look for answers to abstract questions.

My thanks to the dozens of *Newsday* reporters who had so skillfully researched and written about this subject before I even began. And to the reporters from the *New York Times*, the weeklies, and *Long Island Business News*, thank you for making my task so much easier.

My thanks to the numerous officials of Long Island companies and organizations who spent hours showing me their world. Thanks to Anne, Mike, Bob, Ellie, P.J., Greg, John, and Doris, to farmers Vernon and Alex, and to the fellow officers of the Press Club of Long Island who picked up the slack when "the book" took time away.

And special thanks to my family for understanding the holidays missed, the calls never made. And to my husband Terry who patiently supported me through the months and months of talking, living, breathing, "the book." We made it, T.K.—time to enjoy those shores of plenty.

Diane E. Ketcham
Long Island, New York

Foreword

Like many before them, my parents moved from New York City to Long Island so that their two young children could have a backyard to play in and a house to call home.

Our family settled in Port Washington, the beautiful North Shore community of rolling hills, seaside restaurants, and Sands Point mansions. Although the mansions were seen mostly from the outside, the restaurants frequented only on special occasions, and the rolling hills a real challenge to a 17-year-old learning to drive, Port Washington was a wonderful town to grow up in. And though I have lived in several Long Island communities since, Port will always be home to me.

I can still recite every word of the Paul D. Schreiber High School fight song and I can still remember my father racing each morning to catch the last car of the Long Island Rail Road (LIRR) train for his daily trek into the City. The comings and goings of the LIRR became as important a part of my life as my grades in school, for my father always seemed to be coming and going. He worked nights, weekends, even holidays so my brother and I could continue our idyllic childhood on Long Island's North Shore.

I took my father's sacrifices for granted as I took Port Washington and Long Island for granted. It wasn't until I went away to college that I realized not everyone could swim in an ocean anytime they wanted, not everyone had a Perry Como living in their hometown year-round and a Paul Newman spending the summer, and not everyone could visit the world's largest department store or see a Broadway show at a moment's notice because the world's most exciting city was right at their doorstep.

Decades later, having lived and worked on both of Long Island's shores, I thought I finally appreciated the island I call home. But after a few weeks researching this book, I realized how much about Long Island I still didn't know, how many places I had never even seen.

And so I learned about Long Island all over again, or maybe really for the first time. This time when I went to Jones Beach, I truly looked at the wondrous park Robert Moses had built. I walked the beaches of Fire Island and tried to imagine a life without the pounding surf of the Atlantic Ocean nearby. I walked through isolated salt marshes, quiet forests, and potato fields. I toured the most advanced high-technology plants, stood on a runway as an F-14 raced past, attended a local ballet, and watched the New York Islanders hockey team practice.

I visited Long Island's mansions and museums, and learned of the history of this region, a history so rich and full of excitement that even Cecil B. DeMille couldn't have done it justice. I rode the Long Island Expressway and actually enjoyed the sights from Queens to the East End. Everywhere I went I looked as if for the first time. I looked at the majestic scenery, the dynamic business operations, and the amazing people.

And I learned Long Island is full of surprises. Try to experience as many as you can.

In writing this book I finally realized why my parents had given up so much so my childhood could be spent here. Never again will I take this wondrous island for granted. And though my father is no longer with us to see a sunset on the Sound or race for that last car on the LIRR, his love of Long Island lives on in me.

This book is for you, Dad. Thanks for giving me Long Island.

On the South Shore, the Fire Island Lighthouse is a welcome site to many an Atlantic Ocean voyager. Photo by Audrey Gibson

PART I
LI, N.Y. Now and Then

14

Office construction in Suffolk County progresses at a rapid pace. Photo by Ken Spencer

I
Modern Times

16

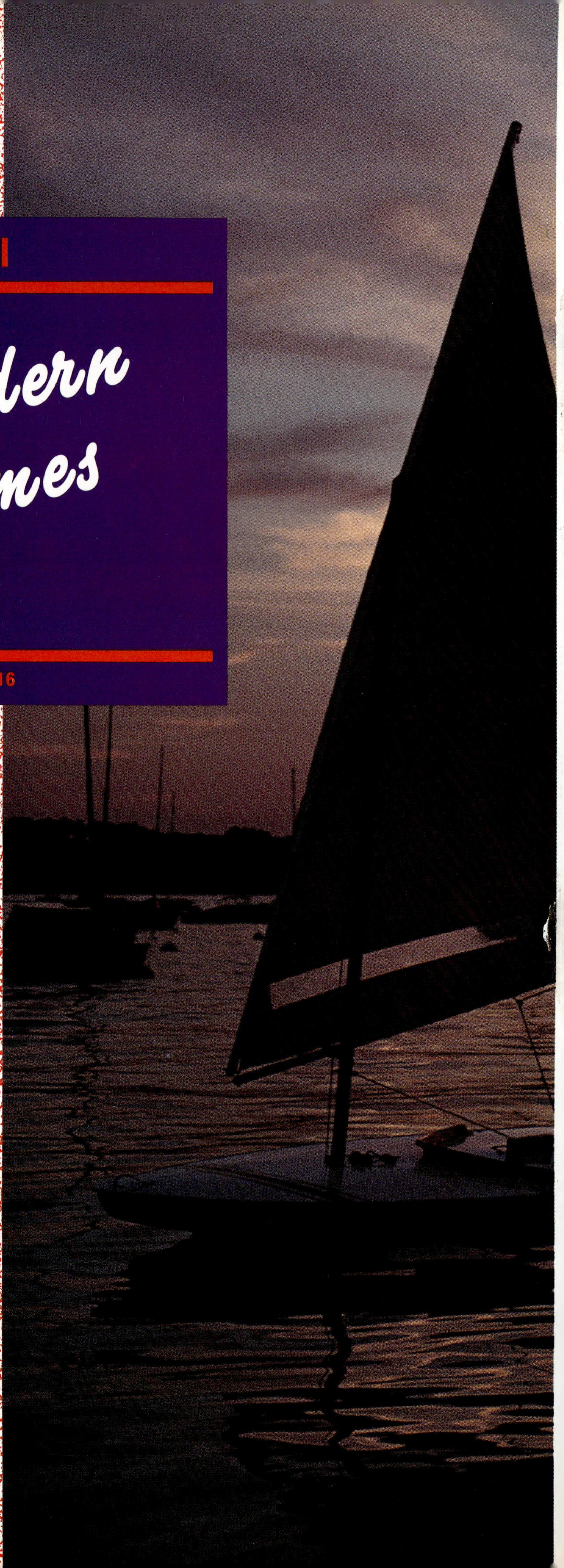

LONG ISLAND

Above: With Jones Inlet appearing in the distance, the sun sets over South Shore wetlands. Photo by Ken Spencer

Previous page: Sailing a sunfish at sunset is a truly relaxing activity. Photo by Ken Spencer

Sea-Beauty! stretch'd and basking! . . .
Isle of the salty shore and breeze and brine!
—from Walt Whitman's *Paumanok*

A sparkle of midafternoon sun bounces off the silver wing of Eastern Airlines flight 750 as it begins its final descent toward the shores of Long Island.

With veteran pilot Norm Wright gently banking the Boeing 727 to the left, passengers see the endless rolling waves of the Atlantic Ocean finally give way to land, splashing on a narrow strip of white sand, a pencil-shaped island with luxurious modern houses facing each shore.

"Long Island?" a passenger may ask, peering down at the small island. No, it's Fire Island, an exclusive summer resort and the quarter- to half-mile-wide barrier island that protects Long Island from the ocean. Long Island's massive shoreline looms to the north.

Heading toward that shore and Long Island MacArthur Airport, its final destination, the Fort Lauderdale jet soars over Fire Island and its miles of pristine beach. The black-and-white-ringed Fire Island Lighthouse blinks a welcome.

The Great South Bay offers a view of one of the world's finest shellfishing areas, where dozens of wooden clamming boats bob in the choppy green waters. It is a seascape rivaling any in the world, but the eyes of most passengers stay transfixed on the landmass ahead. Long Island is so much bigger than they realized.

"Visitors are continually surprised by Long Island's size," said George Fey of the Long Island Tourism and Convention Commission. "There's a perception that you can walk from shore to shore."

To the east, airline passengers see the sandy shores of the Hamptons, another popular oceanfront resort and some of the most expensive real estate in the world. To the north are acres and acres of farmland, and miles of miniature pine trees, Long Island's pine barrens—nature's protection for the region's pure underground drinking water.

To the west the flat topography of the South Shore offers a view of wetlands and meadow grass and attractive waterfront homes on narrow canals, which give way to schools, office building complexes, industrial parks, shopping centers, and highways, including one of the most famous ribbons of concrete, the Long

MODERN TIMES

Island Expressway. But even though there is an ample supply of homes and businesses, everywhere below it is green. Trees seem like huge umbrellas of green, expansive lawns like carpets; trees and lawns seem to be everywhere.

Further north, past the rolling hills and the secluded estates of the North Shore, the passengers can just make out the edge of the Island's northern boundary: another huge body of water, Long Island Sound.

At 120 miles long and 20 miles wide, Long Island is the largest island adjacent to the United States. There are more than 1,180 miles of coastline, and just about every type of natural environment—with the exception of mountains—is on display. From the air the view is spectacular.

Unfortunately, airline passsenger Esther Lurrie doesn't see much of it. The former resident of East Meadow, now of Coconut Creek, Florida, is lost in thought as she returns to Long Island via flight 750.

Lurrie and her husband, Sol, raised their family on Long Island and then retired to Florida. Now Lurrie is coming back to meet her newest grandchild, two-day-old Heather, born to daughter Sheila Lohr of Commack. Her other daughter, Rhonda Lalia of Brightwaters, waits at the airport.

The Long Island that Lurrie is returning to is far different from the Long Island where she raised her family. Even the airport she's arriving at is a new experience.

No longer is there an hour or more car ride to and from one of New York City's hectic air terminals for her and her waiting daughter. "MacArthur Airport is so convenient; it's only 15 minutes from my home," Lalia said. "It's much easier to come here or take off from here."

Long Island's major airport is now a modern jetport with nonstop service to Chicago, Florida, Washington, D.C., Pittsburgh, and North Carolina and connecting flights to just about everywhere else. Forty years ago MacArthur was a tiny general aviation airfield.

But then, 40 years ago, eastern Long Island was considered to be just potato fields and western Long Island was the home of the brand new Levittown, the ultimate suburb, a bedroom community for New York City.

In 40 years Long Island has changed remarkably. "The Island," as it's known to residents, is now a thriving region, separate from its prestigious city neighbor

Privacy abounds for those who live in the mansions of the North Shore. Photo by Ken Spencer

to the west. New York City was once Long Island's lifeline, but no longer.

Geographically, Long Island consists of four counties: Brooklyn, Queens, Nassau, and Suffolk, and up until the early 1900s, that was Long Island. But ever since Brooklyn and Queens became part of the five counties that make up the City of New York, Long Island has consisted of just Nassau and Suffolk counties.

The distinction became official in 1972, when Nassau and Suffolk counties were made a separate SMSA, or Standard Metropolitan Statistical Area. In 1980 the two counties became the first suburban region in the nation designated as a separate U.S. Economic Development District. The designations are important, as they finally allow separate statistics to be drawn about an area that many say was lost for too long in the shadow of the world's most exciting city.

Now Long Islanders officially know that they live in the wealthiest region of the country. Long Island has the highest disposable median income in the U.S., the highest retail sales per household in the U.S. (the two counties' retail sales average is greater than that of

LONG ISLAND

Left: From the air, the lush greenery of East End farms proves to be a visual feast. Photo by Ken Spencer

Facing page: In the 1980s, through the efforts of concerned Long Islanders, the Fire Island Lighthouse was restored and relit. Photo by George Michell

26 states), and the wealthiest zip codes in the U.S.

How much wealth is there on Long Island? In 1984 *Forbes* magazine reported that more than 17,000 millionaires lived there. The figure is even higher today.

Three of the 10 wealthiest communities in the United States (Great Neck, Roslyn, and Manhasset) are on Long Island's North Shore, and the North Shore hamlet of Mill Neck was considered the country's most expensive community in 1987. A survey reported the average price of a Mill Neck house was $1.2 million. Nearby Laurel Hollow was sixth highest in the country at $900,000; Muttontown was tenth at $770,000. Residents of the communities took exception to the figures. They said the amounts were too low.

The North Shore of Long Island has been home to the Vanderbilts, Woolworths, Whitneys, Morgans (as in J.P.), and hundreds of others of the nation's wealthiest, including railroad financier Otto Kahn, who, wanting to live on the highest point on Long Island, built his own hill, and who put $1,000 bills into his Easter eggs to make the annual egg hunt a little more exciting.

But you don't have to be a millionaire to live on Long Island. With 2.67 million residents, a population larger than that of 21 states, it is home to an incredibly diverse society. Retired senior citizens, young married couples, and a strong and vibrant middle class are all happy to say, "I'm a Long Islander."

"You have the baymen, the farmers, the 16th Lord of the Manor, the New York arts scene transplanted in the Hamptons—they're all successfully molded together on Long Island," said Lee Koppelman, executive director of the Long Island Regional Planning Board.

More than 90 percent of the Island's population is white, with Hispanics, blacks, Asians, and American Indians also represented. The median age is 33.6, but in recent years the population has been aging. By 1990 13 percent of the residents will be over 65.

But then, the Island itself is aging.

Thanks to Long Island's first family, the Gardiners of Gardiner's Island fame, Nassau/Suffolk celebrates its 350th anniversary in 1989. Back in 1639, only 19 years after the Pilgrims first stepped on Plymouth Rock, Long Island's first real estate deal took place. Lion Gardiner paid "a few dogs, a gun, some powder, some rum, some trinkets, and a pair of blankets" to Wyandanch, the Indian chief or sachem of the Montauk Indians, for a lovely island off the eastern end of Long Island. A Gardiner has owned and lived on Gardiner's Island ever since.

"I'm the only lord of the manor who still has a manor," said 77-year-old Robert David Lion Gardiner, the 16th Lord Gardiner and, as the proprietor of Gardiner's Island, the owner of the oldest estate in North America. "History to me is not a bunch of dates," Gardiner said. "It's my family's life."

During the last 350 years the Gardiners have been joined by millions of other proud Long Island home-

MODERN TIMES

owners. Eight out of 10 Long Island families live in single family homes. "The whole pattern of suburbia was invented here on Long Island," Koppelman said. "From 1950 to 1960 Nassau County was the fastest growing county in the United States. Then the 1960 census came out and Suffolk took over."

"With its substantial economic opportunites and high quality of life, Long Island has achieved in its pattern of development something very close to the American dream," said Jim Larocca, president of the Long Island Association, the Island's largest business and civic group. But not everybody knows about the Island's exceptional life-style or its thriving business climate.

"Long Island has a low profile because it's been in the shadow of New York for so long," said Charles F. Dolan, chairman of Long Island's Cablevision Systems Corporation, which owns cable franchises on Long Island, and in Chicago, Boston, and Cleveland, making it one of the largest cable companies in the nation. "Yet Long Island is one of the most remarkable areas from both a demographic and a natural resources point of view. I can't think of an area where I'd rather be doing business than here on Long Island."

Most of his neighbors agree. Rather than commuting to jobs in "the City," as most Long Islanders did for decades, 80 percent of Long Islanders now work on the Island in the service industry, high-technology field, defense industry, manufacturing, or as farmers of the land and the sea.

In the last decade the Island's economic activity has increased by 30 percent. By 1988 less than 3 percent of Long Islanders were unemployed. Long Island experienced the nation's third largest increase in jobs from 1980 to 1986 with 220,000 being created, five times the national average.

And what a diversity of jobs. Working on Long Island is, and always has been, exciting. The Island was home to the first American cowboy (on Deep Hollow Ranch in Montauk in 1747) and the first airmail pilot, who flew from Mineola to Garden City in 1911.

The great blue yonder has always held a special fascination for Long Islanders. The Island is known as the "Cradle of Aviation," with even the Wright Brothers having come to the area to learn a thing or two. That pioneering aviation spirit has continued into the Space Age. The lunar module, the vehicle that put the first man on the moon, was made on Long Island.

America's first jockey rode on Long Island. (The Hempstead Plains was the site of the nation's first horse racing track.) From Long Island the first guided missile was launched, by Lawrence Sperry from Amityville in 1918, and the Island can boast of the first supermarket checkout clerk (the first self-service supermarket was opened by King Kullen in 1930), not to mention a president, Theodore Roosevelt, and a great poet, Walt Whitman.

Long Islanders have won Nobel and Pulitzer prizes, baseball and football world championships, hockey's Stanley Cup—four times—and Grammys, Emmys, and Oscars. They set world records in fishing almost every year, although that isn't surprising given the Island's surroundings.

THE ISLAND

Shaped like a giant fish with two flukes, or tails, Long Island appears on a map to be nibbling on the shores of the Eastern Seaboard. The Island forms a 90-degree angle at its near junction with New Jersey and New York Harbor.

Since the Atlantic Ocean flows toward the Island at a 45-degree angle, always in an easterly to westerly movement, the tidal action erodes the eastern end of the Island while adding sand to the west. Consequently, the easternmost tip of Long Island, Montauk Point, is now more a stub than a point. On the barrier isle of Fire Island, however, one can see the dramatic exam-

LONG ISLAND

ple of the western shifting sands. The Fire Island Lighthouse, the westernmost point of Fire Island in 1858, the year it was built, now stands five miles away from the western edge of land and the Fire Island Inlet.

While the modern-day Long Island of Nassau and Suffolk counties is more a peninsula than an island, the unusual aspects of island life still apply.

First, as Samuel Taylor Coleridge wrote, there's "water water everywhere." The Island's southern and eastern borders are the ocean—Long Island is the only part of New York State with Atlantic Ocean frontage. Flowing into the ocean are numerous bays, the Great South Bay being the largest. On the north, sheltered harbors and bays flow into Long Island Sound, Long Island's answer to the Mediterranean. The Sound, more than 100 miles long, is very similar to an inland sea since the body of water is almost completely surrounded by land yet filled with the salty water of the Atlantic Ocean.

Long Island Sound is considered the largest boating center in the country. More than 95,000 sailboats and power boats from New York and Connecticut are said to cruise its waters on a nice summer weekend.

At the edge of Long Island's waterways are thousands of acres of salt marshes, the breeding grounds and habitat for the tens of thousands of ducks, geese, egrets, swans, raccoons, otters, ospreys, hawks, muskrats, and beavers that make Long Island's wetlands their home. The wetlands also prevent flooding by absorbing the rise of nearby waterways, and at the same time help to recharge the underground water tables. Ninety percent of New York's wetlands are located on Long Island, and the wildlife located there and in the waters nearby is a nature lover's delight. The Island's horseshoe crabs, for example, are considered the oldest living fossil known to man; they look the same today as they did 200 million years ago.

Since the Island at its widest is only about 20 miles, no one is ever far from the water, and contact with the sea, whether in the form of boating, swimming, fishing, or just walks on the sandy beaches of the South Shore or the rocky beaches of the North Shore, are an important part of the Long Island way of life.

The Island also has an abundance of inland waterways. Besides the many ponds, streams, and creeks,

Above: Children have played on the shores of Long Island for many past seasons, and will continue to do so for seasons to come. Photo by Ken Spencer

Right: Long Island sailors take on the Atlantic Ocean in the "Around Long Island Regatta." Photo by Ken Spencer

Azeleas bloom in one of the many nature preserves on the Island. Photo by Ken Spencer

Nassau County has two lakes—Lake Success, actually a kettle hole left from the glacier that formed Long Island, and Hempstead Lake. Suffolk boasts of the Island's largest lake, Lake Ronkonkoma, which is also a kettle hole formed by the glacier. Suffolk is also home to Long Island's four major rivers: Connetquot, Carmans, Nissequogue, and the longest, the 12-mile-long Peconic. (Many of Long Island's natural phenomena were named by or for the Indians that first settled the region.)

For the ultra water lovers, there are the Island's islands. In Nassau there are the barrier islands of Jones Beach and Long Beach. In Suffolk, there are Fire Island and the East End islands: Shelter Island with its rolling hills; Gardiner's Island, the private island of the Gardiner family; and the smaller islands of Plum, Gull, and Fishers. There are also dozens of small undeveloped islands that dot the Island's South Shore.

To get off Long Island requires navigating the water. You can go over it, under it, or through it. Five bridges and two tunnels connect the western end of the Island to Manhattan. The East River, which is not really a river but a strait or channel connecting Long Island Sound with New York Bay, separates the island of Long from the island of Manhattan. The Whitestone and the Throgs Neck bridges connect Long Island to the Bronx and more northerly points. To leave Long Island any other way means you either fly, sail, or rev up the boat engines.

Landlubbers can feel at home on Long Island, too. Besides the rich smelling farmland at the eastern end of the Island, both counties have forests where deer, fox, and turkeys roam free, and of course there are the many, many parks. Long Island has some of the largest parks in the country. "Open space" is important to Long Islanders, and local government has responded to that concern by preserving thousands of acres.

"With farmland preservation, pine barrens acquisitions, and parks, the various levels of government have set aside probably 15 percent of the land. When we're done 25 percent will be permanently protected," said Koppelman.

WEATHER

There isn't really a time of year when you would want to leave Long Island. All four seasons offer scenes and scents that delight. On a summer day you can breathe the salty clean air of the ocean as you sunbathe at one of the world's most beautiful beaches, or you can smell the freshly turned soil in Long Island's farm country. Walk through the woods on a crisp fall day and experience the brilliant reds and yellows of Long Island's fall foliage. Cross-country ski or sled on freshly fallen snow in one of Long Island's many parks during its gentle winters. Smell the new grass and budding flowers on a Long Island spring morning.

Long Island's weather is influenced by the bodies

LONG ISLAND

of water that surround it. The Island is cool in the summer—the prevailing wind is southwest, bringing ocean breezes over the South Shore, and warm in the winter. Further north the winters are more severe. Further south there's no change of seasons. Long Island offers delightfully versatile yet comfortable weather.

The interesting time of year is hurricane season. An island sticking 120 miles out into the Atlantic Ocean can expect some barometrical bounces, and in August and September eyes look south to see what storms are brewing. Eight major hurricanes have hit Long Island shores in the last 250 years. The one that's still talked about is the hurricane of 1938. That September storm devastated the East End, killing 70 people—28 in Westhampton Beach alone. The hurricane broke through Long Island's barrier beach, forming the Moriches and Shinnecock inlets.

While storms have caused inlets to come and go in the barrier islands throughout Long Island's history, a storm some time before 1670 is said to have formed one that endured—the Fire Island Inlet. A major storm in the early 1700s created the Jones Inlet.

Long Islanders' most recent brush with exciting weather was in 1985, when Hurricane Gloria raced across the Island, tearing up tens of thousands of trees and knocking out electricity in some areas for 11 days. But Long Island's hurricane season is a small price to pay for the joy the Island's geography brings to visitors and residents alike.

ISLAND LIFE

Home to what many consider to be the world's greatest beaches, Long Island is one of the most popular summer resorts. Many choose not only to visit Long

Winter marks the quiet time of waiting at boatyards like this one in Glen Cove. Photo by Ken Spencer

MODERN TIMES

Island but to buy a vacation home there. Consequently there's no other place in the world that has such an interesting mix of resort life and suburbia.

With its combination of wealth, natural beauty, and a booming economy, Long Island is one of the finest places to live in the United States. The Island "appears routinely in surveys of great places to live," stated *Money* magazine when it rated Long Island the sixth best place to live in 1987 and the fourth best in 1988. Long Island is always near the top of the list according to *Money* magazine because of its "well-regarded schools and colleges, health care, waterfront, strong economy, and proximity to New York."

In 1985 *American Demographics* magazine rated Long Island the *best* place in America to live. That year Rand McNally had rated the Island the sixth best place and *American Demographics* took strong exception to the lower ranking. In terms of economic growth, climate, crime rate, housing costs, education, health care, and recreation, Long Island was tops, according to *American Demographics*.

Whether treading for clams on the Great South Bay or bicycling down the woodsy country lanes of the North Shore, whether working on the complex F-14 jet built by the Grumman Corporation or lifeguarding at Jones Beach—for work or play the Long Island lifestyle is hard to match.

What Long Islanders Have to Say About Long Island Today

Lee Koppelman, executive director, Long Island Regional Planning Board:
Long Island is a microcosm of the United States. We have every pattern of development, every environmental concern. And yet we have the joys of island living while we're located next to one of the most exciting cities in the world. The museums, theater, Broadway, restaurants in New York—the diversity of experience for everyone from the very sophisticated to the naive is exceptional. Long Island, with New York City close by, offers it all.

Norm Wright, Eastern Airlines pilot for 22 years. Garland Jones, Wright's first officer. Both fly to Long Island but are based in Florida. About Long Island in the fall:
Jones: From the air the color of the trees is spectacular. It's truly a mosaic.
Wright: Last month the colors were so beautiful, the flight engineer ran out to the parking lot here [at MacArthur Airport] looking for a tree. He took some leaves back to Florida so his son could use them for show and tell.

Jogging the picturesque trails and streets of Long Island makes exercising a joy. Photo by Ken Spencer

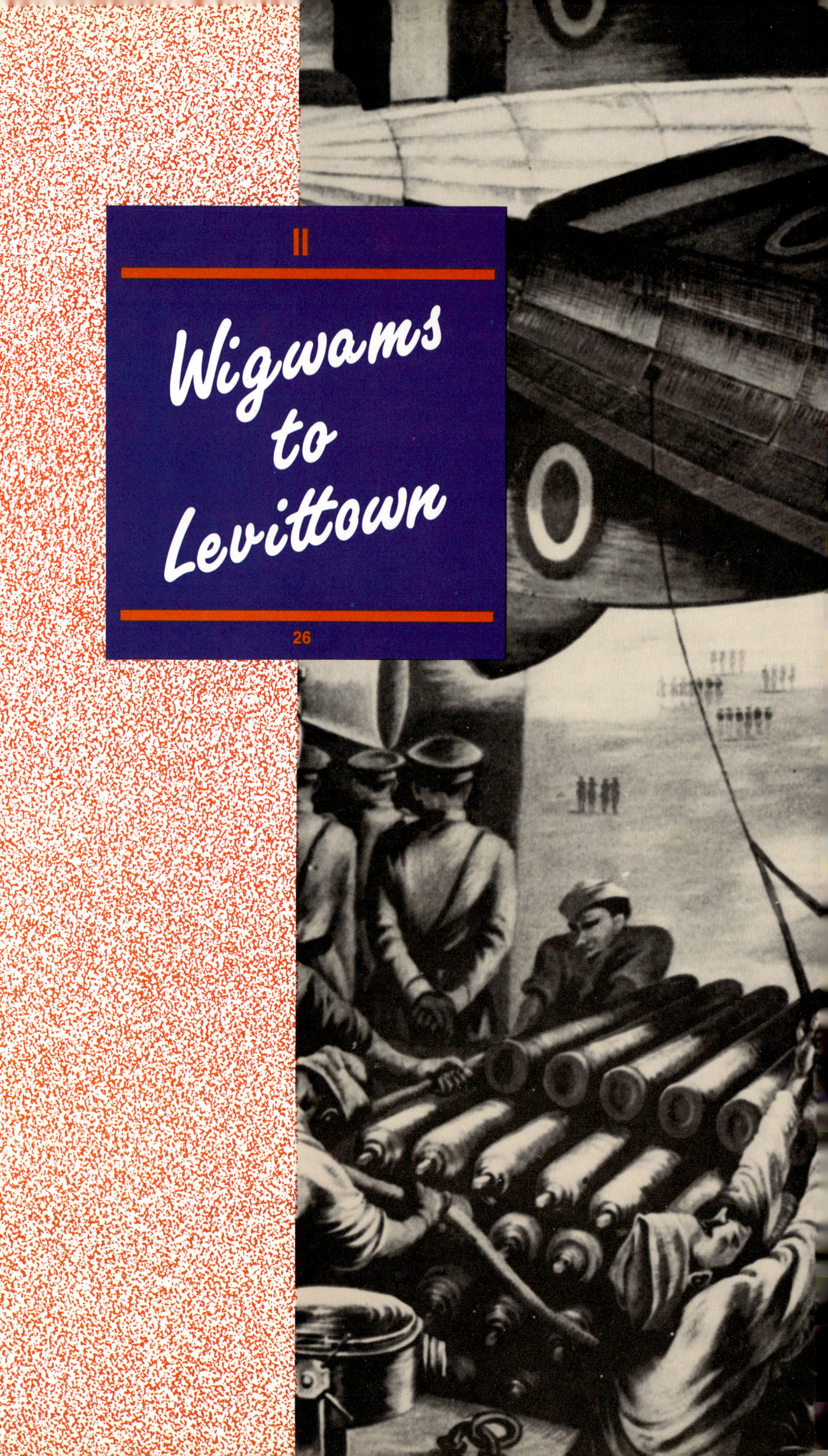

II

Wigwams to Levittown

26

LONG ISLAND

Above: Stephen Pharoah, a Montauk Indian, was a legendary long-distance walker who won a number of competitions across the country. This portrait was taken circa 1875. Courtesy, Smithsonian Institute

Previous page: Painted in 1937 for the Hempstead post office, this mural illustrating the arrival of the first airmail delivered by the British dirigible R34 in 1919, was part of a larger government effort to counteract severe unemployment during the Depression. Courtesy, National Archives

If you don't like the Long Island accent, blame it on the Dutch. It was Adriaen Block, sailing for the Dutch East India Company in 1614, who was the first to call the lengthy island he circumnavigated "Lange Eylandt." With various inflections, Lange Eylandt has been Long Island ever since.

Although Block, of Block Island fame, is considered the first European to sail around Long Island and the first to map out the boundaries of the Island, the Dutchman was not the first to set foot on Island shores. That honor goes to one of Henry Hudson's crew. In 1609 Hudson, an Englishman working for the Dutch, was looking for a route to China. He discovered Coney Island instead.

Anchoring his ship, the *Half Moon*, off the coast of Brooklyn, he sent a few of the crew ashore to meet Long Island's native Indians. All did not go well. One of Hudson's men was killed by a Canarsie Indian, giving the *Half Moon* crew the distinction of being the first Europeans to set foot on Long Island and the first to die there.

Long Island's history is filled with adventure stories like Hudson's. With explorers, Indians, pirates, the American Revolution, whaling, Teddy "Rough Rider" Roosevelt, the birth of flying, Charles Lindbergh, bootlegging, hurricanes, and German spies in World War II, the Island's history suffered from no lack of excitement.

JOYS OF DISCOVERY

Long Island's age of exploration goes back even further than Henry Hudson. The English claimed that John Cabot sailed along the South Shore of Long Island in 1498. The French said it was Giovanni Verrazano, an Italian explorer sailing for France, who was the first European to explore Long Island waters in 1524.

Regardless of who arrived first, what the Europeans found was a bit of paradise. There were beautiful sheltered coves, plenty of water, forests, and the massive Hempstead Plains—60,000 acres of meadow without a single tree. The Island's climate was much milder than the more northern settlements. And with hunting, fishing, and shellfishing, food from the land and sea was plentiful.

Most importantly, the Indians of Long Island were generally peaceful and anxious to trade. And trading was important, for it turned out that Long Island was

WIGWAMS TO LEVITTOWN

Dome-shaped Shinnecock Indian wigwams consisted of vertical poles set in a circle, which were bent and tied into arches, then reinforced by horizontal poles. Animal hides or woven mats were usual coverings. A bench, serving as bed, chair, and table, was found inside. Smoke escaped from the central fireplace through a hole in the roof. Courtesy, Department of Library Services, American Museum of Natural History

to become the wampum capital of the New World.

Wampum, polished shell beads made out of whelks (periwinkles) and quahogs (hardshell clams) had been used by the Indians as a form of tribute to their warlike neighbors. Since Long Island, especially the South Shore, had plenty of clams and therefore plenty of shells, and since Long Island Indians had plenty of warlike neighbors, it became a gold mine for wampum.

Indians referred to the Island as Seawanhacky, "Island of Shells." And because so many of the wampum beads left the Island to keep peace with the Pequots in Connecticut and the Narragansetts in what is now Rhode Island, the Island was also called Paumanack, "Land of Tribute."

European settlers soon joined the Indians in using wampum as a form of currency. Long Island became the colonial mint for wampum, so widely distributed that it was found in church collection plates. It is said Long Island wampum even wound up on the Pacific Coast, where John Jacob Astor used it for fur trading. The black or purple wampum from the South Shore's hardshell clams were more valuable than the white periwinkle variety. Wampum is on display today at several Long Island museums, including the Garvies Point Museum in Glen Cove.

INDIAN LIFE

The Long Island Indians were a band of Delaware Indians belonging to the Algonquin tribe. They were considered separate groups, not tribes, each with their own language. Because of the various languages, and the fact that the Indians had no written language, different spellings are used today for Long Island Indian names. Paumanack, for example, may also be seen as Paumanok and Paumanacke. And pronunciation of Indian-named communities like Quogue, Hauppauge, and Commack continues to be a challenge to visitors and residents alike.

Most of the Island's 13 Indian groups were named after the geographic area in which they lived. From west to east, they were the Canarsies, the Rockaways, the Merricks, the Matinecocks, the Massapequas, the Nesaquakes, the Secatogues, the Setaukets, the Patchogues, the Corchaugs, the Shinnecocks, the Montauks, and the Manhassets, who lived on what is now Shelter Island— nowhere near the Nassau County community named after them.

They were ruled by a *sachem* or chief. The two most famous Long Island chiefs were Wyandanch, the ruler of the Montauks, the most powerful Indian group on the Island, and Tackapausha, sachem of the Massapequas.

Unlike modern day Long Islanders with continuously changing hair fashions, the hairstyles of the Long Island Indians carried great significance. Indian men shaved their heads using clam shell razors. They left scalp locks, which some historians claim was to defy their enemies, in essence saying, "Come and get it." The women braided their hair; two braids meant they were unmarried and one braid meant they

LONG ISLAND

were wed.

Wigwams, Long Island's first homes, looked like warm-weather igloos. The Indians made them out of young trees bent over in the shape of a dome and then covered with grass.

Approximately 6,500 Indians lived on the Island in the 1640s when the first European started calling Long Island home. Less than 100 years later only 400 were left. Smallpox and other diseases brought by the Europeans killed many of Long Island's natives. The Indians had no natural immunity to European diseases and no tolerance to the alcohol that was so widely distributed to them by the settlers.

The last full-blooded Long Island Indian died in 1905. Today two Indian reservations remain on the Island. The Shinnecock Reservation in Southampton has approximately 350 Shinnecock Indians on its 800 acres. Founded in 1703, the reservation is reported to be the oldest, self-governing Indian reservation in the United States. The 170-acre Poosepatuck Reservation in Mastic is home for about 100 Unkechaug Indians.

SETTLING IN

The Dutch and English started settling Long Island about the same time, but at opposite ends. While the Dutch settled the western portion of the Island, the English founded communities on the eastern end. The North and South forks' ties with Connecticut and New England date back to the 1640s, when Englishmen crossed Long Island Sound from New England to settle Southold, Southampton, and East Hampton.

Thanks to the English and Dutch, Long Island will celebrate some important anniversaries in the years ahead. Southold and Southampton, the oldest towns on Long Island, will mark their 350th anniversaries in 1990. Other East End communities and several Nassau towns will do the same as the 1990s unfold.

The Island itself will celebrate 350 years in 1989. Many historians consider the beginning of Long Island history to be 1639, the year Lion Gardiner purchased his East End island from Wyandanch, sachem of the Montauks. The lives of the Gardiners, Long Island's first family, established many historic milestones. Elizabeth Gardiner was born on the family's island in 1641, the first English child born in New York State and the first European born in Suffolk.

Lion Gardiner and Chief Wyandanch became close friends, actually Indian brothers. The relation-

Above: By the 1800s the remaining descendants of the once-numerous Long Island Indian groups were concentrated on two state-recognized reservations at Mastic and Southampton. Approximately 450 Indians currently live on the reservations. Courtesy, The Nassau County Museum

Facing page, below: With this deed dated July 14, 1659, Chief Wyandanch conveyed as a gift to Lion Gardiner a tract of land between Huntington and Setauket. Wyandanch's mark can be seen at bottom right, along with that of his son, Wiandanbone, and his wife, known as "the Sunck Squa." Courtesy, Long Island Historical Society

ship developed when Gardiner successfully ransomed back the chief's only daughter, Heather Flower, from the Narragansett Indians. She had been kidnapped on her wedding day. In gratitude, Wyandanch, who was then the head of most of Long Island's Indian groups and called the Grand Sachem of Paumanack, gave Gardiner much of eastern and central Long Island.

Gardiner eventually ceded some of this land to Richard Smith of Smithtown fame. Smithtown residents like to believe that Smith got his property from the Indians after he was promised all the land he could cover in one day's travel upon his bull, Whisper. Most historians, however, say the bull story is just that—they dispute the tale.

The Gardiner family also holds an unusual place in Long Island history because of their run-in with the notorious pirate, Captain William Kidd. Captain Kidd buried some of his treasure on Gardiner's Island and supposedly warned the Gardiners he would kill them if they ever revealed the location. Some wishful Long Islanders haven't given up hope that part of the pirate's booty remains buried there or on Fire Island.

While the English were developing the East End, the Dutch settled the tiny village of Breukelen. The Dutch also allowed English settlers to live in New Amsterdam, and in 1643 Long Island's first feminist, Lady Deborah Moody, established Gravesend. Gravesend holds title to many firsts. It was the first English settlement in Brooklyn, the first settlement headed by a woman in the New World, and the site of the first recorded Quaker meeting in America.

Above: While Long Island, and especially Suffolk County, remained close to its agrarian roots into the twentieth century, important changes were taking place. A growing population clamored for property, causing farm acreage to drop. The major focus for the remaining farmers thus became market production of potatoes, rye, and corn for the expanding New York City market. Courtesy, SPLIA

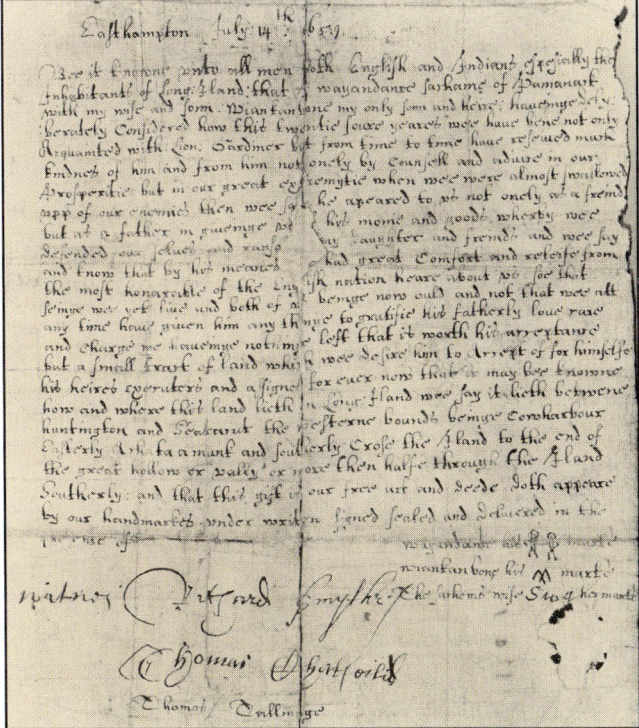

The Dutch and English divided the Island in 1650, signing a treaty that set up an "international line" located near today's Nassau/Suffolk county border. But 14 years later the English had taken over, and New Amsterdam became New York.

The Dutch left us a colorful legacy—quaint community names such as Flushing, the legend of Santa Claus, ice skating, and the Dutch door. They also have the dubious distinction of having introduced slavery to Long Island.

The Island's farming heritage dates back to

LONG ISLAND

Above: William Floyd came from a wealthy family which settled in Long Island in 1655. A signer of the Declaration of Independence, a state senator, and a New York delegate to the Continental Congress, Floyd supported American independence and was forced to flee his home at Mastic during the Revolution. This portrait shows the confident and straightforward gaze of a wealthy gentleman farmer and highly respected citizen. Courtesy, Independence Historical Park, Philadelphia

Facing page: Slavery was introduced to New Amsterdam by the West India Company, which furnished slaves to landowners as an inducement to colonization. Traders paid about $60 a head for slaves in Curacao and sold them in New York for as much as $150. It was said that a strong male could bring $250. Courtesy, Picture Collection, New York Public Library

colonial days when 80 percent of Long Islanders were farmers. The Hempstead Plains were ideal for grazing cattle and sheep, so Long Island became one of the leading cattle areas of the colonies. For a glimpse of this period of Long Island history, the Old Bethpage Restoration Village is well worth a visit.

THE WAR OF INDEPENDENCE

The era of the American Revolution, the only war to be fought on Long Island soil, was one of the most intriguing and yet most difficult times for the Island. Conflicting loyalties split the colonists, even dividing families. The patriots or rebels were strongest in the eastern end. Suffolk towns were almost unanimous in their support of the rebel cause. For some, especially in the western end, ties to England were not easily broken. Those loyal to the king were called Tories, and Long Island had many.

Oyster Bay residents voted 205 to 42 against having anything to do with the revolutionary government. Division was so strong in Hempstead that in 1775, Hempstead patriots seceded, making the northern section a new community called North Hempstead. South Hempstead was later named Hempstead once again.

All through the seven-year occupation by the British, from 1776 until 1783, Long Islanders never unified behind either cause, but by 1776, many had joined the rebels. William Floyd of Mastic was the first New Yorker to sign the Declaration of Independence. The rest of Long Island didn't have long to wait before it too was caught up in the war.

The first big battle of the American Revolution, the Battle of Long Island, was fought in August 1776. Many historians believe it would have been the last battle of the revolution if George Washington hadn't retreated so cleverly.

That first summer of the war, 400 British ships sailed into New York Harbor carrying 24,000 British troops and 8,000 German Hessian soldiers. General Washington's 10,000 American troops took their position in Brooklyn. The British came ashore at Gravesend and drove the Americans back to Brooklyn Heights. British general William Howe surprised the rebels by sending part of his army through Jamaica Pass, cutting them off. It appeared as if the Americans were trapped, but nature intervened.

A stiff wind and rain prevented the British from

bringing their ships forward to bombard and finish off the rebels. When the storm ended, a thick fog appeared. Under the cover of darkness and fog, Washington silently evacuated his troops to lower Manhattan. The British had been only 600 yards away.

Although the American army lived to fight another day, Long Island was soon occupied by the British. Of the 30,000 Island residents, 5,000 left Long Island to avoid the occupation. They took temporary residence in the rebel stronghold of Connecticut. Throughout the seven-year occupation, patriots came across Long Island Sound for nightly assaults against the British, known as "whaleboat raids."

On the Island, even though many residents were happy with the British, rebel spying was a daily occurrence. Nathan Hale, a native of Connecticut, was caught spying in the Huntington area. Before he was hung in New York City, he is said to have uttered the immortal words: "I regret I have but one life to lose for my country."

The black petticoat of Nancy Strong, a resident of Crane Neck near Stony Brook, also became a symbol of the rebel cause. Strong was part of the patriots' spy ring, and if her wash was hung a certain way—the black petticoat followed by a certain number of white handkerchiefs—the spies knew where to meet.

After the rebels won their war of independence, Long Islanders went back to their farms and resumed their daily lives. But a new era and a new industry was dawning for the Island. Whaling would give Long Island and Sag Harbor worldwide recognition.

TO THE SEA

The colonists learned onshore whaling from the Indians. When a finback or right whale came close to the shores of Long Island, the Indians used arrows and spears to kill the mammal. The colonists soon followed suit. In the 1600s Southampton divided its beachfront into wards. Residents of each ward were entitled to whales washed ashore within their boundaries.

The Indians also introduced the beginning of offshore whaling, using their dugout canoes to chase whales that came near the shore. By the nineteenth century, sea-loving Long Islanders were venturing far out into the Atlantic Ocean looking for the more elusive sperm whale. The larger whaleboats soon needed a protective harbor to dock and unload, and Sag Harbor filled the bill. It became the third largest whaling port in the world, surpassed only by New Bedford and Nantucket.

Whale oil was used for lamps and whale bones for buttons. Scrimshaw, carvings from whales' teeth, also became fashionable. Consequently, whales were in big demand. Long Islanders began to search even farther for them. It was not uncommon for whaleboats to be at sea for several years. Long Island's whaling industry reached its peak in 1847.

Due to several events, including the discovery in Pennsylvania of petroleum oil, a lamp oil which was cheaper and easier to get, and the gold rush in California which beckoned to many of the more adventurous Long Islanders, Long Island's whaling industry came to an end. By 1871 the expression "thar she blows!" had become part of Long Island history. Harpoons, scrimshaw, and a whaling boat are today on display at the Cold Spring Harbor Whaling Museum and at the Sag Harbor Whaling Museum.

BLACK HISTORY

Many whalers were Indians and former black slaves. Slavery had existed on Long Island since the Dutch introduced it there in 1626. By the end of the 1700s, there were approximately 5,000 slaves on Long Island, 15 to 20 percent of Suffolk's population. But by the time New York passed a law ending slavery in 1827, most of

LONG ISLAND

Left: Spring and fall were fox-hunting seasons on Long Island. Elaborate breakfasts and elegant dinners and balls were part of the overall aura of excitement. Theodore Roosevelt, an enthusiast of any outdoor sport, and the smartly dressed members of the MeadowBrook Hunt prepare for a meet at Roosevelt's summer estate, "Sagamore Hill" in Oyster Bay, 1895. Courtesy, MeadowBrook Club Album

the Island slaves had already been freed.

Even so, it wasn't an easy time for blacks on Long Island. In 1860 a statewide referendum to "give equal voting rights to people of color by eliminating the requirement that they own property" was overwhelmingly defeated by Long Islanders. As late as 1947, when William J. Levitt built Levittown, racial bias was still a concern on the Island. There was a covenant in Levittown's bylaws that stated no blacks were allowed except as "domestic servants."

Today Long Islanders are proud of the contributions blacks have made to the Island's heritage. Island history boasts several prominent black Americans, including Lewis Lattimer of Queens, an assistant to Thomas A. Edison in the development of the light bulb, and the nation's first black poet, Jupiter Hammon of Lloyd Harbor, a slave owned by the Lloyd family. The African-American Museum in Hempstead has a permanent display of black history on the Island.

SUBURBIA

Suburbia and Long Island—for decades the two have been synonymous. The roots of suburban Long Island can be traced back to the 1800s when a few Brooklynites traveled by ferry to Manhattan, becoming Long Island's first commuters. By 1883, when the Brooklyn Bridge was completed, many Brooklyn residents worked in the City. Nassau residents were soon to follow.

Alexander Turney Stewart envisioned a dream suburbia. In 1869 he purchased more than 7,000 acres on the Hempstead Plains for $55 an acre. Stewart, for whom Stewart Avenue is named, began work on a new model suburban community called Garden City, one of the first planned communities in the country. The homes built there were to be rented, with Stewart continuing to own the property. But he never lived to see Garden City completed—he died in 1876 with only a few homes having been built. (The project continued on with other architects.) Partially as a memorial to Stewart, his wife had the majestic Cathedral of the Incarnation in Garden City erected. Stewart's body was to be interred there but in 1878 the body was stolen from the churchyard it had been temporarily placed in while the cathedral was being built. A $25,000 reward was offered for Stewart's corpse, and a few years later a body was ransomed back. But in one of Long Island's odder mysteries, several Garden City historians question whether the body was indeed Stewart's.

During the 1800s another suburban landmark, the Long Island Rail Road, made its debut. Today the LIRR is the third oldest railroad in the world still in operation. Strange though it may seem, the nation's busiest commuter railroad was not built to bring Long Islanders to New York City, but so that New York City riders could get to Boston, Massachusetts.

Crossing the flatlands of the Island to Greenport, ferrying the passengers across the Sound, and then hooking them up with a train in northern Connecticut made more sense to railroad officials than trying to lay track through the hilly regions of southern Connecticut. On July 27, 1844, the LIRR made its inaugural run from Brooklyn to Greenport, and then, in stages, on to Boston.

CRADLE OF AVIATION

Airplanes soon became as common on Long Island as trains. In the early 1900s, while Long Islanders were proudly watching their colorful native son Theodore Roosevelt lead the land, the flat Hempstead Plains

Like so many other coastal communities, Greenport was adversely affected by the decline of the whaling and shipbuilding industries. During the early 1900s it turned to cod fishing, oystering, and light industry, such as paint oil manufacturing. Once one of the busiest whaling ports on Long Island, Greenport still offers the sea as a major attraction, although the boats moored at dock are pleasure boats, not schooners. Courtesy, G.B. Brainard Photo, The Brooklyn Public Library

LONG ISLAND

became known as the ideal site for aviation.

Wilbur and Orville Wright may have started it all in 1903 at Kitty Hawk, North Carolina, but within 20 years Long Island had become the Cradle of Aviation.

The first international aerial tournament was held on the Island in 1910. In 1911 the first airmail flight in history—from Mineola to Garden City—was noted in the record books. Harriet Quimby of Mineola, America's first female pilot, took off from the Hempstead area in 1911. The Island's aviation achievements were capped in 1927 when the *Spirit of St. Louis* made its historic flight from Roosevelt Field. Charles A. Lindbergh made aviation and Long Island history in his 33½-hour solo flight across the Atlantic from Long Island to France. And in 1938 "Wrong Way" Corrigan made another kind of history when he took off from Long Island, heading for California. He wound up in Ireland instead.

The aviation bug had taken over Long Island. Leroy Grumman began building planes in a rented garage in Baldwin in 1929, and the Grumman Corporation was born. The Republic Aviation Corporation soon followed.

THE 1920s, 1930s, AND 1940s

The Roaring Twenties was a time of excitement everywhere in the country, but especially so on the Island. North Shore mansions were playgrounds in which millionaires and celebrities like writer F. Scott Fitzgerald and his wife Zelda danced the night away. Fitzgerald's *The Great Gatsby* was written about this raucous time on the Island.

These were the years when Long Island's coastline gained notoriety as "Rum Row." During Prohibition

Right: Long Island's country estates were the sites for banquets, balls, and weddings, such as this one at the Pratt estate in Glen Cove. In conjunction with the Island's fashionable country clubs, magnificent estates were the focal point of the summer "season." The members of this group summered together on Long Island or at Newport, spent the fall in Europe, entertained each other at their New York townhouses, and often intermarried. Courtesy, Lawrence and Anne Van Ingen

Bottom right: Charles Lindbergh and his *Spirit of St. Louis* captured the wonder and imagination of a generation of Americans when he flew from Long Island on May 20, 1927, and landed in Paris 33½ hours and 3,640 miles later. With this first transatlantic flight the potential of the early "sport" of aviation became a reality. Courtesy, The Nassau County Museum

The Vanderbilt Cup races held on Long Island from 1904 to 1910 attracted huge crowds. However, the mounting number of accidents and deaths to both racers and spectators eventually led to the termination of the event. Courtesy, Vanderbilt Museum

boats anchored offshore, past the three-mile limit, with every type of liquor available. At night the rumrunners would come out and select their wares, hoping to race back to some Long Island waterfront community without being caught. Greenport, because of its location, became a popular docking area for the bootleggers. The liquor was then shipped by car to Manhattan. Long Island road chases between mobsters, hijackers, and the local police were not uncommon. James Cagney would have had a field day.

It was also during the 1920s that the Ku Klux Klan became extremely active on Long Island. It's reported that one out of every eight residents of Nassau and Suffolk counties was a member of the Klan in the early twenties. Island Klan members were bigoted against Catholics, Jews, blacks, and all foreign born. Freeport was one of the Klan's most active communities, and a Klan parade there in 1924 saw 30,000 line the streets. A rally in Central Islip the year before had attracted 25,000. As the twenties wound down, so did the Klan's membership on the Island.

In the late 1930s another controversial group surfaced on Long Island. Nazi sympathizers took residence at Camp Siegfried, a 45-acre site near the community of Yaphank. Streets there were named after leading Nazis such as Adolf Hitler and Hermann Goering, and Nazi propaganda and swastikas were in abundance. Fifty thousand Nazi sympathizers were said to visit Camp Siegfried for the Sunday afternoon rallies. When World War II erupted, the camp became only an unpleasant memory.

World War II placed Long Island on the alert. As in World War I, Camp Upton in Brookhaven—the inspiration for Army Private Irving Berlin's "Oh How I Hate to Get Up in the Morning"—was used to house troops on their way to Europe.

Grumman and Fairchild were turning out thousands of war planes, and because of its vast coastline, there was concern about Long Island's vulnerability to the enemy. The fears were well-founded. On June 12, 1942, a coastguardsman patrolling a beach in Amagansett happened upon four figures speaking German. They offered the young coastguardsman a bribe, which he pretended to take—there being four of them and only one of him—and then he quickly returned to his lifeboat station to report the incident.

Coast guard officers raced back to the spot, but the German spies had disappeared. Later it was discovered they had taken the Long Island Rail Road to Manhattan. The four Germans were part of a group of saboteurs—

Coney Island continued to draw huge summer crowds after World War II, as seen in this view from the parachute jump at Steeplechase Park in 1950. Courtesy, National Archives

four more landed in Florida a few days later—brought to this country to blow up plants, bridges, and railroad tracks. A massive manhunt was initiated, but the group's leader surrendered to the FBI in Washington, D.C., about a week after the Amagansett incident.

GROWING, GROWING . . .

It was after the war, with the return of the veterans, that Long Island experienced its massive population explosion.

Nassau County holds the title as the first major suburb in the country, and William J. Levitt gets the credit for giving Nassau that distinction. In the construction of Levittown, Levitt devised a system of assembly-line house building that hasn't been equalled since. With 15,000 workers on the job, 35 houses were completed in a day. By 1951, 17,447 Levitt houses had been constructed on the Hempstead Plains.

Levittown typified suburbia. A community survey in the early 1950s asked residents to name their major complaint about life at the moment. The number one answer? "Too many dogs are running unleashed on the lawns." The number two response? "World communism."

Nassau's population continued to skyrocket after Levittown. It rose 93 percent in the 1950s. By 1960 the population of the county was 1.3 million people. Finally the migration slowed down. By 1980, the census figure for Nassau was just under 1.3 million, almost exactly the same as it had been 20 years earlier.

Suffolk's growth has always been a few years behind Nassau's. The eastern county's population shot up 142 percent in the 1950s. By 1960 it was 666,784, half of Nassau's. But people continued to flock to Suffolk. By 1980, 1,284,231 people lived there.

With this tremendous influx of people, Long Island's character changed radically. By 1973 only 7 percent of Nassau County land was vacant. Areas like Hempstead had gone from rural to suburban to almost urban in what seemed like overnight. Suffolk County in the 1980s saw farmland decreasing rapidly as new housing and condominium projects sprung up on former potato fields. Long Island became much more independent with this growth; people looked to the Island rather than to Manhattan for employment and entertainment. The term "suburbia" no longer seemed to apply to Long Island. But the region suffered enormous growing pains in the process. With the massive population and business increase, local officials wrestled with the problems of affordable housing, waste disposal, and adequate energy.

As housing prices have escalated, the young and old have found it more and more difficult to find affordable housing. Long Island, with its dependence on the automobile and home heating oil, was especially hard hit by the 1970s oil crisis. And the battle over whether or not Long Island Lighting Company's Shoreham Nuclear Power Plant should have opened consumed Long Islanders in the 1980s. So did the question of what to do with the tons and tons of garbage that 2.6 million people disposed of daily. The notorious Islip garbage barge of 1987 and its unwanted cargo will surely take its place in Long Island history.

So will Hurricane Gloria, which in September 1985 caused a power outage of up to 11 days for some residents, and $300 million worth of damage. The storm also uprooted tens of thousands of Long Island's oldest trees. Like the hurricane of 1938, Gloria reminded Long Islanders once more just how fragile their wonderful island existence can be.

What Long Islanders Have to Say About the Island's History

Rufus Langhans, Huntington town historian:

My favorite period of history was the American Revolution. At the end of the Revolution the state legislature fined Long Island 10,000 pounds for lack of enthusiasm for the war. I thought that was most unfair because you don't have too much enthusiasm when the British troops are stationed in your own house. You sort of have to temper your enthusiasm, you know. We had to pay that fine. I asked for it back during the Bicentennial, but I didn't get anywhere.

I would go back to the eighteenth century if I could bring penicillin and plumbing. I hate the twentieth century; there are no Indians or British. It's very dull. All suburbia. After Teddy Roosevelt it was downhill for Long Island history.

Michael F. Smith, Shinnecock Indian; trustee, Shinnecock Indian Reservation:

Historically we were whalers. We earned our living from the sea and the soil, and we continue to do that. The sea and the soil are natural elements of this community, and we have lived off of them for generations and generations.

I'm most proud that, in spite of what's gone on around us, we've maintained our land base for 350 years, drawing upon the strength of our elders. And we continue to go on, in spite of external pressures to exploit our natural resources.

III

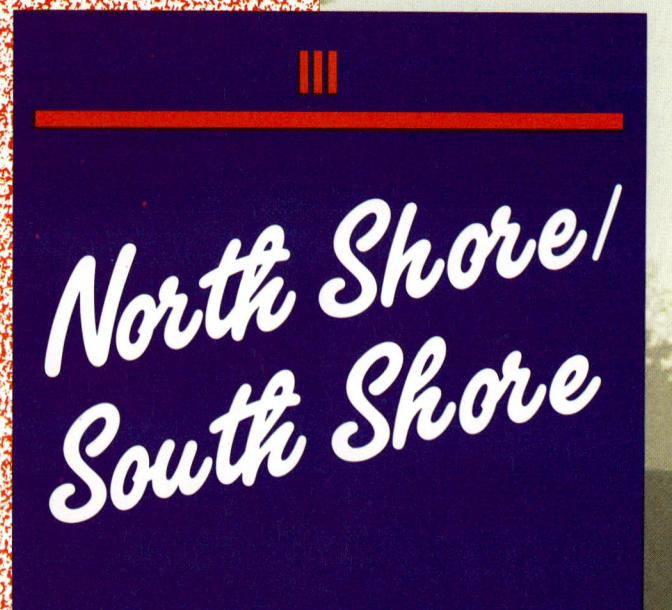

North Shore/ South Shore

40

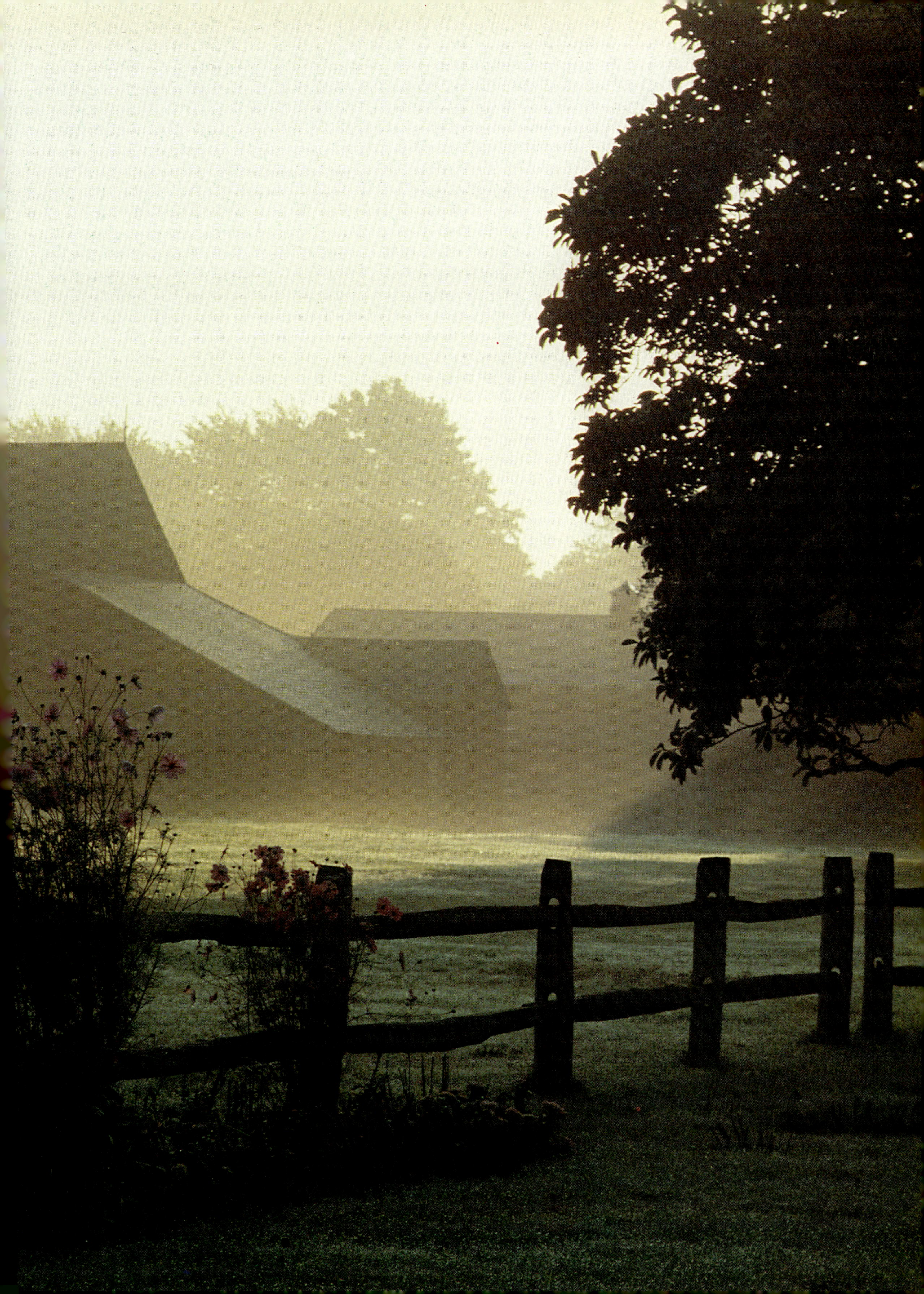

LONG ISLAND

Above: The sun sets over Execution Rocks Lighthouse and the shores of Sands Point. Photo by Ken Spencer

Previous page: This charming country barn was photographed amidst the early morning fog in East Hampton. Photo by Ken Spencer

Facing page: From the air the North Fork, with Orient Point in the background, appears to be an island. Photo by Ken Spencer

North Shore/South Shore, North Fork/South Fork, Five Towns or Three Village area—Long Island is a region of regions. Long Islanders are not only proud of their island and its local communities, but the geographical areas they live in as well. Why choose the North Shore over the South Shore, or vice versa? A Long Islander won't be shy in explaining his preference.

The Island has no shortage of official boundaries. With 2 counties, 13 towns, 2 cities, fire and school districts galore, and hundreds of local communities, some of which are villages, some unincorporated areas, political entities abound on Long Island. A recent tally puts the figure at 815.

Because of its diverse geography and the contrasting life-styles that it offers, Long Island is also divided into unofficial "preferred" areas. You can live by the ocean or on the Sound, near the City, or just a ferry ride from New England. Neighborhood landscapes can include woodlands, wetlands, farmlands, or seaside cliffs.

No governing body rules these "preferred" locales. Their borders may be defined simply as "north of Jericho Turnpike," "south of Montauk Highway," or "on the East End." To a Long Islander, however, these regions can be as separate a domain as any town, county, or state.

To know Long Island you have to understand the geographical and social differences of living on the North Shore versus the South Shore, or near the City rather than on the East End.

THE GOLD COAST VS. THE OCEAN COAST

Thanks to the Ice Age, and specifically the Wisconsin Glacier, Long Island's North and South shores have distinct physical differences. The glacier's southerly movement twice reached Long Island. The first time it stopped right in the middle of the Island, leaving debris behind which created the hills of Hauppauge and Farmingville. The second time the glacier only reached the Island's northern coast. As it receded it left rubble and rocks, carved out peninsulas, and gave the cliffs to Sea Cliff, the port to Port Washington, and the coves to Glen Cove.

The glacier never reached the South Shore, leaving that area flat, sandy, and, in many sections, marshy. Home to some of the world's finest beaches, the South Shore's southern border is the Atlantic Ocean. The area runs west to east from the first Nassau community of Valley Stream to the Hamptons on the South Fork. The Long Island Expressway is the northern boundary.

The North Shore of Long Island, known for its mansions and millionaires, has Long Island Sound as its northern border. The western boundary line begins with the Nassau community of Great Neck. Where the eastern boundary lies is subject to debate.

Purists consider the North Shore to encompass only the Nassau County portion of the Island's northern coast. Some allow Huntington to fit under the title. But recent arrivals to the Three Village area—the northern Suffolk communities of Stony Brook, Setauket, and Old Field—have been known to call the North Shore home, and geographically these communities are on the north shore of the Island.

In defining today's Island, it's easier to refer to Nassau County's northern shore by its other nickname, "The Gold Coast," so named because of the wealthy who settled there in the early 1900s. Let the North Shore of Long Island include every community in Nassau and Suffolk north of the Long Island Expressway out to the Town of Riverhead. That's where the East End's North Fork begins.

Since the Island has such a long, narrow shape, there's no real middle section and no strong proponents to create one. (If you live on an island, who wants to boast about living in the middle of it?) So Long Islanders live either in the hilly northern area, or the flatlands of the south, and loyalties are displayed accordingly.

The dispute over which shore is better dates back to colonial days—even George Washington got into the fray. After a trip to both shores in April 1790, our first president wrote:

The Island, as far as I went, from West to East, seems to be equally divided between flat and hilly land. The former on the South, next to the seaboard, and the latter, on the North, next to the Sound. The highest, they say is the best and most productive, but the other is the pleasantest to work, except in the wet season.

North versus South—Long Island style. The Expressway has been the Mason-Dixon line for years. Why choose one picturesque area over the other? Get your scorecards ready. Here are a few of the debating points.

43

LONG ISLAND

North Shore residents like the hills and seaside cliffs of the north coast. Trees are taller; the landscape more picturesque, they say. South Shore residents say they have attractive areas, too, and there's no worry about getting into steep driveways in snowstorms.

South Shore residents boast of their sandy beaches and the beautiful Atlantic Ocean parks, Jones Beach, and the Fire Island National Seashore. North Shorians acknowledge the rocks and pebbles on their coast, but brag of the luxurious private beaches that abound in the numerous harbors and coves.

With the breezes off the ocean, the South Shore is cooler in the summer, South Shorians say. The North Shore's warmer summers mean more use of swimming pools, and almost a month longer growing season, North Shorians say. "Want proof?" they ask. Look at the fall foliage. When the leaves have turned red and brown on the South Shore, they're still green on the North Shore.

The dispute over which shore is better is even more heated when it comes to boating. South Shore power boaters prefer the Great South Bay with the quick jaunts to Fire Island and the easy access to the Atlantic Ocean available through the several inlets. Sailors there say the Great South Bay is less subject to calms, and some will even throw in the old wives' tale that North Shore sailing has been ruined by New York skyscrapers cutting off the breezes.

North Shore sailors strongly prefer Long Island Sound. The Sound is deeper and wider than the South Shore's Great South Bay, and much better for sailing, they say. North Shore power boaters talk of "shooting over" to Greenwich and the Connecticut shore.

Different life-styles are a part of the North/South difference, too. With former residents such as Harry Guggenheim, F.W. Woolworth, J.P. Morgan, C.W. Post of Post Cereal fame, William K. Vanderbilt, and Otto Kahn, the railroad financier, the North Shore is known as the Island's wealthiest region. Several North Shore communities even rank higher than Beverly Hills in median income. (The South Shore resort areas of Fire Island and the Hamptons don't have as many year-round wealthy residents.)

In the 1920s, the Gold Coast's heyday, approximately 1,000 mansions dotted the rolling hills of the North Shore of Long Island. Today the number is less than 500, but huge estates are still plentiful. The western South Shore has its millionaires and mansions too, but contemporary ranches and split-levels are more common.

Of course everything is relative when it comes to Long Island's blue bloods. Since Lord Robert David Lion Gardiner's family founded the East End and Gardiner's Island 350 years ago, he considers the Vanderbilts and such the "nouveau riche."

"The Fords, the Rockefellers—sure, they can go to Sotheby's and buy a piece of Paul Revere silver for $100,000," said Gardiner. "We have Paul Revere silver too. The difference is Paul Revere made the silver for our family."

Years ago the stereotypical image of a North Shorian was an aristocrat draped in European fashions enjoying a catered lawn party. Dances at private country clubs, even full-fledged balls, were part of the entertainment calendar.

South Shorians were perceived as the middle-class barbecue crowd, or as baymen with pants legs rolled up. But those images don't fit the reality of today's Island. There are extremely rich Long Islanders on the South Shore, and baymen and barbecues are plentiful on the North Shore.

In today's mobile society the Island's old North/South stereotypes are quickly fading. But as to which shore is better, don't throw your scorecards away just yet.

THE EAST END

On the East End of Long Island, where the Island splits into two forks, the North and South coasts reverse roles. With quaint villages and rolling farmland, the East End's northern coast is home to most of Long Island's farmers, and people who today still take pride in the conservative views of their New England Puritan ancestors. Money on the North Fork is not on display. It's in the bank.

The South Fork, site of the world-famous Hamptons, is much more open in displaying the many riches of the area. Although the laid-back residents of Montauk and Sag Harbor and the year-round residents of the Hamptons may be as conservative as their North Fork counterparts, they are overshadowed by the rich and famous who make the Hamptons their summer home.

There is so much wealth in the Hamptons that some joke that the village communities should be rated by the following scale: Westhampton Beach is new

Old Westbury Gardens, along with its mansion, is one of several North Shore estates now open to the public. Photo by Audrey Gibson

LONG ISLAND

money, Southampton is old money, and East Hampton takes the most money. It can cost $200,000 to rent a Hamptons oceanfront home just for "the season."

The East End's South Fork has only two towns, Southampton and East Hampton, but the towns are made up of numerous communities, some actual villages, and some unincorporated areas. For example, in the town of East Hampton, there is also a separate village of East Hampton and unincorporated areas such as Wainscott, Amagansett, and Montauk. Southampton also has a village of Southampton and communities including Bridgehampton, Quogue, and Hampton Bays.

The North Fork offers a much quieter life-style, residents there say. The area resembles New England. There is the picturesque fishing community of Greenport and the lovely town of Southold. Thousands of acres of potato, cauliflower, and corn fields, flowering fruit orchards, vineyards, and horse farms make up the landscape. In the spring and summer, farm stands pop up on practically every corner, similar to other farming

Above right: Accessible only by ferry, Shelter Island offers a quiet life. Photo by Audrey Gibson

Right: The Hamptons are a mixture of magnificent mansions and the artless beauty of nature. Photo by Audrey Gibson

Facing page: Beachfront homes in Southampton offer all the amenities. Photo by Ken Spencer

areas. But Long Island farming is unique in that a North Fork farmer can ride his tractor in the morning and then spend a summer afternoon taking his wife and children out on the family boat.

Boating and fishing are available on Long Island Sound or the many bays on the south side of the fork. Shelter Island, a beautiful, hilly island with attractive cliffside homes, can be reached only by ferry from either the North or South forks. Shelter Island residents tend to align themselves with the more conservative views of the North Fork.

The South Fork also has farms and farm stands, but it is the lovely, chic villages of East Hampton and Southampton, and the luxurious mansions by the ocean, that make the South Fork the place to be for so many people. Art galleries, museums, and trend-setting retail shops, all catering to the summer population, make this area a visitor's haven between May and September. The year-round residents consider it a haven once the summer people go.

Who's who in the Hamptons? Take out any social register or movie magazine, and it's safe to assume the names featured there have either vacationed in the area or have homes there. From Jacqueline Kennedy Onassis, who was born in Southampton and raised in East Hampton, to rock star Mick Jagger, who has summered in Montauk, the East End has played host to just about every American celebrity.

The only area on Long Island that rivals the Hamptons for top summer resort honors is Fire Island, which is known for its untouched beauty and individualistic communities.

The summer people, most of whom come from Manhattan, often debate over which Long Island resort area is better, Fire Island or the Hamptons. And which community is the best? Water Mill in Southampton? Wainscott in East Hampton? How about Ocean Beach or The Pines on Fire Island?

The mildest temperatures on the Island are recorded on the South Fork because of its proximity to the ocean and other waterways. The area offers boating and fishing on the Atlantic and in Shinnecock and Moriches Bay. While you'll see flocks of sailboats on the North Fork waterways, because of the South

Shore's shallower bays, power boats of the large, racing variety are more common in the Hamptons and off the shores of Fire Island.

The South Fork is not only East, South, or West Hampton. There is the quaint, former whaling community of Sag Harbor, and at the farthermost tip of Long Island sits the rustic community of Montauk, with its internationally recognizable Montauk Lighthouse, said to be the most photographed lighthouse in the world.

For many years a fishing village, Montauk now draws more of the wealthy crowd trying to avoid the hectic summer social scene of the Hamptons.

In 1926 a plan to turn Montauk into the Miami Beach of the North was hatched by Carl Fisher, creator of Florida's Miami Beach. He spent $1 million building the 200-room Montauk Manor, plus all the accessories that went with it—polo field, golf course, and a seven-story office building. The resort concept never took off, although today Montauk Manor is divided into condominiums, most of which are used in the summer. Today the residents of Montauk, who at dawn can walk the ocean beach with only an aimlessly wandering seagull as company, are probably delighted Fisher's plan failed.

The East End of Long Island, especially in the winter, offers a far different life-style than that of Nassau County. New York City is more than two hours away, and most of those who choose to make the East End their year-round home have no ties with the City. That's true for many of the residents of the Eastern Suffolk towns of Riverhead and Brookhaven, too.

NASSAU AND THE FIVE TOWNS

The proximity to Manhattan is an important consideration for many Long Islanders in choosing where to live. Residents of the Five Towns area of Nassau County say its location just over the Queens border is perhaps its strongest selling feature.

Woodmere, Hewlett, Lawrence, Cedarhurst, and Inwood make up the Five Towns region. An area of luxurious homes and exclusive retail boutiques, the Five Towns is prime real estate. In 1987 one local official said, "You can't buy a shack here for less than $200,000."

Unlike the acres and acres of open space in middle and eastern Suffolk, Nassau County has very few vacant parcels left, and housing plots can run as small as 60 by 80 feet. But many Long Islanders prefer Nassau because the area is settled. The new ranches, split-levels, and colonials of the 1950s and 1960s are now secluded by tall trees and shrubs, and people have added on and repainted, eliminating the new development look. In Suffolk new houses and developments continue to spring up, especially in Brookhaven, the fastest growing town.

THE GOVERNING BODY

Nassau and Suffolk counties also differ in their forms of government. Both have county executives elected every four years, and town supervisors. Suffolk has an 18-member County Legislature while Nassau is governed by a six-member Board of Supervisors. In keeping with the proverb, "the grass is always greener on the other side of the fence," there have been attempts in both counties to switch to each other's form of government, but it hasn't happened yet.

Politics is a way of life for many Long Islanders, but understanding the levels of government on the Island requires concentration. There is no Long Island governing body. There have been cries for statehood, but no recent movement in that direction. Regional authorities such as the Long Island Housing Partnership, however, which would bring together Nassau and Suffolk leaders to focus on issues of concern to all Long Islanders, have been promoted.

Nassau's Board of Supervisors is made up of a presiding supervisor from Hempstead (because it is the largest town) and town supervisors from Hempstead, Oyster Bay, and North Hempstead. Two cities, Glen Cove and Long Beach, also are represented on the board. The Nassau cities have their own governments. So do the towns. And then there are the villages with their mayors and village trustees, and the school, library, and fire districts with local school boards, library trustees, and fire commissioners.

In Suffolk, besides the county government, there are 10 towns: Babylon, Islip, Huntington, Brookhaven, Smithtown, Riverhead, Southold, Southampton, East Hampton, and Shelter Island. Each town has its supervisor and town board. Villages and school and fire districts are plentiful, just as they are in Nassau.

THE NAME GAME

The variety of Long Island's taxing districts is nothing compared to the variety of Long Island community names. Most of the older localities received their names from the English, Dutch, and Indians. More modern-day communities such as Levittown or Shirley were named after the builder who created them.

The origin of some community names are more easily understood than others. Rocky Point, Sea Cliff, Bayport, and Oyster Bay, for example, are all descriptive names. When you have an island with 1,180 miles of coastline, water-based names are bound to be common. Bayville, Bay Shore, Ocean Beach, Great River, Brightwaters, Seaford—the list goes on and on.

Long Island also has a large number of Indian-named communities. From Massapequa to Manhasset, just about all of the 13 original Indian groups on Long Island have some locale named after them. So do a few Indian sachems, like Wyandanch. Some town names are derived from Indian words that are descriptive of the area. Rockaway, for example, means "the sandy place."

There are a few Dutch-named communities like Flushing, and many communities are named after the hometowns of the English settlers or the leading English peerage of the 1600 and 1700s. Nassau, Suffolk, Islip, and Southampton are just a few examples of English-named areas.

Add to these names all the communities that start with North, South, East or West: 36 in all. Southold is one of the northernmost towns on Long Island. It was settled by the English from New Haven, Connecticut; thus, it was the southernmost land for them. Long Island also has its share of centers: Centereach, Centerville, Centerport, and Centre Island. There's even a biblical community name—Babylon.

Then there are the communities which understandably weren't happy with the names originally given to them. Skunk's Misery is now Malverne. Punk's Hole is Manorville. Mosquito Cove became Glen Cove. But for some names, there's just no figuring. East Marion is a puzzle, because there is no Marion on Long Island. The community was originally called Rocky Point, but residents discovered the name was taken. They came up with East Marion instead.

By the late 1980s, condominiums were the popular choice for waterfront home development. These condos, complete with boat dock, are in Northport. Photo by Ken Spencer

THE PEOPLE

Like most Americans, Long Islanders tend to settle in communities where they find people of their own religious, ethnic, or economic background. Long Island is incredibly diverse in its population. Just about every nationality, religion, and occupation is represented.

Italians are the most populous ethnic group. Long Islanders of Italian heritage can be found in every com-

"Home Sweet Home"
by John Howard Payne

Born in 1791, John Howard Payne was raised in East Hampton. He wrote "Home Sweet Home," his ode to Long Island, in 1823.

Mid pleasures and palaces though I may roam,
Be it ever so humble, there's no place like home.
A charm from the sky seems to hallow us there,
which, seek through the world, is ne'er met with elsewhere.

An exile from home, splendor dazzles in vain,
Oh give me my lowly, thatched cottage again!
The birds singing gaily, that come at my call!
Give them, with the peace of mind, dearer than all.

How sweet 'tis to sit 'neath a fond father's smile,
And the cares of a mother to soothe and beguile!
Let others delight 'mid new pleasures to roam,
But give me, oh! give me the pleasures of home.

To thee I'll return, overburdened with care,
The heart's dearest solace will smile on me there;
No more from that cottage again will I roam,
Be it ever so humble, there's no place like home.

Chorus

Home! Home! Sweet, sweet home!
There's no place like home.
There's no place like home.

munity on the Island, but according to the 1980 census the hamlets of Massapequa, North Babylon, and Copiague have exceptionally large Italian populations. The Irish, the second largest group, also call just about every Long Island community home. However, Garden City, Rockville Centre, and the Sayville-Bayport area have the most residents of Irish heritage.

Germans are the third largest group. There's an area dubbed Germantown in Yaphank, and the German population is strong in the Three Village area, Northport, and Centerport. There are Poles in Riverhead who call their area Polish Town, U.S.A., and Russian Jews in Great Neck and the Five Towns. Those with English heritage are found everywhere, but especially in East Hampton and Shelter Island.

Roman Catholicism is the predominant religion on the Island. More than one million Long Islanders are reported to be Catholic. The Diocese of Rockville Centre is the eighth largest Roman Catholic diocese in the United States. (Brooklyn is number seven.) Jews are the second-largest religious group. In 1982 a *Newsday* poll estimated 10 percent of Suffolk County residents and 25 percent of Nassau County residents were Jewish.

Once considered an area of young families, Long Island's population is aging. Those over 55, who accounted for 14.5 percent of the population in 1960, were 20.5 percent in 1980, and the East End of the Island has the oldest average population. The North Fork now has a higher median age than the state of Florida. Southold's, for example, is 43.1, compared to Florida's 34.7. Shelter Island tops the list with a median age of 50. The Nassau/Suffolk median age is 31.9 years. Only Long Beach, with its condominium boom and the influx of young married couples, has had an age decrease in its population during the last 10 years.

No matter what the age, religion, ethnic group, or community in which they live, Long Islanders stand together in their strong feelings about the island they call home. They are proud of the diversity of the Island and the many pleasures it affords.

It was with Long Island in mind that John Howard Payne wrote the song "Home Sweet Home" in 1823. Local historians say the immortal work applies to East Hampton, the town where Payne was raised. But "Home Sweet Home" can serve as the theme song for all Long Islanders. "Be it ever so humble, there's no place like home"—a Long Island home, that is.

What Long Islanders Have to Say About the Island's Regions

Peggy Phipps Boegner, a resident of Old Westbury. Mrs. Boegner is the daughter of John Shaffer Phipps, whose family made its fortune in steel, and Margarita Grace Phipps, a member of the W.R. Grace & Company shipping line family. The Phipps family owned the estate now known as Westbury House at Old Westbury Gardens. Mrs. Boegner was raised there. On North Shore living:

I never heard the term Gold Coast. We never used it. Everybody around here was rich. There were some who led a more flamboyant life-style. They were always entertaining the duke of this or the king of that. But we all enjoyed having lovely gardens, fine clothes, and servants. We didn't connect it with money. It was a way of life. It was really quite common for the time.

We're definitely seeing the end of that era.

A Long Island cocktail party conversation:

"You can't beat the South Shore. We have the ocean, sandy beaches, and it's warmer in the winter, cooler in the summer."

"There's no comparison. The North Shore is much more scenic—the rolling hills, beautiful harbors, attractive homes. And the wealth . . . I'll take the North Shore any day."

Facing page: The sun sets over Long Island's North Shore. Photo by Ken Spencer

IV

At Your Service

52

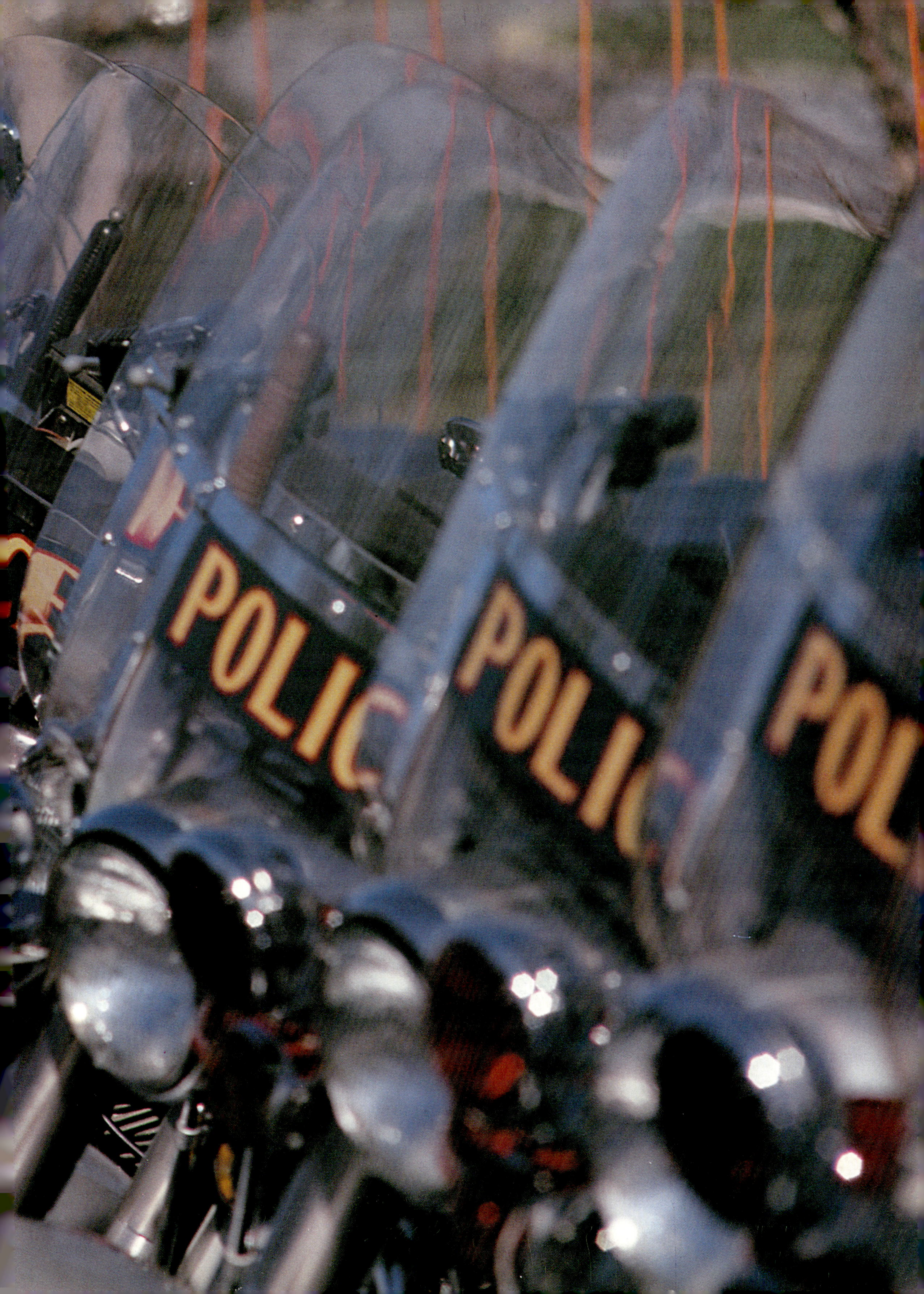
POLIC
POLIC
POL

LONG ISLAND

Above: Dining on Long Island can be casual or formal. These Port Jefferson diners opt for the former. Photo by Ken Spencer

Previous page: The Nassau and Suffolk county police forces are considered the best in the country. Photo by Bruce Bennett

Right: Gosman's Dock in Montauk is a popular stop for East End shoppers. Photo by Ken Spencer

Facing page: Smaller eating establishments do well on Long Island because of its fast-paced life-style. Photo by Jeff Greenberg

The story goes that, as a child, Ralph Waldo Emerson happened upon a man sawing logs. Young Emerson realized that cutting wood was beyond his strength, but, wanting to be of service, he thought of a way he could help. "May I," he asked, "do the grunting for you?"

Now that's service, and service is what Long Island is all about. Long Island businesspeople may not go as far as Emerson, but they can supply assistance in just about every other way, for service is Long Island's number one industry.

In the last few decades, the national economy has seen a tremendous shift from reliance on the manufacture of goods to the supply of services. Business analysts call it the "Second Industrial Revolution." Nowhere is this revolution more apparent than on Long Island.

From a small boarding house in Orient to the Island's largest hotel, from a mom-and-pop grocery store to Roosevelt Field—legal services to catering, automotive repair to banking, advertising, architecture, public relations, government, retail, communications, real estate, landscaping, brokerage houses, public utilities, accounting, health care and restaurants— the Island's service industry covers a broad range of categories.

Just what is a service business? Economists usually define manufacturing as the production of goods resulting in a tangible product, whereas services result in something intangible that requires the direct interaction between the servicer and the customer.

While Long Island still has a thriving manufacturing or goods-producing base, it's the increase in service jobs that has boosted the economy; 70,000 new service jobs were introduced into the Island's work force during the first half of the 1980s, and that figure doesn't include the retail trade. Many of those new jobs were in Long Island's number one service industry, tourism.

TOURISM

"From Sound to Sea, the place to be!"
"Nassau County, A Peach Of A Place Next To The Big Apple"
"Suffolk County, A Place To Live"
"Long Island, The Sunrise Homeland"
"Do It On Long Island"
"Visit Long Island"

—Long Island slogans

No matter what slogan is used or how it's promoted, Long Island has been a major people attraction for hundreds of years. The Island welcomed an estimated 25 million visitors in 1987, and every one of them needed a place to stay, a place to eat, and a place to go for recreation. That's why tourism is the number one service industry on the Island.

Tourism pumped $5 billion into the Island economy in 1983. Today the figure is $7 billion. (The total includes the ripple effect of all businesses the tourism industry helps support.)

The Long Island Tourism and Convention Commission estimates that between 3,000 and 5,000 local companies are involved in travel and tourism, employing more than 96,000 Long Islanders. That makes the Island number two in New York State in tourism employment, just behind the state's biggest attraction, New York City.

Long Island is also one of the top three attractions in New York. And many visitors who list New York City as their primary destination include a day or two on Long Island in their travel plans. Who are these visitors and why do they come to the Island? In a 1983 Long Island Tourism Commission survey, 14.5 percent of Island tourists were international travelers, 49.6 percent were from New York State, and 31.9 percent came from other states. A majority, 53.7 percent, were repeat business. The survey found most of those visitors had come to the Island for vacation.

According to the Tourism Commission, in the 1970s, 85 percent of Long Island tourism was on the East End and seasonal. Today only 20 percent of the visitors to Long Island travel to the East End come summertime, while 80 percent choose the year-round destination of Nassau or the western end of Suffolk. That's because today there are two diverse segments of the Long Island tourist trade: resort and commercial business travel, business travel being on top. Of everyone who visits Long Island, 60 percent now do so for business.

EATING OUT

Tourism's major revenue producer is the food and beverage industry. Long Island's fine restaurants cater not only to visitors but to residents as well. The Island boasts more than 4,000 eating places, and every type and ethnic variety of food is offered. Seafood is a specialty, of course, with much of the fish and shellfish coming from Long Island waters. With locally grown vegetables, fruits, and even ducks, you know you're getting it fresh when you order a Long Island meal. And many like to top it off with a glass of one of Long Island's many fine wines.

Whatever the choice in cuisine, from Chinese to Italian, Greek to German, or continental to good old-fashioned American, Long Island restaurants have it all. Choose an elegant eating establishment or a folksy seaside cafe. And if it's a larger group that needs to be wined and dined, the Island offers some fine catering halls and has abundant room in hotel ballrooms and country clubs. Eating in style, whatever the mood, is part of Long Island's appeal.

SLEEPING OVER

You can also sleep in style. Once the majority of overnight accommodations in Nassau and Suffolk were one- or two-story courtyard motels. But no longer.

With Long Island's immense popularity as a vacation spot and business destination, the demand for first-class hotel rooms has never been higher. Hotel development follows commercial development, and since Long Island's commercial development has been booming, so has the hotel business. Large hotels are cropping up all over the Island. That's a recent phenomenon, and the area is considered the last virgin territory for hotels in the United States, according to Joel Mounty, a vice president of the Carlin Organization, which built the Royce Carlin in Melville.

Boarding houses and seaside hotels were common at the turn of the century and in the early 1900s, when the shores of Long Island first became a popular beach resort. Most of the large guest houses were demolished, however, as Long Islanders started claiming the coastline for themselves, building homes or establishing public parks on the ocean, bay, or sound. It wasn't until the 1980s that the Island saw a resurgence in hotel construction, and today hotels are being located near major roadways, not picturesque beaches.

Hotel occupancy rates, which average 65 percent across the nation, can exceed 90 percent on Long Island. There were 12,575 hotel/motel rooms in 1987 on 300 properties—4,000 in Nassau and 8,575 in Suffolk. In 1988, 14 more hotels were in the planning or construction stage for an additional 3,800 rooms. Officials of the State University of New York at Stony Brook were even talking about putting a hotel on the campus grounds.

And it's not enough. Hotels in Nassau and western Suffolk estimate that 70 percent of their business is weekday businesspeople. With more office space being developed in the busy Route 110 corridor in Melville and Veterans Memorial Highway in the Bohemia/Ronkonkoma area, and more business visitors expected, many predict more hotels will be needed.

The Island's largest hotel is the Long Island Marriott Hotel in Uniondale. An additional 250 rooms may soon be added to its 391 rooms. The Island also has a Sheraton Hotel in Smithtown, the Royce Carlin in Melville, and the 280-room Islandia Hilton. Hempstead has its Grand Royal Hotel with a huge ballroom, and Westbury is home to the Island Motor Inn. There are seven Holiday Inns, two Ramada Inns, and three Howard Johnson's Motor Lodges. Just about every major hotel chain is or soon will be represented on the Island.

The elegant Garden City Hotel, with 280 rooms, has perhaps the most interesting history. The original hotel, built in 1874, was rebuilt at the turn of the century after a fire. The newer version was on an even grander scale, with luxuries like a marble swimming pool. The hotel registry read like a social register, with such prominent last names as Vanderbilt, Morgan, and Astor. Charles Lindbergh even rested there before he took off for Paris in 1927. The building was torn down in 1973, but the new Garden City Hotel opened on the same grounds in the 1980s.

On the Island's East End, visitors have their choice of resorts as well as hotels and motels. There's the 50-year-old Gurney's Inn in Montauk—1,000 acres with a private beach, international health and beauty spa, and four dining rooms. Many smaller resort motels can be found on the East End, too. Some include marinas, where visitors may choose to sleep on a boat's bunk rather than in a bed.

Another important industry that falls under the tourism category is transportation. To enjoy Long Island you have to be able to move around. Many Islanders service visitors and residents alike, working for the LIRR or at one of the Island's airports or ferry companies. There are taxi companies, limousine services, car rentals, boat dealers, marinas, and bicycle rental shops.

Although attractions may realize the least amount of revenue in the tourism industry, they are no less important. The parks, beaches, museums, and historic homes are the reason people come to the Island. Most Long Island attractions, however, are not-for-profit. The Island has no Disneyland, although some people say Jones Beach in the summertime can be a strong rival, crowd-wise. But the state, county, and federal parks are

AT YOUR SERVICE

a big summertime employer for the area's youth.

After a day in the sun, visitors and residents may take a quick ride to a nearby movie theater, race track, bowling alley, night club, local arts event, or one of the large arenas such as the Nassau Veterans Coliseum or Westbury Music Fair. Long Island offers exciting night life and a wide variety of daytime fare, and that's all part of the service industry.

RETAIL INDUSTRY

Long Island is the place to buy, and Long Islanders love to shop—statistics bear that out. The Island ranks ninth in the nation in total retail sales, and first in the large metropolitan markets in per-household retail sales at more than $22,000 per household. Nassau County is the second and Suffolk the third highest retail sales county in New York. Only Manhattan tops them.

Although the Island has more than 30 million square feet of retail space in regional, community, and neighborhood shopping centers, retailers have difficulty finding store space to rent. The Island's retail store vacancy rate is only 2 percent, compared to the national average of 7 to 11 percent.

Smaller shopping centers are currently going up as fast as single-family housing went up after World War

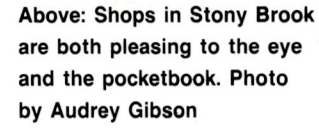

Above: Shops in Stony Brook are both pleasing to the eye and the pocketbook. Photo by Audrey Gibson

Left: The Garden City Hotel is one of the many fine hotels serving visitors to Long Island. Photo by Mary Ann Brockman

II, and older shopping centers are getting face-lifts. In the 1950s and 1960s giant regional malls were being constructed. Today it's local neighborhood shopping centers. They've become popular because Long Islanders like personalized shopping.

But Long Island's large, modern shopping malls still draw the biggest crowds. The largest shopping center is Roosevelt Field in Garden City, which opened in 1955. With 10,000 parking spaces and 2.2 million square feet of floor space, the 185-store complex is one of the largest indoor shopping malls in the country.

Green Acres Mall in Valley Stream isn't far behind. It has 1.6 million square feet, with 210 stores on 95 acres and 7,400 parking spaces. The Broadway Mall in Hicksville is the Island's third largest mall. Smith Haven in Lake Grove is fourth. They're followed in size by Sunrise Mall in Massapequa, the Walt Whitman Mall in Huntington Station, and the South Shore Mall in Bay Shore.

Other popular shopping spots are the Miracle Mile in Manhasset, Franklin Avenue in Garden City, Great Neck Plaza in Great Neck, and, of course, all the local Main Street shops in the many Island communities.

What's the number one store chain on Long Island? Abraham & Straus has the largest physical area of retail space—1.84 million square feet in seven Long Island branches. TSS-Seedmans has the most branches, with 10 stores taking up 1.799 million square feet, and Macy's is third with five stores and 1.6 million square feet.

The thousands of smaller retail stores, selling anything from cigars to living-room furniture, complete the shopping picture on the Island.

SUPERMARKETS

The Island also has numerous food stores and the distinction of serving as the site of America's first supermarket. In 1930 Michael Cullen opened his first King Kullen in Long Island's Jamaica. The public referred to it as a warehouse grocery. One pound of coffee sold for 25 cents; a pound of sirloin steak went for 29 cents.

From those bargain days the supermarket industry has grown by leaps and bounds. Sales from local checkouts are now more than $2.6 billion, and more than 24,000 Long Islanders are employed in the area's supermarkets.

King Kullen still has the most stores on the Island: 47. Waldbaum's, however, is narrowing the gap. It currently has 45 stores. New Jersey's Pathmark is third, followed by A&P and Foodtown.

REAL ESTATE

One of Long Island's first service industries was real estate. In 1639, when Lion Gardiner received the deed for his island, the Montauk Indians were witness to Long Island's first real estate transaction.

Today buying and selling Long Island real estate is big business. The Long Island Board of Realtors is made up of 7,500 licensed members from approximately 1,700 real estate offices, the largest real estate board in New York State. And those real estate brokers and agents specialize in residential real estate. There are hundreds of other brokers on Long Island who concentrate on commercial real estate.

A whopping 72 percent of all real estate licenses in New York State are in New York City and Long Island. That's because the Long Island real estate market did incredible business in the 1980s. Long Island is second only to Boston in the Northeast in the average selling price of houses. By early 1988 the average price of a home in Nassau County was $205,000, and in Suffolk it was $185,000, according to the Long Island Board of Realtors. Homes were appreciating at 15 percent a year for most of the 1980s.

Even though prices were the highest ever, businesses and individuals flocked to Long Island. And many Long Islanders stayed put. Three out of four homes sold in Nassau or Suffolk are sold to a Long Islander. While there is concern that affordable housing for young families and senior citizens is becoming scarce, Long Island continues as the place to be, and the Island's realtors are delighted.

MEDICAL CARE

Long Island is also the place to be if you become ill. It's no longer necessary to travel for special treatment. The Island boasts some of the finest health professionals in the world, and most of them are just a short car ride away.

Long Island has five private and 24 nonprofit hospitals, three of which are supported by government funding: the federal Veterans Administration Hospital in Northport; University Hospital at the State University of New York in Stony Brook; and one of the Island's largest hospitals with 644 beds, Nassau County Medical Center in East Meadow.

More than 40,000 nurses and almost 9,000 doctors are registered in the two counties. Long Island physicians cover every specialty. Doctors in Long Island hospitals are certified to perform intricate operations, including open-heart surgery and organ transplants. Some hospitals have extensive burn-care centers. Many have advanced diagnostic equipment, and five Long Island hospitals are so well recognized for their state-of-the-art surgical and research facilities that patients come to them from all over the world.

These hospitals, known as tertiary-care facilities, are: North Shore University Hospital in Manhasset, which is affiliated with Cornell Medical School and is the largest hospital on the island with 844 beds; Long Island Jewish-Hillside Medical Center in New Hyde Park, with its 150-bed Schneider Children's Hospital specializing in childhood diseases; St. Francis Hospital in Roslyn, known for its exceptional pediatric and adult-cardiac diagnostic and surgical programs; Nassau County Medical Center, which is home to the Long Island Poison Control Center; and University Hospital, part of the Health Sciences Center at the State Univer-

Top: The Port Jefferson shorefront is a popular tourist attraction. Photo by Ken Spencer

Above: The Montauk Point Coast Guard Station is one of several area Coast Guard facilities assisting thousands of Long Island boaters. Photo by Ken Spencer

Right: Many Long Islanders work in government positions. Serving as a park ranger on Fire Island is one of the more pleasant federal service jobs. Photo by Ken Spencer

59

LONG ISLAND

Above: Some of the Island's energy needs are met by this LILCO plant in Glenwood Landng. Photo by Ken Spencer

Facing page: EAB Plaza in Uniondale is perhaps the most recognizable office building complex on Long Island. Photo by Jeff Greenberg

sity of New York. The 19-story Health Sciences Center combines teaching, research, and hospital facilities. There are schools of medicine, dental medicine, nursing, allied health professions, and social welfare. More than 2,000 Long Islanders work there.

GOVERNMENT

Whether it's at the federal, state, county, or local level, government service is also an important part of the Island's service industry. More than 220,000 Long Islanders—about 18 percent of the Long Island work force—are government workers.

The federal government has several offices on Long Island, the largest being the Internal Revenue Regional Center—the Brookhaven Service Center in Holtsville. Come tax time, 4,000 Long Islanders are busy poring over 8.7 million tax returns there. The Brookhaven Service Center is responsible for all returns from New Jersey, New York City, Westchester, Rockland, Nassau, and Suffolk counties. On just the one day of April 16, 1986, the center sent $1 billion worth of tax checks to the bank.

But a greater amount of money comes back to the people. About three out of four taxpayers get refunds, so the thousands of Long Islanders who work at the IRS center aren't viewed by the public in quite the hostile way that revenue agents who also work on Long Island are.

Postal workers are another large segment of the Island's federal work force. It's Nassau, Suffolk, and local town governments, however, that are the backbone of government work on the Island. Whether park worker or county policeman, social worker or elected official, local government is a big employer on Long Island.

PUBLIC UTILITIES

Long Island's two large utilities, the Long Island Lighting Company (LILCO) and New York Telephone Company, probably offer the most important services to the Island. They certainly have the most customers.

More than one million electricity customers and 450,000 gas customers are serviced by LILCO's 6,300 employees. The utility has 46,000 miles of line and supplies power through five oil-fired power plants located in Northport, Port Jefferson, Glenwood Landing, Island Park, and Far Rockaway. The company's first nuclear plant, the Shoreham Nuclear Power Plant, has been the subject of debate for decades.

AT YOUR SERVICE

Long Island's power company is the biggest taxpayer on Long Island. In 1988 LILCO paid more than $258 million in property taxes to Nassau, Suffolk, and local communities.

New York Telephone also has a major impact on the Island's economy. With 7,600 employees, the telephone company's annual Long Island payroll is $238 million. And like LILCO, just about every Long Islander comes in contact with New York Telephone. With 532,000 residential customers in Nassau, 483,000 in Suffolk, and almost 120,000 business customers, New York Telephone company executives say Long Island, particularly Suffolk County, is the fastest-growing part of New York State for telephone service.

The area's telephone company has 50 local centers in Nassau and Suffolk, and in addition to offering telephone service to homes or businesses, New York Telephone has placed 25,000 pay phones at various locations on the Island.

FINANCIAL SERVICES

When you have the attractive mix of commercial business and affluent individuals that Long Island has, service businesses thrive. And so it is with the Island's financial industry. Banking, accounting, brokerage houses, and insurance companies are all finding Long Island a fertile territory for doing business. The headquarters for the financial services industry are centered in the communities of Melville, Woodbury, Lake Success, and Jericho.

BANKING

With such an affluent population, whose consumption and credit needs are among the highest in the country, Long Island is a popular site for the banking industry. The big banks, the large New York City money institutions, have all become part of Long Island's financial services. Chemical Bank, with over $3 billion in Long Island deposits and more than 80 local

LONG ISLAND

Small businesses are the backbone of the Long Island economy. Photo by Deborah E. Sarabia

branches; Citibank, the bank with the largest assets; Chase Manhattan; Manufacturers Hanover Trust Co.; Bank of New York; and Albany's Norstar Bank are all represented on the Island.

Long Island has also been called the bank back-office capital of America. With a quality work force and lower costs for office space than the financial capital of the world, nearby New York City, Long Island is the natural outlet for large banks to place their office personnel. European American Bank (EAB) is an example. Most of the EAB workers are based in EAB Plaza in Mitchel Field, which consists of two office buildings, each 15 stories high, and more than one million square feet of office space for its tenants.

Banking on Long Island, however, is not comprised of just large commercial banks. The independent local commercial banks offer hometown service, and thrift institutions, savings and loans, and credit unions are numerous, too.

ACCOUNTING AND INSURANCE

More than 7,000 certified public accountants do business on the Island. The nation's "Big Eight" accounting firms all have Long Island headquarters, and independent accountants abound. The reason accountants find the Long Island market so lucrative is that many Island companies are small entrepreneurial businesses, not large public corporations. Because they're small and privately owned, perhaps by a family, these businesses often require outside consulting—the bulk of the Long Island accounting business.

A CPA's major work on the Island is accounting and auditing—doing tax returns, checking the ledgers, etc.—but the large accounting firms now also offer management consulting, inventory management, and tax planning. But some things never change. While computers have started to play a major role in Long Island accounting firms, "the good old-fashioned calculator is still king," said Mike Borsuk, managing partner of Coopers & Lybrand.

In the 1980s Long Island had the largest concentration of national, regional, and branch insurance offices in all of New York State. Most are based in Woodbury.

Major insurance companies have come to Long Island because of its skilled white-collar workers and the desire to service the Island's small independent agencies, which numbered 1,250 in 1987. With much to protect, Long Islanders need a lot of insurance. Both personal and commercial life are handled by the Island's insurance companies.

LEGAL SERVICES

Long Island is known for its exceptional attorneys. Most of the large law firms on Long Island are based in Nassau County, where 5,300 lawyers belong to the Nassau County Bar Association. Suffolk lends itself more to the single practitioner, according to Suffolk County Bar Association statistics. The Suffolk association has 2,070 members.

More and more attorneys are hanging out their shingles in Nassau and Suffolk, thanks to the Island's law schools, Hofstra University and Touro, which are steadily adding to the Island's supply of bright young lawyers.

Long Island's attorneys are not only engaged in the private practice of law, but are also involved in public service. An example of this commitment is a local project that offers poverty-level Long Islanders free legal help. Known as the Pro Bono Project in Suffolk and the Volunteer Lawyers Project in Nassau, the effort consists of more than 1,000 private attorneys who volunteer to work without pay for indigent clients.

AT YOUR SERVICE

More than 5,000 Long Islanders have received help since the project first began in 1982. The Pro Bono effort is considered a trailblazer in the legal profession, and similar projects are beginning around the country.

ADVERTISING AND PUBLIC RELATIONS

Long Island's advertising and public relations agencies no longer sit in the shadows of their big-city counterparts. The high cost of Manhattan's Madison Avenue advertising agencies and the City's large public relations firms have brought business to the Island, and once there, clients stay.

Long Island's larger advertising agencies have become full-service agencies, offering broadcast campaigns, direct mail, and other state-of-the-art techniques. National and international clients now use Long Island businesses for their advertising needs. The smaller agencies offer quality work as well. Industrial advertising and trade publications are a large part of their business.

The Long Island Advertising Club has more than 600 members, making it fourth in the nation in membership size. Its annual BOLI (Best on Long Island) awards are as coveted by the local advertiser as an Emmy or an Oscar.

SMALL BUSINESS

The entrepreneurial spirit is alive and well on the Island. New businesses with growth potential are born every day, and most of them are in the service industry.

The glue that holds Long Island's economy together is the vigor and resoluteness of the small entrepreneurial firms. Of all the Island's companies, 90 percent are considered small businesses. More than 60,000 firms have only one to nine employees.

Long Island has so many successful small businesses, and so many ingenious entrepreneurs coming up with new ideas for businesses every year, that a complete list of small-business categories will probably never be compiled.

From the Island's automobile dealers, who sold more than $3.5 billion worth of cars in 1985, to the printing and graphics companies, the mail order businesses with 3.7 billion pieces of bulk mail shipped through local post offices, and the banner-towing operation of a small aviation company, the small businesses of the Island's service industry continue to thrive.

It's service with a smile on Long Island.

What Long Islanders Have to Say About The Service Industry

Kenneth Kenigsberg, M.D., pediatric surgeon, on why he chose to practice on Long Island:

Long Islanders have a high priority on medical care for children, and the hospital facilities are very good. And the Island is very beautiful. Long Island is just a nice place to practice, and it's easy on the eye.

C.R. "Rick" Merolla, president and CEO of Bank of Long Island:

I'm extremely bullish on Long Island. I think banking has a challenge on Long Island, the likes of which it's never had before. The fact that the Island's economy is booming and probably will continue to for the next five years creates a lot of excitement and challenge with regard to innovative loans and the demands for more types of service from the public.

Banking on Long Island is completely different than it was 10 years ago. We used to accept deposits, mostly in savings—we didn't have money market accounts or CDs to speak of—and we'd take those funds and put them into automobile, personal, or mortgage loans and that was it, a simple procedure.

From there we've now gone into commercial loans, lease financing, different types of mortgage loans, cash lines, credit cards, IRAs. There are so many different services that have been added to the menu, and the challenges of what more we can do, continue.

Douglas Ryder of Bay Shore, 16, food preparer at Robert Moses State Park (his first summer job):

I cooked the hamburgers and the hot dogs. I'm not going to do this stuff for the rest of my life—I hope to be a lawyer or a stockbroker—but it's pretty nice working at the ocean in the summertime. I'd like to work my way up to a "blue shirt"—those are the counter workers and the cashiers. They make more money.

Jeffrey Ryder (Doug's brother), 14 1/2, Newsday carrier:

I like being my own boss. I can deliver my 30 papers any time I want after school, and most of the people are nice. I guess I average about 10 cents a day tip from each house. And then there are the Christmas tips. I live for the Christmas tips.

V

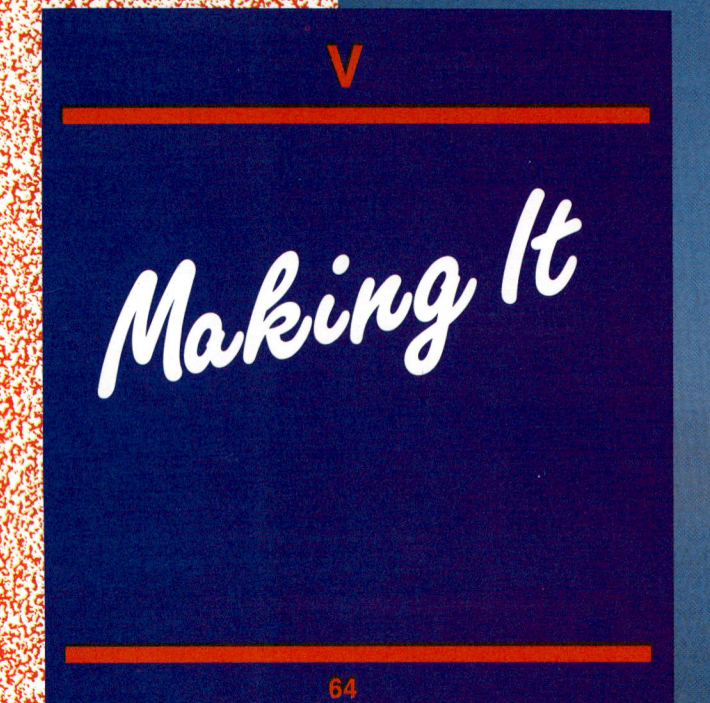

Making It

64

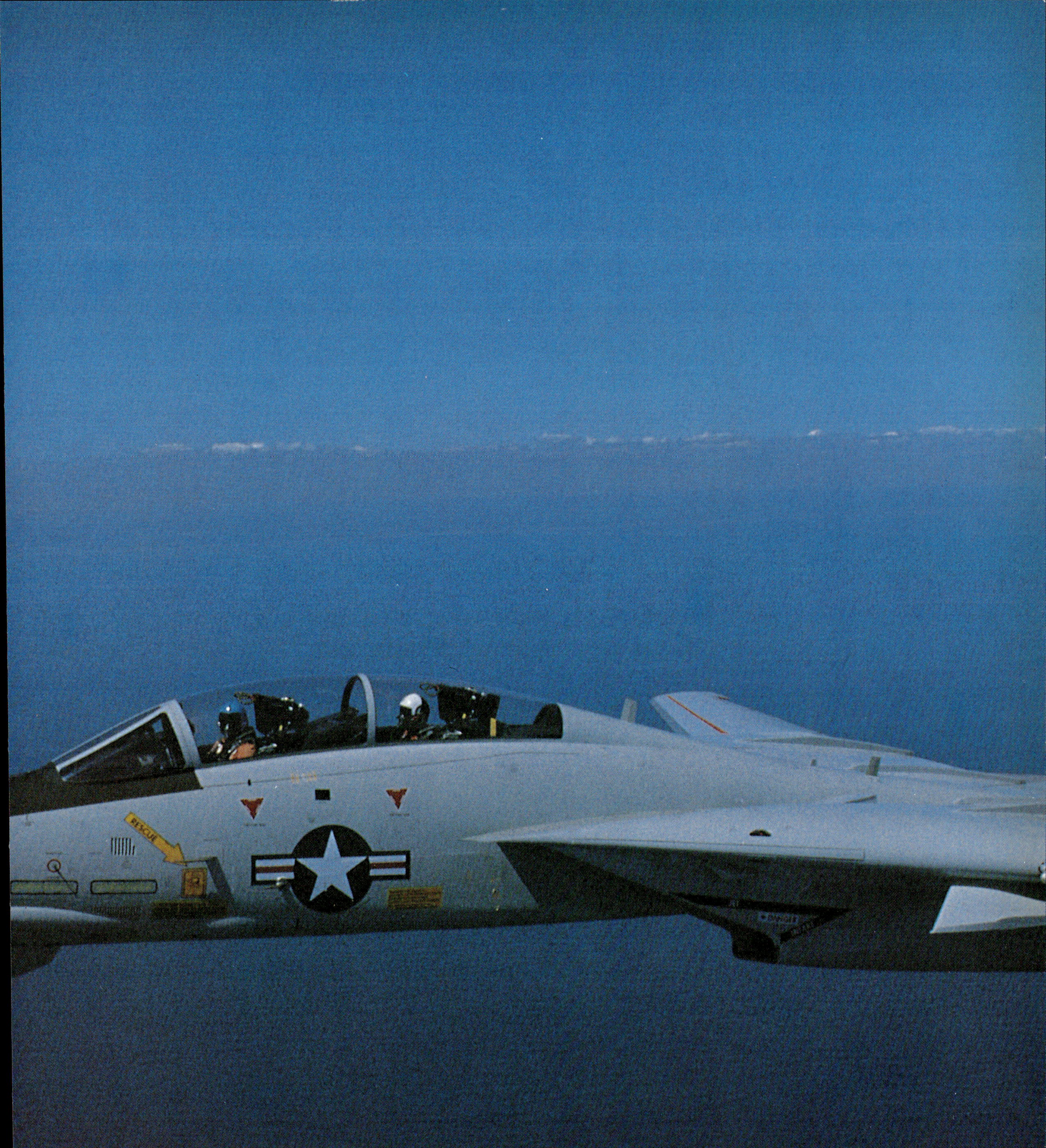
RESCUE

LONG ISLAND

Above: Although the Long Island economy is diversifying, defense contractors still constitute an important segment of the business community. Photo by Jeff Greenberg

Previous page: A Grumman F-14 soars over the Atlantic Ocean. Photo by Ken Spencer

Dressed in orange flight suits, their faces hidden behind large oxygen masks and hoses, the two naval officers crisply saluted as they taxied past in the battleship-gray fighter plane. A bright blue delivery truck with "Grumman" emblazoned on the side tagged behind.

Down to the end of the 10,000-foot runway adjacent to Grumman's Calverton plant the small caravan traveled, while a fire truck, several Grumman employees, and a visitor watched its progress. Now a distant gray speck, the F-14 turned and then stopped. It was time. The Grumman truck circled the $26-million aircraft for one last inspection.

"Get ready, this is going to happen fast," said Skip Conlon of Grumman's Calverton operation. "You may want to cover your ears, the sound is really something."

A low roar erupted from the end of the runway. "I think it's moving—yes, it's moving," Conlon shouted. "Here it comes!"

The speck of grey was suddenly a giant bird/plane racing forward, its arched-neck cockpit and twin tails about to take flight. Seconds later the F-14 was airborne, but stayed only a hundred or so feet off the ground as it gained speed and more speed until, with a roar of sound and power that vibrated through the body and made the hands go to the ears involuntarily, the supersonic aircraft tore past the small gathering on the taxiway. The twin afterburners glowed with fire, like the underside of a space shuttle rocket during its launch.

Gaining altitude, the fighter plane banked sharply to the left as it roared over the tower and soared into the blue sky above. It all had taken less than a minute.

"You want high-tech? That's high-tech," Conlon said.

Several miles away at Brookhaven National Laboratory in Upton, speed and power were also being measured, but in terms that challenge one's basic understanding.

Accelerating protons within one percent of the speed of light shared the stage with the world's most intense x-ray and ultraviolet light source. A dome-shaped nuclear reactor, Long Island's only operating nuclear plant and one of the most advanced research reactors in the world, was spewing out neutrons for scientific research.

Just another high-tech day on Long Island.

TECH ISLAND

Neutrons and protons, F-14s, computer software, semiconductors, lasers, and assorted advanced electronic and telecommunication equipment—that's manufacturing the Long Island way.

Long Island is Tech Island. Of the 26 high-tech industries listed by the U.S. Bureau of Labor Statistics, all but one are represented on Long Island. The only industry missing is oil petroleum refining. (As of yet, no major oil finds have been discovered off the shores of Long Island.)

The Island has the highest concentration of high-tech employment in New York State. More than 1,000 Long Island firms deal in high-tech manufacturing or research, and the Island ranks seventh nationwide in the number of high-technology manufacturing workers. The region was one of the few areas of the Northeast that increased manufacturing jobs during the early 1980s, and most of those jobs were in high-tech fields.

Long Island is also considered Tech Island because of its combination of high-technology businesses and support systems. There are 11 research and testing labs, 20 colleges and universities, and 23 technical associations.

The large number of high-quality educational institutions, the availability of venture capital, and the proximity to research facilities has put Long Island alongside Silicon Valley in California and the Route 128 corridor in Massachusetts as one of the country's high-tech leaders.

But unlike companies in Silicon Valley or on Route 128, the Island's high-tech firms are spread out over a far greater distance. For 100 miles, from the New York City line to the borders of the East End's farmland, research and development firms flourish alongside other Island businesses. This lack of geographical concentration is one reason Long Island's high-tech industry hasn't received the recognition it deserves. High-tech on Long Island is such a changing industry that 50 percent of the Island's high-tech companies surveyed by Chemical Bank said their products would become obsolete five years after production.

"You have to invest heavily in research and development," said Jack Carroll, a vice president of the Grumman Corporation. "It's 15 years from the day you start a brand new airplane until the first time it flies, and during that time technology is racing onward. The only way to keep up with it is to heavily support research and development, and we do."

ON THE DEFENSIVE

"DEE-fense" is a chant heard at many a New York sporting event. But it also has served for many years as the foundation of Long Island's economy. Much of the Island's high-tech business has come from the the United States government, particularly the Department of Defense, known in government parlance as the DOD.

Twenty-five years ago 20 percent of Long Island's entire economy was based on defense work. Today it's only 10 percent and the type of defense work is changing. As Paul Schreiber, *Newsday*'s high-technology writer puts it, "Long Island is making fewer airplanes but more innards." Contracts are shifting from the manufacturing of airplanes to electronics.

The change in Long Island's defense industry results from changes in Defense Department strategy. The military has been upgrading electronics and existing hardware rather than buying new airplanes. Priorities have switched as billions of dollars go into the Strategic Defense Initiative, or "Star Wars." Long Island defense companies are trying to keep up with that change.

While Long Island recently lost one of its major defense contractors—the Fairchild Republic Corporation—the Island still has a good mix of defense contracts and contractors, both prime and subcontractors. Small Long Island firms that once relied for subcontracting work on the Island's three prime contractors—Grumman, Sperry, and Fairchild—are going out on their own, and defense subcontracting firms are growing in number and in status.

ELECTRONICS AND AEROSPACE

What are those defense and other high-tech companies making? Aircraft and parts, communication equipment, and electronic components are the three categories that make up most of high-technology manufacturing on the Island. But George Soos, president of LIFT, The Long Island Forum for Technology, Inc., an unofficial lobbying group for the Island's high-tech industry, says a fourth category may soon be added.

"Biotechnology is going to play a significant role in the future of Long Island's high-tech industry," he predicted.

For now about two-thirds of the field is in electronics. Hazeltine, Unisys, the AIL division of the Eaton Corporation, and Harris Corporation are a few of the

LONG ISLAND

Above: Grumman employees work on the complex innards of an F-14. Photo by Ken Spencer

Facing page: A Grumman F-14 undergoes a final inspection before heading down the runway at Calverton. Photo by Ken Spencer

larger Long Island electronics firms that have helped make the area fifth in the nation in number of electronics companies. Avionics, computer peripherals, circuit boards, lasers, semiconductors, and satellite links are just a few of the wide variety of electronics manufactured on Long Island.

UP, UP, AND AWAY

Making airplanes is a Long Island tradition. The Island wasn't dubbed the "Cradle of Aviation" without good reason. Besides all the early flying feats that took place over Nassau County, Long Islanders were also building planes as early as 1909.

Modern-day airplane manufacturing began when Leroy Grumman founded his company in 1929 in a rented Baldwin garage. By World War II, airplane building was one of the major industries on Long Island.

"Rosie the Riveter" was alive and well on Long Island. Almost 90,000 Long Island men and women, many of the women doing assembly-line work for the first time, worked on the airplanes built during the war. Republic-Aviation Corporation (later Fairchild Republic) was the largest wartime producer of fighter aircraft. Grumman followed closely behind, and the Bethpage company was able to turn out 600 planes in just one month during the war.

Today about 29 percent of the Island's work force is employed in the manufacturing of aircraft and its parts. The aerospace industry pumps about $4.6 billion into the local economy. But there have been major changes in the Long Island aerospace industry.

Sperry Corporation in Great Neck, which made bomb sights during World War II, is now part of the Unisys Corporation. Sperry merged with Burroughs in 1986 to form the new company, and although its 5,100 employees in Great Neck are still working on defense electronics, submarines rather than planes are their main focus. Today Long Island Unisys employees work on guidance control systems for the Trident Submarine.

One of the sadder chapters in Long Island aerospace history occurred in 1987 when Fairchild Republic shut down after the Air Force decided to discontinue the T-46A jet trainers. It was the end of an era for loyal Fairchild workers. Only the Grumman Corporation, Long Island's largest employer, is still turning out airplanes like they were in the good old days.

MAKING IT

GRUMMAN

"The name Grumman on a plane is like sterling on silver," said a navy combat officer during World War II. Forty-five years later a Grumman-built plane still carries that reputation.

Hovering over their charges like doctors in a giant operating room, the aircraft assemblers at Grumman's Calverton plant are busy putting together newer versions of the most complex of military aircraft.

Lined up on one side of the massive assembly hangar are planes in the A-6 Intruder family, including the A-6E, an all-weather attack plane that can carry missiles or bombs. Across the aisle are the navy's fighter planes, the Tomcats, the F-14 and the F-14A+, the latter a newer version with an upgraded engine. The F-14D, due in 1990, will be even more advanced, with new digital avionics.

The F-14s, covered with a yellowish-green prime coat, sit in various stages of assembly as Grumman specialists add the high-technology components, including 31 miles of electrical cable that tie into 18,000 terminal points. Unlike an auto-assembly plant, the airplanes don't move down the line. It would be a little tough shifting 25 or 30 supersonic aircraft around each day. Instead, teams of assemblers come to the planes. The aircraft aren't moved until it's time to add the wings or put on the final coat of paint.

Walk down any Grumman airplane assembly line, and you'll see signs everywhere asking the workers to check for "FOD," foreign object debris. Cleanliness is next to godliness when you're building sophisticated aircraft. A small item dropped in the wrong place on an F-14 could not only mean the loss of a $26-million aircraft but "more importantly," as one Grumman official said, "people's lives." Apollo astronauts' lives were certainly on the line when they first landed on the moon on July 20, 1969. However, Grumman's lunar module landed them there safely (and returned them, too), making space history at the same time. Grumman employees have also built the space shuttle's wings and manufactured the shuttle training aircraft.

"Space has played a major role in Grumman's past, and it's important to our future," said Grumman's former chairman of the board, John C. Bierwirth. And so company officials were delighted when Grumman was recently awarded a new NASA contract to support the design and development of a space station. The contract could be worth $1.2 billion.

Although faces and projects have changed on the Grumman assembly line, being part of the Grumman "family" remains the same. Long Island's largest private employer has 25,000 Long Islanders currently working at its various locations—corporate headquarters in Bethpage, the data systems division in Brookhaven, and manufacturing plants in Bethpage, Calverton, and Great River. Just about every Long Islander knows somebody who's worked for Grumman, and many have shared in feasting on a Grumman Christmas turkey, or gotten the time from a Grumman retiree's gold watch.

"It's very easy to find three generations in a family working at Grumman," said Jack Carroll. "Sometimes people will ask, 'What do you want your kids to do when they grow up?' and the answer will be, 'Well, I don't want them to do what I do.' It's quite the opposite at Grumman. A lot of our people fully expect that when their kids grow up, this is where they're going to come to work."

If they do, they may not be working on the same project as their parents. Like other Island aerospace manufacturers, Grumman is diversifying. The company's other businesses include the manufacture of trucks, emergency vehicles, and data processing systems. Sales for all its divisions was $3.5 billion in 1986.

Grumman's business also has a major ripple effect on the Long Island economy. The corporation supplies much subcontracting work. Hundreds of small- and medium-size Long Island companies are doing business thanks to Grumman contracts.

For decades business observers have said, "As Grumman goes, so goes Long Island." In the 1980s many still felt the same way.

RESEARCH

From stomping feet to smashing atoms, an isolated area in the town of Brookhaven has served as the site for unusual goings-on. Camp Upton was a training camp for both world wars. Young GIs, including Irving Berlin, came to eastern Long Island to learn their "left, right, lefts" before being shipped off to Europe. After World War II, the army site became the headquarters of one of the nation's leading research labs.

Brookhaven National Laboratory, also known as Brookhaven, BNL, and simply, The Lab, sits on more than 5,200 acres of mostly scrub pine, just north of the Long Island Expressway. Only 800 acres of the property are currently being used, creating an expansive buffer zone that makes the lab a world all its own. With casually-dressed scientists bicycling past acres of green grass, tennis courts, a gymnasium, a hospital, and cafeteria, Brookhaven reminds one of a huge college campus. But as Anne Baittinger, a Brookhaven public relations official said, "There are very few ivy-covered walls here."

Most of the lab's buildings still look like army

barracks. That's because about one-third of them are. Former Camp Upton buildings now serve as office space for the lab's administration. And some barracks are still used for housing, but not for the likes of World War I Army Private Irving Berlin and his friends; 1,500 to 2,000 visiting scientists and educators now stay on the grounds of Brookhaven Lab each year.

Cooperative research is what the lab is all about, and visiting scientists, many from universities, use the lab's "big machines," as personnel refer to them, to do research not possible at their smaller institutions.

Brookhaven Laboratory, established in 1947, is about as high high-tech as you can get on Long Island. The lab, run by Associated Universities, Inc., and under contract with the U.S. Department of Energy, carries out research in basic and applied nuclear science, biomedical and environmental sciences, and energy technologies.

At Brookhaven, 3,200 employees work in facilities that are valued at almost $2 billion. The world's first nuclear reactor designed for peacetime research started up there in 1950. The lab was also the site for one of the first particle accelerators in the world. Atom smashing is a way of life at Brookhaven.

"There is a science culture here," said Dr. Bill Marcuse, head of the lab's Office of Research and Technology Application. "It's very hard for the world at large to recognize that there are people who really get their kicks out of finding out more about how atoms are connected or how molecules interact on the surface of a given kind of structure. They'd rather do that than maybe make another $50,000 a year applying themselves in other ways."

With synchotrons, polarized protons, ion beams, and an abundance of acronyms (BNL is just the start), it's almost as if they speak a different language at the lab. But scientists there tend to humanize their experience. White coats are kept to a minimum, and the individuality of some of the world's most brilliant scientists is always on display.

"Physics is good for you" reads the bumper sticker on a wall inside the High Flux Beam Reactor, a 60-megawatt, dome-shaped nuclear reactor that provides intense beams of thermal neutrons for research purposes.

A pink flamingo and mylar balloons adorn the ceiling in the National Synchotron Light Source, the source of the world's most intense x-ray and ultraviolet light. And huge goldfish-like carp swim in an aquarium in the control room of the Alternating Gradient Synchrotron (AGS), where protons race around a half-mile-long ring at energy levels of 33 billion electron volts, almost the speed of light.

If you loved physics in school, you'd love Brookhaven. Physics programs are the largest part of BNL's budget, and five scientists have won Nobel prizes for their physics work there.

Above: Some of the world's most prominent scientists have walked the grounds of the Cold Spring Harbor Laboratory. Photo by Colin Photographics

Facing page: Research facilities on Long Island, like the Cold Spring Harbor Laboratory, offer scientists the opportunity to work in historic settings. Photo by Colin Photographics

LONG ISLAND

COLD SPRING HARBOR LAB

Nobel prize winners are also in abundance in another renowned Long Island research facility, the Cold Spring Harbor Laboratory on the wooded North Shore of Nassau County. The lab claims the highest concentration of resident Nobel Laureates in the world.

While huge advanced-technology machines may be the order of the day at Brookhaven, microscopes are more the norm for Cold Spring Harbor scientists. It's a much more intimate scientific facility. The 300 employees, 90 of whom are scientists, work in picturesque nineteenth-century buildings, and most of the scientists live year-round on the 100-acre waterfront property.

Established in 1890, Cold Spring Harbor Lab carries out biological and cancer research. The lab has been at the forefront of DNA research since 1952, when scientists there proved that DNA is a molecule of heredity. A few years later the structure of DNA was discovered.

Each year the lab hosts the Cold Spring Harbor Symposium on Quantitative Biology, considered the most prestigious gathering of molecular biologists in the country. But Cold Spring Harbor administrators believe in reaching beyond the scientific community. Today the lab is bringing its DNA knowledge to the public. "We like to share the excitement of DNA science with the nonscientific public," said David Micklos, a spokesman for the lab. That's why, he added, the lab created two DNA mobile vans that make summer tours of high schools and colleges spreading the DNA word. Administrators have also established a DNA museum right on Main Street in Cold Spring Harbor.

Long Island is home to several other research facilities. Much research is done on the waters that surround the island and the marine life that lives there. And situated a little more than a mile off Orient Point is the mysterious Plum Island.

The 800-acre island is the site of the Plum Island Animal Disease Laboratory, which is run by the United States Department of Agriculture. The facility is the only location in the United States where highly contagious animal diseases not present in this country can be studied.

With about 250 employees, the Plum Island Laboratory is one of the largest employers for Suffolk's North Fork, but not many residents get to see its inner workings. Security is tight on the island that has conducted research on hoof-and-mouth disease, African Swine fever, and numerous human diseases such as Hong Kong Flu, Swine Flu, and AIDS.

ISLAND ALMA MATERS

Tucked away down a quiet country lane in Glen Cove is perhaps the world's smallest college. Webb Institute of Naval Architecture graduates approximately 20 students a year.

Talk about knowing your classmates. The entire student body at Webb usually averages less than 90. There's no tuition, the students pay just room and board, and everyone takes the same courses because everyone is training to be "the Frank Lloyd Wright of the shipbuilding world," according to Vice Admiral C. Russell Bryan, the former head of the college. Webb trains students to design ships and marine structures such as oil-drilling platforms. The student body at the four-year college is made up of some of the brightest college students in the country.

Webb Institute is just one of the 20 colleges and universities on Long Island where exceptional students and specialized degree programs abound. Long Island today has one of the most highly skilled and educated work forces in the nation. Much of the credit goes to local educational institutions.

Long Island colleges have been changing their programs to meet the growing needs of specialized personnel for the Island's high-tech businesses. For many years schools and businesses have worked together to keep the island's unemployment rate down. In 1912 New York State opened the first public college on Long Island in Farmingdale. Later mandated to meet the employment needs of the Island, Farmingdale State became the New York Agricultural and Technical College. Today, "Agricultural" is no longer a part of its name.

Most of the students at Farmingdale and at the majority of the Island's colleges are commuters. Parking is as important on a Long Island campus as obtaining books. Adelphi University in Garden City even took college commuting a step further, setting up Adelphi-on-Wheels via the Long Island Rail Road. The Adelphi LIRR classroom offered MBA study during the morning and evening rush hours through most of the 1980s.

Long Island has five public colleges and universities. Nassau Community College, a two-year school, has the largest enrollment, with more than 20,000 students; Suffolk Community College, another two-year school, is second with over 18,000. The State University of New York (SUNY) has campuses in Farmingdale; at Old Westbury, which is the only four-year public arts and sciences college in Nassau; and at Stony Brook, the Island's premier public university.

MAKING IT

Stony Brook has 11,500 undergraduates, 4,500 graduates, and a 1,400-member faculty. With its support staff, the university is the second-largest employer in the town of Brookhaven. The university ranks in the highest category of U.S. research campuses, and many consider it the Berkeley of the East. Its Health Sciences Center, where degrees are offered in medicine, nursing, and dentistry, includes University Hospital, the leading medical center in Suffolk County.

Stony Brook is working to be the site of an incubator facility for newly formed high-technology companies. The university plans on leasing space to between 15 and 30 high-tech entrepreneurs. A new company will work with college scientists and students, sharing high-tech knowledge until it reaches the point where it can function alone. Then it will move out and a new operation will occupy the incubator slot.

Hofstra University in Hempstead, with a student body of more than 11,000, is a private Long Island university that has achieved national recognition. The "Flying Dutchmen," as the students of Hofstra are nicknamed, have access to one of the finest college libraries in the country with more than one million volumes. Hofstra also has outstanding progams in law, business, and theater arts, and a television program that offers students the use of a new 35,000-square-foot building housing some of the

Above: Hofstra University is known for its cultural and educational contributions to the Island. photo by Mary Ann Brockman

Below: The C.W. Post campus of Long Island University is built on a former North Shore estate. Photo by Mary Ann Brockman

most advanced broadcasting equipment in the country.

Another fine university system is Long Island University. LIU has three campuses in Nassau and Suffolk counties: C.W. Post Center in Greenvale, which had an enrollment of 8,000 in the 1988-1989 school year; Southampton College in Southampton, with 1,320 students; and the LIU Brentwood campus, which had 1,065 students in 1988-1989, 715 of whom were graduate students.

LIU has been at the forefront of academic advances on the Island. In the fall of 1989 the University implements its LIU Plan, a "blueprint of change in higher education," according to Steve Bell, a C.W. Post official. LIU will offer alternating trimesters of classroom study and professional work experience. "It's a great first for a four-year institution in the metropolitan New York area," Bell said.

Other private colleges on Long Island include Adelphi University in Garden City, Long Island's first degree-granting liberal arts college; New York Institute of Technology, with campuses in Old Westbury, Commack, and Central Islip; Polytechnic Institute of New York in Farmingdale, which specializes in high-tech programs; Dowling College in Oakdale; Molloy College in Rockville Centre; St. Joseph's College in Patchogue; Friends World College in Lloyd Harbor; Five Towns College in Seaford; New York Chiropractic College in Old Westbury; and The Touro Law School in Huntington.

The Merchant Marine Academy in Kings Point rounds out Long Island's higher education institutions. Known as Kings Point, the academy is one of the nation's service academies similar to West Point or Annapolis. Situated on the former Walter P. Chrysler Estate, the academy is under the jurisdiction of the U.S. Maritime Administration. Cadets enrolled there will eventually go to sea on U.S. Merchant Marine ships.

PICKLES TO APPAREL

While high-tech gets the spotlight on the Island and research labs and college programs support that industry, Long Island offers other types of manufacturing. Machinery, apparel, metal products, printing and graphics, pharmaceuticals, and boats are just a few of the goods that can be stamped "Made on Long Island."

The Island may have been passed over during the Industrial Revolution because of a lack of falling water, but the area has more than made up for its slow start in manufacturing.

For the past seven years Suffolk County has been New York State's leading county in the number of manufacturing jobs. Industrial parks are as common in Suffolk as are beaches, and just about every type of product is being manufactured in those parks.

All kinds of things have been created on Long Island. Hicksville was once known as the Pickle Capital of the World. The H.J. Heinz pickle factory started operations there in 1898, processing not only pickles, but sauerkraut and ketchup as well. Hicksville's air must have had an interesting aroma in the early 1900s.

Shipbuilding was a major Island manufacturing industry during the 1800s. Port Jefferson was renowned as the Island's premier shipbuilding community, and the industry was also strong in Cold Spring Harbor and Greenport. Some of the famous China Clippers were built on the Island. And in the Brooklyn Navy Yard, where many Nassau residents worked, the Civil War battleship *Monitor* and the ship whose sinking led to the Spanish-American War, the *Maine*, were constructed.

Because of its proximity to Manhattan's garment district, Long Island has been one of the major centers for clothing manufacturing since the 1930s. The whirring sound from hundreds of sewing machines still can be heard in many of Suffolk's South Shore communities. From Christian Dior brassieres to Pierre Cardin suits, dresses to coats, lingerie, swimwear, sweaters, and sportswear, every type of clothing has been made on Long Island. But the 1980s were not the best of times for the 120 or so Long Island apparel contractors. Imports have hurt the industry and so has the shortage of seamstresses.

It has been a good time, however, for the Island's printing and graphic manufacturers and suppliers. Some say Long Island is becoming the printing and graphic capital of the United States. There are currently more than 800 printing-related manufacturers and publishers on the Island, from the one-man, fast-print shop to large publishing companies like Doubleday in Garden City.

CONSTRUCTION

It has also been a good time for the Island's construction business. Residential and commercial building is booming. New home and condominium construction remains strong, and new office buildings and industrial parks are popping up all over the Island.

In Uniondale, Mitchel Field, with its 1,265 acres set aside for office buildings and industrial plants, has seen much activity. It's one of the Island's major commercial/industrial centers.

While companies once viewed Melville as eastern Long Island, the Route 110 corridor is now considered Long Island's Main Street. Construction continues on just about every available inch of that roadway. The rest of the major commercial building is taking place to the east. Land and water is more available in Suffolk, and commercial builders are focusing their attention on Hauppauge, considered by many the industrial center of the Island, and on the Veterans Memorial Highway in Islip, where 9 million square feet of office and industrial space has been built in the last decade.

Brookhaven, Long Island's largest town—bigger in size than all of Nassau County—is experiencing tremendous growth. "Now is an excellent time to build in Brookhaven," said Jack Kulka, one of the Island's leading commercial builders. The town, which used to be considered Outer Mongolia by City folk, is welcoming new home buyers and businesses at a rate similar to Nassau County in the 1950s. A commercial acre in Brookhaven in 1984 cost $35,000; in 1988 it was $100,000.

Brookhaven is considered the Island's last frontier for commercial development. "No businessman is going to go out any further on the Island unless they build a high-speed monorail," Kulka said. But then decades ago builders said that about Huntington, now considered the center of the island.

EXPORTING

Exporting is an important part of Long Island manufacturing. In the early 1980s almost 41 percent of Long Island businesses were involved in international trade, and experts say the figure has increased since then. The Island is the second largest exporting area in terms of work force in the country, second only to Los Angeles.

Some of the exporters have set up in Long Island's Foreign Trade Zone, a 52-acre industrial park located in the southeast corner of Long Island MacArthur Airport in Islip.

The Trade Zone is considered to be outside the country for purposes of U.S. Customs, so companies can bring in goods for storage, assembly, or manufacture without paying duty or taxes. Duty is paid, however, if the goods are later shipped to a destination in the United States. Manufacturing on Long Island, whether for export or domestic distribution, and whether involving the newest of technologies or standard products the public has come to trust, continues to be a major employment base for the Island's work force. "Made on Long Island" is here to stay.

What Long Islanders Have to Say About High-Tech

John J. "Jack" Carroll, vice president of community affairs, Grumman Corporation, on the changes in aircraft manufacturing:

It used to be that we'd be competing for a new plane every year. Now the competition for new planes comes along every 8 to 10 years, and the projects are so costly and so complex, an individual company can't bid alone. You put together a team of companies to bid.

On Grumman leaving Long Island:

The greatest misconception people have is that we're going to move off Long Island. You could move the bricks and the machinery, take the fence down from around our plants, but what makes Grumman are the 25,000 Long Islanders who work here, from the guy who gets to work at 3 a.m. to butter the rolls, to the guards, to the engineers, to the secretaries. They're not a transportable asset. We're a community and you can't move that.

Dr. Bill Marcuse, head of the Office of Research and Technology Application, Brookhaven National Laboratory, on bringing business and research labs together:

Historically there's been a hostile or alienated relationship between government laboratories and industry. On the one hand the industrial side has its negative view. And on the other, scientists, just because of the nature of their culture, have not been interested in potential applications. We're trying to change all that.

Brookhaven Lab is being proactive, setting up workshops with industry and lab officials. Somehow, to maintain our competitive position, we've got to get the products that come out of government laboratories into commercialization early enough to be ahead of the rest of the world.

VI

Farming the Land and Sea

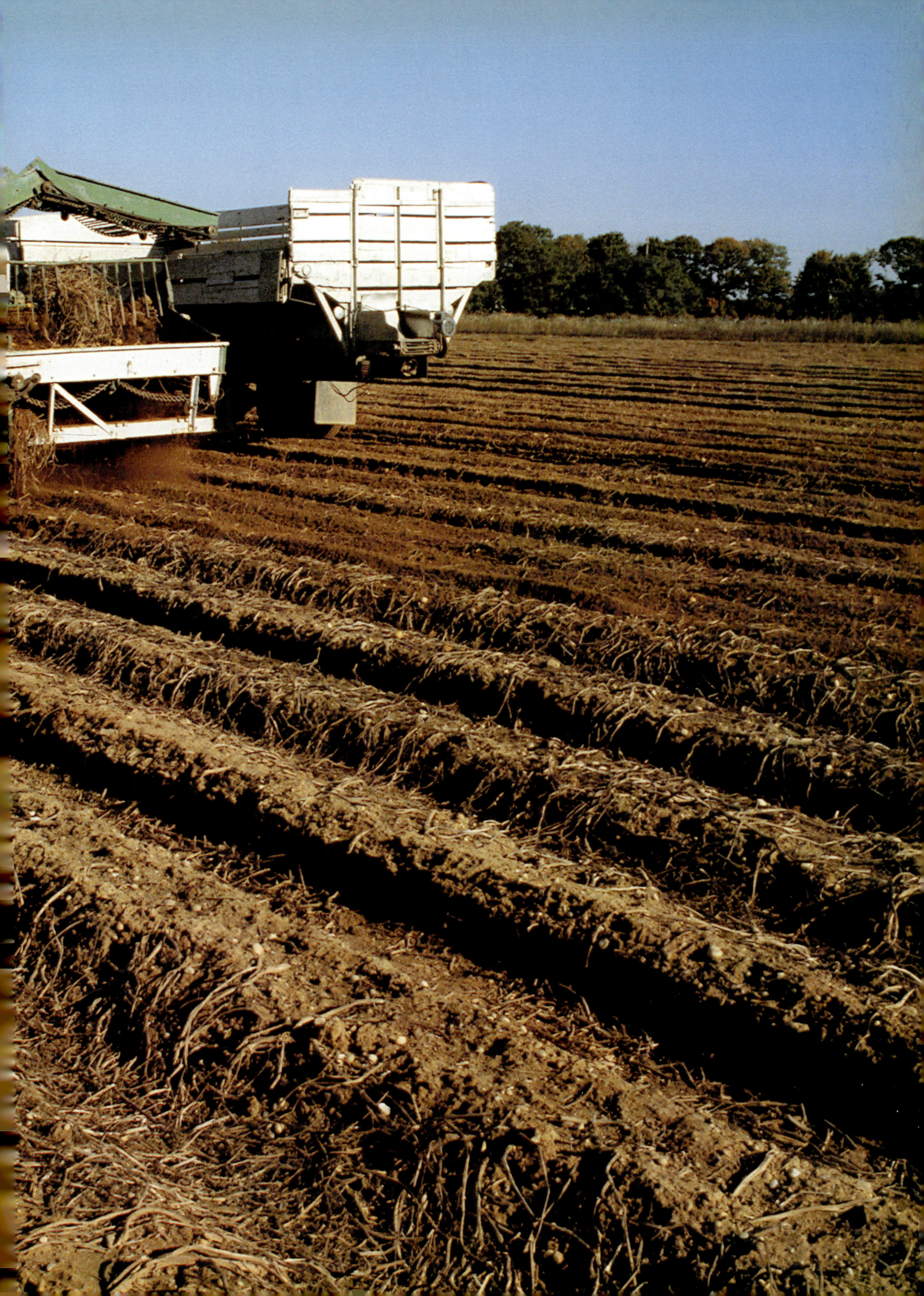

LONG ISLAND

Above: From Fort Salonga to Orient, apple orchards are a common sight. Photo by Ken Spencer

Previous page: It's potato harvest time on the Wells Farm in Riverhead. Photo by Ken Spencer

Facing page, top: From the air a North Fork farm forms an oasis in the midst of plowed fields. Photo by Ken Spencer

Facing page, bottom: Fruit is a popular Long Island crop. These peaches are from the orchards of the Wickham Farm. Photo by Ken Spencer

A ball of red fire, the August setting sun cast crimson highlights on the already red hair of Long Island potato farmer Vernon F. Wells, Jr., as he pulled a bushy green potato plant from the soil.

"Here they are," announced the 57-year-old, freckle-faced farmer as six pale brown potatoes popped out of the earth. "There should be more; it's early yet."

It's the beginning of potato harvest time on Long Island. The beginning of another season of hope—hope for a good crop, hope for a good price. Potato farmers like Wells of Riverhead have done their fair share of hoping these past few years. With potato prices fluctuating, the potato, once the mainstay of Long Island farming, isn't always the farmer's pride or joy these days.

Forty years ago Long Island farming meant potato farming. Tens of thousands of acres of potato fields blanketed the Nassau and Suffolk landscape. Long Island was one of the top three potato-producing regions in the country, and the spud was king, even queen. A Long Island Potato Queen reigned over the Potato Blossom Ball.

Long Island was farm country back then, 145,000 acres worth. The Island was known for the products it harvested both on the land and in the sea. Duck farms shared the spotlight with potato farms, and the Island's waters were home to some of the world's finest clams, oysters, and scallops.

But with development came change. The potato farms of Nassau gave way to Levittown and other suburban communities. In Suffolk, New York State's leading agricultural county, potato acreage shrunk to only 9,000 of the 40,000 acres still used for agriculture in 1988. The shellfish industry, hurt by water pollution and the mysterious brown tide or algae bloom, fell upon hard times. Duck farms shrunk in size, too.

Long Island farming is not dying, however. It's just changing. Long Island's farmers "are undergoing an evolution," according to Bill Sanok of the Suffolk County Cooperative Extension Office. "Industries have to evolve if they wish to survive," he said, and so the Island's farming industry is doing just that. Diversification is the key.

Horse farms and vineyards are replacing the old potato farms. The East End of Long Island is "the ideal spot" for vineyards, according to Alex Hargrave of the Hargrave Vineyard in Cutchogue. Cauliflower, cabbage, and corn are popular and profitable Long Island crops. And along with the $100-million Long Island agricultural food industry, $50 million more now comes from horticulture—nursery stock, flowers, and sod farms.

SOUND AVENUE

Drive along Sound Avenue on the North Fork in the late summer or early fall and you will see, smell, and breathe the new farming on Long Island. This two-lane, curving road has been called the Island's agricultural Main Street, and come harvest time, green or yellow tractors swirl up dust and slow down traffic as they make their way to cultivated fields or rural side roads. Farm stands, large and small, dot every available vacant piece of land.

It is on this modest east-west thoroughfare that the changes in Long Island farming are most apparent. Wells' farmhouse and parts of his potato farm still sit on Sound Avenue. So do other vegetable farms. But Sound Avenue is also home to newer horse farms, like the expansive Big E Farm surrounded by its acres of brown fencing. And further down the road, where it expands to four lanes and changes names, there are grapes growing in places like Hargrave's 50-acre vineyard. Old and new farming sit side by side on Sound Avenue.

FARMING'S PAST

The first farms on Long Island date back to the first Long Islanders. Wells, a 10th-generation Long Island farmer, still cultivates part of the land where his ancestors turned the earth in 1661. The Wells farm on Sound Avenue is the oldest continuously running farm in New York State. But before the Wellses and other settlers arrived, Long Island's first farmers, the Indians, were growing corn. And they were using their dugout ca-

79

LONG ISLAND

noes for fishing, which also makes them the Island's original baymen.

European settlers are credited with introducing livestock to the Island's agricultural community. Sheep and cattle thrived on the massive 60,000-acre Hempstead Plains, a natural pasture region, Long Island's home on the range.

Long Island became the Texas of colonial America. In Hempstead the cow was so much a part of daily life that it was a unit of exchange. Taxes were paid in cattle "delivered alive."

Cows and sheep also munched away on the meadows of Montauk, which was the site of the country's first cattle ranch and home to the first cowboy in 1747. The Island's peninsulas made natural cattle and sheep pens, and nearby marsh grass was used as fodder. Each year on the second Tuesday of September, a gala sedge grass harvesting day was held. Livestock owners from all over the Island came together to harvest the salt grass for their animals.

Wheat, oats, and rye were grown on the Island also. On eastern Long Island you can still see windmills where grain was ground to flour. But by the mid-1800s the cheaper lands out West were preferred for growing wheat and raising livestock. The sea then became the site of the Island's harvest. Whaling put the communities of Sag Harbor and Cold Spring Harbor on the map, and the shellfish industry of the Great South Bay soon had an international reputation.

Blue Point oysters, named after the South Shore waterfront community in whose waters they were found, were famous the world over. At the turn of the century New York City residents were spending more money on Long Island oysters than on meat. When the Great South Bay oysters died off in the 1930s, clams, previously thought of as "the poor man's shellfish," came into favor. Then the Peconic Bay Scallop joined the gourmet's most favored list. Long Island shellfish were soon in demand everywhere.

Back on land, potatoes were introduced in the early 1900s, and farming once again took off. Decades later cauliflower, cabbage, and other vegetable crops made truck farming a popular business. Farmers with small plots would grow different types of vegetables and then truck the produce into the city or to various farmers' markets on Long Island.

THE POTATO FARMER

Certain names are synonymous with Long Island farming—Wickham, Hallock, Talmage, and Wells. Like their ancestors before them, Vernon F. Wells, Jr., and his sons—Dan, Craig, and Todd—are potato farmers, although Vernon is quick to add, "We grow a lot of cabbage and just about everything else." Today the family farms about 650 acres. They own 200 acres and

Left: On the North Fork, farm workers load a truck with boxes of fresh produce. Photo by Ken Spencer

Facing page, top: The Long Island potato has been a staple of Long Island farming for fifty years. Photo by Ken Spencer

Facing page, bottom: Long Island grapes ripen in the sun. Photo by Ken Spencer

rent the rest. Most of their potatoes are sold to Puerto Rico, according to the senior Wells.

The only son of Vernon F. Wells, Vernon Jr. stayed in farming, he said, "because I never knew another way of life, and as an only son, there was plenty to do."

There still is. Wells and his three sons work 11 hours a day, almost every day. "The work now is more demanding than when I was young," said the red-haired farmer, now a grandfather. "It was Dad and me with 150 acres, and we had time to enjoy ourselves. I could go fishing. Now we have 650 acres and there's never time to do anything. The farm owns us instead of us owning the farm."

But the reserved and cautious Wells softens when he speaks of his love of farming. "There are times when you see a beautiful crop, and you feel like you're providing something people are going to get a great benefit out of—then it's all worthwhile," he said. "I can't see myself moving to Florida when I retire. I'll stay here and watch my sons farm."

Tax increases and the high cost of living, along with the higher value of land, have hurt the potato farmer. "If you can get $100,000 an acre on the South Fork there's no way you can justify putting potatoes on it," Wells said. That's true of the North Fork as well.

But agriculture experts say potato farming will survive on Long Island. "We'll see potatoes forever on Long Island, but it's going to decline to specialty farming," predicted Ron Leuthardt, the former executive secretary of the 2,500-member Long Island Farm Bureau.

Vernon Wells symbolizes the old-time Long Island farmer. He's not pleased with the direction farming is going. "Things keep changing. You can't spray from the air in some places because of development, and sometimes it takes 10 minutes to get across the road with my tractor."

"Sometimes I feel like an Indian," Wells said. "This was Indian country for so long and then with the changes they were forced out. It may be the same with us farmers."

THE GRAPE GROWER

Long Island's modern farmer is epitomized by erudite grape grower Alex Hargrave of Cutchogue. The lanky six-foot, six-inch vintner, who has a master's degree from Harvard in Chinese languages, said: "Agriculture is as much an art as a technical science."

Hargrave lives with his wife, Louisa, and children, Anne and Zander, in an attractive modern home, complete with swimming pool, behind his 50-acre vineyard. The first modern-day wine grape grower on the North Fork, Hargrave started his vineyard in 1973. He chose the area, he said, because of the "total climate and sandy soil. Long Island is like Bordeaux, it's surrounded by water. The soil is light, sandy, and pebbly—just what the grapes want. It's the most ideal spot you can find," he said.

Hargrave became animated when he talked of his type of farming. "The beauty of wine as a product is that you can follow it after the harvest," he said. "It doesn't rot in three months like other crops. It assumes another life—the transformation of harvest."

And what's special about Long Island wine, according to Hargrave, is that "Long Islanders have the chance to see and follow the wines and the wine

LONG ISLAND

personalities in the seasons they've lived through." The wines of 1985, for example, are the year of Hurricane Gloria. "Long Islanders can understand more about the wine because they've been there," Hargrave said. "There aren't many people that reside in the Napa Valley."

The vintners of Napa Valley are watching Long Island grape growers like Alex Hargrave. California currently produces 75 percent of all domestic wines. But Long Island, with its 40 vineyards, 10 wineries, and one million bottles of wine produced annually, is becoming a force to be reckoned with.

The Island's vineyards are located mostly on the North Fork, but a few do well on the South Fork, and Villa Banfi is harvesting grapes in Old Brookville just 45 minutes from Broadway. Several of the wineries offer tours for the public. Long Island's fine wines are winning prizes and gaining in reputation. The Island's largest vineyard, Pindar Vineyard in Peconic, is beginning to distribute its wines nationwide. And last year Pindar and Lenz Vineyards came out with Long Island's first champagnes.

"Long Island wines can stand on their feet the world over; they have the ripeness and smoothness of any great wine," Hargrave said. "The wines of Long Island have earned a place on the banquet table of agriculture."

DUCK FACTS

The Long Island duckling has been a star on the agricultural banquet table for decades. The succulent White Pekin ducks first came to Long Island in 1873—by boat. A sea captain brought five of them all the way from Peking, China. The Pekings, their name shortened to Pekins—the Long Island accent strikes again—were given to a local farmer. They obviously adapted well to the Island, for 20 years later there were 200,000 of them. By 1922 there were 2 million, and by 1940 more than 7 million White Pekin ducks, 60 percent of the ducks sold nationwide, were being raised each year on Long Island

In 1948 a virus hit the Island's duck farms and almost 90 percent of the birds died. Duck farmers recovered from that disaster but soon were fighting development and environmental concerns. "There were 125 duck farms in 1940, 26 in 1976, and by 1988 you'll probably see only a few," said Leuthardt of the Long Island Farm Bureau.

"Duck farms declined because of environmental reasons," he continued. "The Department of Enviromental Conservation came in and said we've got to clean up the bays and creeks but at the expense of the duck grower, not the public."

The Long Island duckling and the Long Island

Left: Alex Hargrave samples his vineyard's wine. Photo by Ken Spencer

Facing page, top: Suffolk County's Big Duck, formerly a roadside food stand and now a preserved landmark, may have as many loyal fans as the New York Islanders. Photo by Ken Spencer

duck industry continues to survive, however, because, as Leuthardt said, "It's a name people have come to respect for good quality."

A few lighter facts about Long Island's commercial ducks: Ducks are called ducks because they duck in and out of the water, but many of Long Island's white ducks never see the water. More and more are being raised indoors. They never swim. They can't fly either. Domesticating ducks weakens their wing muscles, making them lazy, and after three or four generations they lose the ability to fly. The white ducks you see at local ponds are Pekins that were either brought there, perhaps Easter gifts that grew unmanageable, or were born there. They'll stay at those ponds until they die or someone carries them away.

Every spring the Center Moriches Chamber of Commerce sponsors a duck race. For a couple of dollars you can rent a Pekin, courtesy of a local duck farm, and race him or her for prizes. Racers aren't allowed to touch the ducks, so you'll see hundreds of adults and children clapping their hands, stomping their feet, screaming, pleading, or crying to get their ducks to move. It's almost as entertaining to watch as it is to race.

"The Big Duck" has been a Suffolk County landmark since the 1930s. The 20-foot-high, 30-foot-long concrete white duck, with Model T taillights as eyes, was originally built as a sales office for a local duck farmer. Today it's a nationally recognized example of roadside architecture.

FARMING FACTS

Want to become a Long Island farm expert? Here are a few miscellaneous facts about Long Island's agriculture.

Farmingdale and Farmingville are no longer farming communities. While a few hundred acres are still cultivated in Nassau County and western Suffolk, most farms are located out east in the towns of Riverhead, Southold, and Southampton.

Sixty-five varieties of vegetables are grown on Long Island, from asparagus to zucchini. There are even farms that specialize in oriental vegetables.

The Island is number one in the United States in fall harvest of cauliflower.

Long Island corn is sold only on Long Island. Residents and visitors buy so much of it at local farm stands and supermarkets that there's no need to ship any off the Island.

Long Island farmers produce not only vegetables. With a 180-day growing season, many fruits are cultivated. There are apple and peach orchards, and strawberry fields. Suffolk was one of the major cranberry-producing sites in the early 1900s. The last cranberry bog closed in 1974, but there has been talk of reviving the industry.

Pick-your-own is a popular Long Island tradition. From the strawberries of June to the pumpkins of fall, young and old enjoy field harvesting on their own the Island's delicious fruits.

HORSES AND HORTICULTURE

With sleek brown Thoroughbreds grazing on fields of green, the horse farms of Long Island are the most picturesque of the agricultural businesses. Horse farms can be found from Suffolk's Montauk to Nassau's North Shore, making Long Island the largest single region in the state for Thoroughbred operations. Nationally the area ranks only behind Kentucky, California, and Florida.

Both Thoroughbreds and Standardbreds, or trotters, are bred and trained on the Island. The Big E Farm in Riverhead, owned by the Entenmanns, the former baking family, is the Island's largest operation. With 450 acres of grazing land, paddocks, stables, and a half-mile track, the horse farm on Sound Avenue is an impressive operation.

With the thriving industry of real estate on Long

Top: A boat, a fishing rod, and a gorgeous sunrise; what better way to spend a Long Island morning? Photo by Ken Spencer

Above: Oyster Bay still holds a fine supply of oysters. Photo by Ken Spencer

Right: Fishing is fine off Montauk. Here, blues are the "catch of the day." Photo by Ken Spencer

Island, the growing and selling of sod, shrubs, trees, and flowers to landscape new homes, condominiums, and office buildings has become an extremely successful agricultural endeavor.

The acres and acres of luscious green sod that make up the Island's sod farms are located on the East End and in Western Suffolk. Suffolk County produces almost 50 percent of New York State's nursery crops—shrubs, evergreen, rhododendrons, azaleas, shade and ornamental trees, and perennial flowers.

THE FARMERS OF THE SEA

A bayman, it's said, is someone who can drop a dime overboard and the next day go back and find it. Long Island baymen know the water like Long Island farmers know the soil.

Shellfishing, like farming, is more than an industry. It's a tradition. From generation to generation, clammers have used the same equipment, the tongs and rakes, even the same boats that their fathers and grandfathers used.

Although the scallop, oyster, and hard clam industries are not what they once were in volume or profit, there is a pride in the baymen of Long Island hard to match anywhere. And the smell of the sea continues to be as great a lure to some Long Islanders as the smell of the soil.

"To understand a bayman you have to understand the desire to catch," said Steven Nyland, a bayman from Sayville. "Catching is everything. There are some who only pursue it for money but for most of us it's the thrill of bringing in the catch."

CLAMMING

For decades clamming Long Island's waters meant freedom—freedom from the structure of a nine-to-five job, freedom to be your own boss, and freedom to be on the water and to bring in as much of a catch as you wanted. All that was needed was a small boat with an engine, some rakes or tongs, and some muscle. Although it can get mighty cold on the bay in December and January, a clammer's life was looked on with envy.

In 1976 Long Island led the nation in commercial clam production. Of the three Long Island hard clam sizes—from the smallest, called littlenecks or necks, to cherrystone size, to the largest chowder clams—750,000 bushels were sold. More than 6,000 licensed clammers, most of them in the Great South Bay, raked or tonged for clams in 1980. Baymen used to joke that on a beautiful summer day you could walk across the bay from clam boat to clam boat and never touch water.

But the glory days of clamming came to an end in the 1980s. Soft clams or steamers all but disappeared and by 1985 only 177,000 bushels of hard clams were harvested. Monetarily the value to the local economy went from a high of $75 million to $41 million. By the end of the 1980s only 2,000 baymen were still clamming.

Overharvesting, pollution, and greater salinity in the bay are some of the reasons the hard clam decreased so dramatically. Clammers now have to deal with certified and uncertified waters and regulations from the state and the town. The once free-spirited clammers are now hard-pressed to make any kind of a living.

OYSTERS

Before Long Island clams became a popular food, Long Island oysters were in favor, specifically the Blue Point oyster from the Great South Bay.

By 1900 oyster bars and oyster restaurants were the rage. Almost 2 million bushels of Blue Point oysters were harvested annually and shipped to markets in New York, San Francisco, Liverpool, and London.

For a variety of reasons, overharvesting and disease among them, oysters died off in the Great South Bay, and Long Island Sound became the harvesting area. The Suffolk Marine Museum in West Sayville has interesting exhibits of what the Great South Bay oystering industry was like.

As late as 1930 there were 50 Island oyster companies and 100 more from Connecticut working the Sound. Today the only full-scale Long Island oyster operation is the 100-year-old company, Frank M. Flower & Sons, Inc., in Bayville and Oyster Bay. Flower & Sons survive because they are involved in mariculture. Oysters are planted in oyster beds and harvested when they reach maturity.

SCALLOPS, CRABS, AND LOBSTERS

The delicate sweet taste of Long Island bay scallops, and specifically the Peconic Bay Scallop, has been a draw for seafood lovers everywhere. But for the last few years the brown tide, made up of small, single-cell algae, has wreaked havoc on the industry.

While sea scallops are harvested by large dredges

and opened by machine, the delicate, smaller bay scallop is harvested by hand-hauled dredges and opened by hand, and the bay scallop has a harvesting season of late September to March 31. In 1981, 200 commercial fishermen and 150 part-timers raced out the first day of scallop season. In 1986 and 1987 there were no seasons. The scallops had all but disappeared because of the algae bloom. No one has yet determined the cause of the brown tide, but in 1988 it moved somewhat from the East End of the Island to Suffolk's South Shore, causing some relief to the scallopers but concern to the South Shore clammers. Marine biologists are hopeful the scallop industry will come back. Scallops are being transplanted from other areas, and recently the brown tide has not been as severe as in past years.

Blue claw crabs from the many sheltered waterways and lobsters from Long Island Sound, although not major revenue producers, complete the Island's shellfish menu.

FISHING

Although many a Long Islander may spend a lazy summer afternoon out on the family boat fishing for flounder, weakfish, or fluke, Long Island's fishing is not just recreational. Commercial fishing is a $40-million-a-year industry, and large fishing vessels go out just about every day from the ports of Montauk, Hampton Bays (Shinnecock Inlet), Freeport (Jones Inlet), the Great South Bay (Fire Island Inlet), Greenport, Mattituck, Oyster Bay, and Port Jefferson. Every type of fish caught by a summer recreational fisherman is caught in quantity by the Island's commercial fishermen. So are other varieties—70 different types of fin-fish in all.

For the past few years, however, striped bass, a popular fish, has not been one of them. Fearful of the possible carcinogen PCB, which has been found in bass, New York State officials put a total ban on commercial striped bass fishing. This has affected Long Island's haul-seiners especially.

Haul-seining consists of casting nets in the water

to trap fish and "hauling" them back to shore. The process started in the mid-eighteenth century with a fish called the menhaden. Long Island was the center for the menhaden industry for more than 150 years. The small, herring-like fish was harvested off the beach and then brought to local factories for processing as fish meal and oil. Menhaden are now caught farther south.

Striped bass then became the haul-seiners' main catch. Although there are other species of fish that can be caught close to the beach, none have the market value today of the striped bass. The bass ban has devastated the haul-seining industry. Long Island fishermen continue to lobby for its removal.

The $2-million tuna fishing business, however, is thriving, thanks to Japan's voracious appetite for sushi and sashimi. The giant bluefin tuna is the rarest and most prized by the Japanese. That and other varieties of tuna are caught off Montauk, and about 70 percent of them are shipped off to Japan.

FARMING'S FUTURE

While shellfishing and farming have had some challenging times in the last decade, local government and industry are working on management programs that should ensure the future of these important Long Island industries.

In the shellfish industry, mariculture or aquaculture programs where clams and oysters are grown under supervision are becoming more popular, and the transferring of clams from polluted areas to cleaner areas where they can purify themselves has also helped the industry.

The Farmland Preservation Act, started in 1976 by then-Suffolk County Executive John V.N. Klein, has helped keep working farms on the farmland of Suffolk County. The first such program in the nation, the preservation project allows the county to buy development rights from the farmers. Local towns have set up preservation programs too. With the money obtained for the rights, many farmers have been able to remain on their land. Those who choose to sell later have covenants which dictate that future land use must remain agricultural.

Although Long Island farming will never die, industry observers say it will never again be dominated by a few crops. "You're going to see smaller farms and more specialities," predicted Leuthardt of the Farm Bureau. "We'll still have open fields and lots of green, but it will be more than just potatoes."

FARMING THE LAND AND SEA

> ### What Long Islanders Have to Say About Farming
>
> *Ron Leuthardt, former executive secretary, Long Island Farm Bureau, on homeowners building near farms:*
> I wish we could have more tolerance from our new neighbors. The blowing dust from the helicopters that spray pesticides at 5 a.m., the guns going off in the vineyards to scare away the birds—a farmer would just as soon sleep as a homeowner. But he has to do these things. If you plow, there's going to be dust. To save your crop you have to spray; these are not permanent things. There's a period of time when the industry creates nuisances, and we know they are nuisances, but it's part of the farming practice. I just wish people would be more tolerant.
>
> *Vernon Wells, Jr., potato farmer, regarding waterfront property:*
> We thought the land by the Sound was worthless, just a junk heap. We would drag a dead cow or horse up to the north end and just leave it there for the foxes to eat.
> *On what the land means to him:*
> My selling a piece of land is like cutting off my arm. You get attached to it. I know every hill and rock of the farm. It's like a good pet.

Facing page: This roadside stand in Southold is one of hundreds selling Long Island's fresh farm produce. Photo by Ken Spencer

VII

On the Move

88

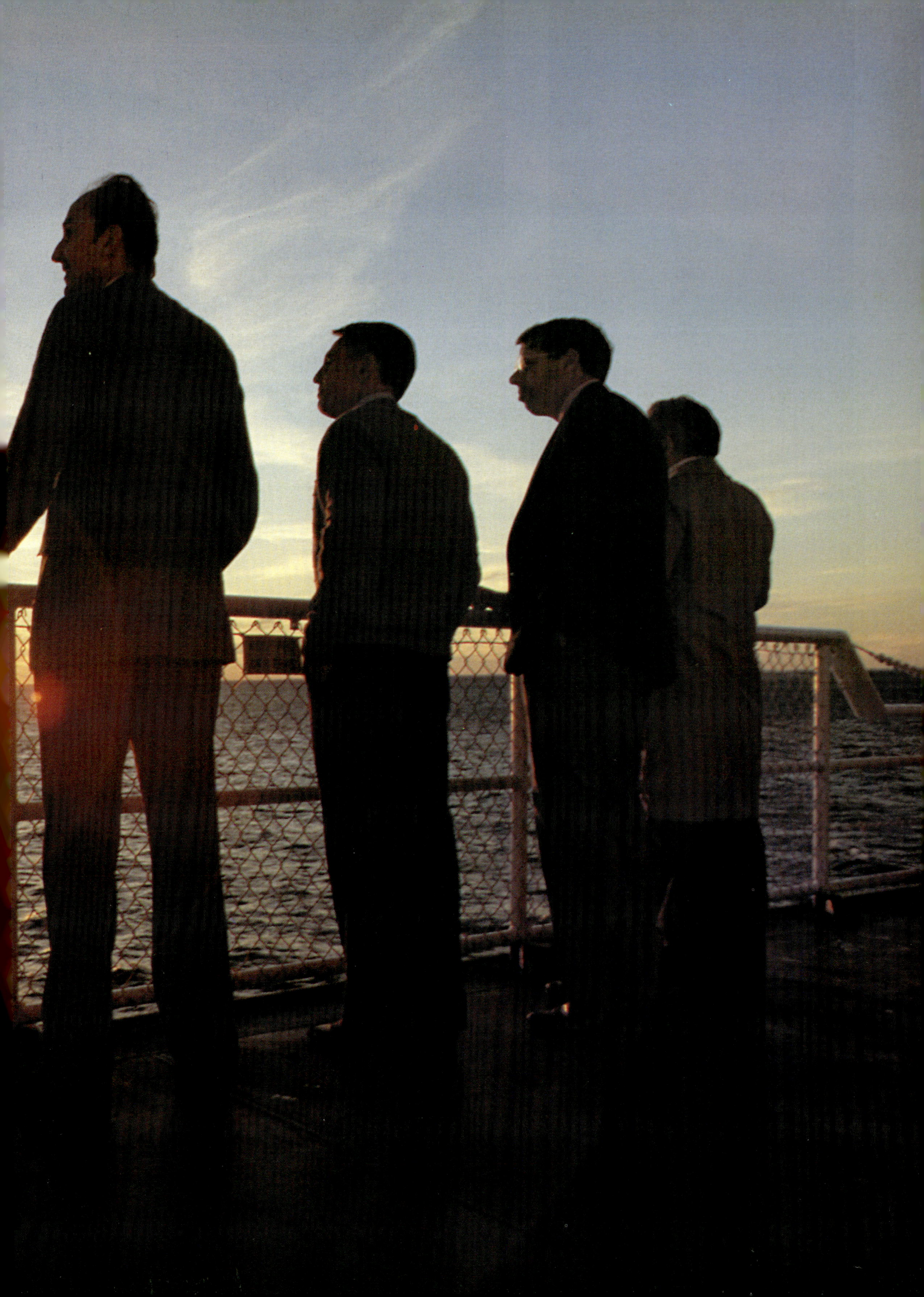

LONG ISLAND

Above: The expressway and the Northern State Parkway cut through the Island like ribbons of concrete. Photo by Ken Spencer

Previous page: For many commuters, taking a ferry from Long Island to Connecticut is the best way to go. Photo by Ken Spencer

Facing page: Nighttime arrives in East Meadow. Photo by Ken Spencer

Although technically it's morning, the moon and stars greet Irv Gordon as he revs up his ever-faithful Volvo and backs out of the driveway of his East Patchogue home. By 6:15 a.m. Gordon is on his way to a teaching job in Roslyn and the beginning of his daily encounter with one of the nation's most famous roads, the Long Island Expressway (LIE).

Irv Gordon can tell you all about the Long Island Expressway. He and his 1966 bright red P1800S coupe have been commuting on the Island's most traveled road for more than 20 years. In fact, in 1987 Gordon's Volvo passed its one-millionth mile, most of which were accumulated on the expressway.

An automobile is to Irv Gordon and all Long Islanders what fire was to the caveman. It's a matter of survival. "There's no other way for me to get to work," Gordon said.

The science teacher travels between exits 64 and 39, about 40 miles each way, making him a typical expressway commuter. With 80 percent of Long Islanders now working on Long Island rather than in the City, many use the expressway for intercounty travel.

But unlike most Long Islanders, Gordon has been commuting in one particular car for 21 years. "I get into my car and it starts, I think another day I'm ahead of the game," he said. And even with all the stop-and-go traffic, he's only had to put in four clutches. "I figure that's 250,000 miles a clutch."

Gordon's trips on the LIE have become a Long Island history lesson. "I've been watching Long Island farmland disappear," he said. "The development in the Route 110 corridor is incredible and the homes that have been going up—it's just amazing."

What affection does Irv Gordon have for the road he spends two or three hours on each day? "None, zero. I have absolutely no affection for this road."

Ah, the Long Island Expressway, the road Long Islanders love to hate. Dubbed "the 4-9-5 Super Slab" by CBers and "the world's longest parking lot" by just about everyone else, the expressway's actual title is Federal Interstate 495. Most Long Islanders simply refer to it as the LIE, pronounced L-I-E.

The LIE has been the brunt of jokes, negative bumper stickers, even satirical poems since its construction began in 1955. Yet "in terms of what it was built to do," said Lee Koppelman, executive director of the Long Island Regional Planning Board, "the Long

Island Expressway is not a failure. It does work."

So for a serious discussion of the expressway, and the transportation systems of Long Island, perhaps we should get some of those Long Island distressway, er, *Expressway* witticisms out of the way right now.

"The Long Island Expressway is to public transportation what Cleveland is to summer resorts."

"We could get peace in the Middle East by putting the Arabs and the Jews on the Expressway at 5 p.m. By the time they got off, they'd be too old to fight." (Alan King, the popular comedian from Kings Point, gets credit for those two.)

There are all sorts of bumper stickers, including "LIE: Long Island's hardening of the artery," and "Pray for me, I ride the LIE."

And *Newsday* columnist Ed Lowe was so moved by his LIE experience that he composed a poem titled "Ode to the Expressway," an excerpt of which appears at the end of this chapter. The Long Island Expressway is Long Island's most traveled road, but it's by no means the Island's only busy road. Every lane, street, avenue, highway, and parkway gets its fair share of cars because the automobile is the transportation vehicle on Long Island.

The Long Island Rail Road, the Island's major public transit and the nation's busiest commuter railroad, goes primarily east and west or to and from the City. Since many Islanders have to travel north and south, a car is a necessity, and more than 2 million motor vehicles are registered in Nassau and Suffolk counties.

Automobiles have been the major means of Long Island transportation since the 1950s. Before that, getting from here to there was an interesting mix of motion.

LONG ISLAND

OLD-FASHIONED MOVING

Long Island's first commuters, the Indians, traveled mostly by water. Canoes were the public transit of the day. Up until the mid-1800s when the railroad came into existence, water remained the quickest way to get to and from the populated western and eastern ends of the Island. (Even during the late 1800s steamboats were still the preferred method of travel from New York to the East End.)

On land the Indians were packing down narrow footpaths, the Island's first roads. As the footpaths grew wider and wider they became public roads, eventually joined by privately built toll roads called turnpikes. Hempstead and Jericho are two of the original turnpikes (minus the toll) still in use today.

Getting from one end of the Island to the other by land meant taking the stagecoach, a three-day trip from Brooklyn to Quogue with two overnight stops. For trips in and out of New York City, one took a ferry from Brooklyn. Prospective passengers would take a conch shell hanging from a tree near where Fulton Street is today and give it a good blow. A ferryman would then come to take the passengers across.

The Long Island Rail Road represented the first major change in land travel. It came into existence in 1834. The oldest railroad in the nation and the third oldest in the world still operating under its original name, the LIRR (pronounced L-I double-R or L-I-R-R) was originally built to take people from New York to Boston. A route across the desolate flatlands of the middle of Long Island was considered easier for construction than building tracks through the marshlands of southern Connecticut. Passengers would complete the journey by taking a steamboat from Greenport across the Sound to Connecticut, then another railroad up to Boston.

Above: These Long Island Railroad (LIRR) commuters head for Syosset and home. Photo by Ken Spencer

Right: The Brooklyn Bridge was once considered the eighth wonder of the world. Photo by Ken Spencer

The LIRR's 96 miles of railroad track from Brooklyn to Greenport was completed in 1844. But four years later a railroad was built through southern Connecticut, eliminating the need for the Long Island route. Since the Long Island Rail Road wasn't built to serve Long Islanders, it wasn't located anywhere near the populated shore areas. Thus, in the 1840s, the only Long Islanders who had contact with the LIRR were the farmers who hated it.

Sparks from the trains set the fields and barns on fire and the noise scared the cows. Farmers shot at the trains, and a woman whose cow had been killed by the railroad was reported to have soaped up the tracks every day, thereby derailing the trains that passed by. The civil disobedience continued until she was reimbursed $20 for her cow.

LIRR officials were also fighting with Brooklynites who didn't like all those dirty steam engines in their community. That prompted the railroad in 1860 to build a line from Jamaica to Long Island City, ensuring another route toward Manhattan. (The opening of the East River tunnels in 1910 completed that route, eliminating the need to ferry passengers across the river.)

Rival railroads began to crop up all over the Island. More than 30 were in operation in the mid-1800s, but by the turn of the century they had all been brought under the ownership of the LIRR.

In 1900 the Pennsylvania Railroad bought Long Island's railroad and operated it until New York State took over in 1966. That was the year Governor Nelson Rockefeller made the famous prediction that he would make the LIRR "the finest commuter line in the country." More than 20 years later Bruce McIver, the current president of the railroad, said, "It's been a long time, but we're almost there." In 1968 the Metropolitan Transit Authority (MTA) was formed and the railroad has been under its jurisdiction ever since.

Ridership on the LIRR peaked in 1929 when more than 118 million riders packed into the trains. Once the subways were completed into Queens, however, the Long Island Rail Road became a commuting line almost entirely for the suburbanites of Nassau and Suffolk counties.

Trolleys were also an important part of the Island's early transportation system. In 1908 the Cross Island Trolley from Huntington to Amityville took about one hour and cost 30 cents. Another popular trolley that ran in Queens and Nassau was called the "Banana Line" because of its yellow color and the "bunch" of cars.

One of the most important transportation developments for Long Island was the opening of the Brooklyn Bridge in 1883. Referred to as the eighth wonder of the world, the bridge was the world's first steel cable suspension bridge and the longest of its kind when built. Most importantly for Long Islanders, it was the first land link to Manhattan.

Another Island first was the construction of the Vanderbilt Motor Parkway, the bulk of which was built between 1904 and 1908. The Nassau/Suffolk highway, creation of auto-racing buff William K. Vanderbilt, Jr., was 48 miles long and 20 feet wide, and the first in the nation to use concrete banked turns, a nonskid surface, guard rails, tollhouses (some of which are still standing as private residences), landscaping, and even special highway police. Vanderbilt has been dubbed the "father of the highway" for his Motor Parkway, part of which is still in use today.

While Vanderbilt created Long Island's first highway, Robert Moses created the Island's highway system and also most of its parks. Nature may have laid out Long Island's physical boundaries, but Moses built its infrastructure.

Moses, who died in 1981, would have seen his centennial year in 1988. Referred to in newspaper accounts as the "Colossus of Roads," he did more to lay out the transportation structure of Metropolitan New York than any other individual.

"He was America's greatest road builder," said Robert A. Caro in his Pulitzer Prize-winning biography of Moses, *The Power Broker*. On Long Island alone Moses built the Cross Island Parkway, the Belt Parkway, the Meadowbrook Parkway, the Wantagh Parkway, the Southern State Parkway, the Northern State Parkway, the Sagtikos Parkway, the Robert Moses Causeway, and the Ocean Parkway, and began the construction of the Long Island Expressway. (Moses lost his last public position of power in 1968 before the expressway was completed.)

Moses was successful in "convincing" Long Island's politicians, townspeople, and millionaires to cede lands for his parks and roads, allowing him to build one of the most innovative highway systems in the country. The irony of it all, as Koppelman points out, is that "the building of the parkway network had nothing to do with the development of Long Island. It was to get from New York to his parks."

Above: Speedy nighttime traffic along Sunrise Highway creates a modern work of art. Photo by R. Settles

THE ROADS OF THE ISLAND

The concept of parkways—scenic routes to parks—was Moses' creation. Today Long Islanders drive those scenic parkways more to go to work than to play.

Only passenger cars are allowed on Long Island's parkways. Commercial traffic to and from the Island relies primarily on the LIE. That's one of the reasons the expressway is always busy. The expansion of Sunrise Highway on the South Shore will relieve some of that congestion, but between 6 a.m.-9 a.m. and 4 p.m.-7 p.m., Long Island's illustrious rush hours, all of the Island's major roads are busy.

Commuter backups on Long Island occur primarily in two directions. It seems the majority of Long Islanders head west in the morning, whether from eastern Suffolk to western Suffolk, or from Suffolk to Nassau, or Nassau to the City, and they head back east at night. You'll find some delays northbound in the morning on routes such as Meadowbrook or Wantagh parkways and the reverse in the evening, but the key to commuting on Long Island, and especially to the Hamptons in the summer, is to find a lightly travelled east-west back road. Those who find such a route covet the information like buried treasure.

The good news about Long Island's road systems is that most of it is free. With the exception of a few bridges and entrances to parks, there are no tolls on Long Island's major roadways, including the expressway.

As the Cumberland Gap and Sante Fe Trail helped settle the west, so the Long Island Expressway helped settle Long Island. Construction started in 1955, and by 1962 the road stretched to the Suffolk line. So did the new homes and businesses that mushroomed up alongside of it. A push by Long Island planners to build a public transit system down the center of the expressway never made it, and by the time the road was completed to Riverhead in 1972, the population of Suffolk had doubled.

Designed to carry 85,000 cars a day, the expressway's traffic load was beyond its intended capacity before the first section was even completed in Queens. On one day in March 1986, 174,300 cars were counted passing between the Community Drive and Shelter Rock Road exits.

In 1983 the entire length was designated a federal interstate, allowing federal funds to be used for its maintenance, and in the late 1980s a traffic system known as IMIS was integrated into the major highway systems on Long Island. Hundreds of sensors are implanted along the roadways to provide information on traffic conditions. The information is relayed as messages on electronic billboards along the road.

Today most of the drivers on the LIE average only an eight-mile trip—a 30-minute drive in rush hour. It's the on-and-off traffic that causes the slowdowns on the Island's major highway. To move the traffic more efficiently, there are plans to add a fourth lane and complete both the north and south service roads, which end abruptly at several points.

The Long Island Expressway, 70 miles of concrete passing through the heart of the Island, is considered by many to be Long Island's lifeline. From the densely populated areas of western Nassau out to the rural farmlands of eastern Suffolk, a ride on the LIE is one sure way to view Long Island and its varied life-styles.

THE LIRR

"Dashing Dan" is still alive and well on Long Island, although today it's more likely to be Dashing Dan and Rushing Ruth. The symbol for the always-in-a-hurry LIRR railroad commuter, Dashing Dan was central to the LIRR's advertising campaign in the 1950s and 1960s. Today, with the Island's railroad having an on-time performance of more than 90 percent, Dan doesn't have to dash quite as much.

The largest commuter railroad in the nation—272,000 passengers ride it daily—the Long Island Rail Road is a vital link in the Island's transportation network. An estimated 75.7 million fares are collected each year from the more than 700 trains that go to and from the City. The fares will increase by more than 3 million, LIRR officials predict, now that the electrification of the Main Line between Hicksville and Ronkonkoma is complete and other improvements are on the way.

"Our ability to provide reliable service has improved greatly," said Bruce McIver, LIRR president. "That comes about from a number of things. One is the tremendous investment that has been made in the physical plant—a new yard on the west side of Manhattan, the electrification to Ronkonkoma, a new shop, work on the tracks, and adding 170-plus cars to our fleet. The equipment of the railroad is in better condition than it's been in many, many years."

"We've placed a tremendous amount of emphasis on providing the best service we can," McIver continued. "We focus on cleanliness and on-time performance, and all of that has helped."

The lines of the LIRR are laid out like a tree. Jamaica is the base of the tree, and eight branches fan out over the North and South shores—the Main Line to Greenport, the Montauk line, Oyster Bay, Port Jefferson, Hempstead, West Hempstead, Rockaways, and Long Beach lines. (Of course, there's the little twig that doesn't fit into this analogy, the Port Washington line, which runs through Long Island City.) The three roots of the Jamaica-based tree go to Penn Station, Long Island City, and Flatbush in Brooklyn.

With millions of dollars being pumped into the railroad for new equipment and renovations, the LIRR is finally on a roll.

ODE TO THE EXPRESSWAY
excerpt

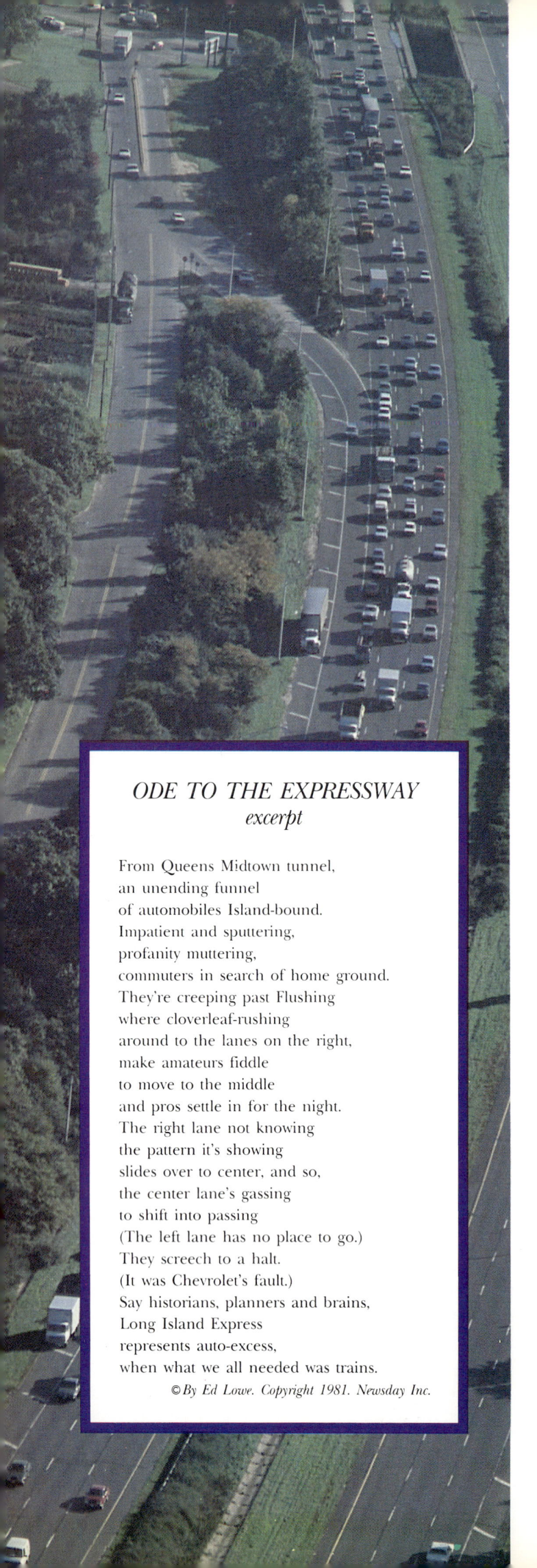

From Queens Midtown tunnel,
an unending funnel
of automobiles Island-bound.
Impatient and sputtering,
profanity muttering,
commuters in search of home ground.
They're creeping past Flushing
where cloverleaf-rushing
around to the lanes on the right,
make amateurs fiddle
to move to the middle
and pros settle in for the night.
The right lane not knowing
the pattern it's showing
slides over to center, and so,
the center lane's gassing
to shift into passing
(The left lane has no place to go.)
They screech to a halt.
(It was Chevrolet's fault.)
Say historians, planners and brains,
Long Island Express
represents auto-excess,
when what we all needed was trains.

©By Ed Lowe. Copyright 1981. Newsday Inc.

BY LAND, SEA, AND AIR

Included in Long Island's modes of public transit is the bus. Long Island buses transport 35 million passengers a year. In Nassau County the bus system is run by the Metropolitan Suburban Bus Authority, with 47 routes. In Suffolk, 67 routes are operated by the county, 10 municipal governments, and independent operators.

You can alway call for a taxicab; an estimated 1,500 taxi companies are in operation, but the key is to call. On Long Island you can't hail a cab; they're prohibited by law from cruising. You either telephone a taxi company or get a taxi at the local LIRR station.

To leave the Island you can go by sea or air. There are two major ferry systems crossing Long Island Sound and connecting the Island to Connecticut—"moveable bridges," Koppelman calls them. You can take a ferry from Port Jefferson to Bridgeport or from Orient Point to New London. A smaller ferry operation is available from Montauk to Block Island, Rhode Island.

Of course, if you want to visit the islands of Long Island, you can take the Shelter Island ferry or the various ferries on Suffolk's South Shore, which take you to scenic Fire Island.

LEAVING ON A JET PLANE

Blue and gray are the morning colors for Long Island's MacArthur Airport. Traditional navy blue and gray business suits are in abundance as Long Islanders wait in line to board their early morning flights to Washington, Chicago, Pittsburgh, or Albany. Business commuters and vacationers have found MacArthur Airport in Ronkonkoma a convenient alternative to New York City's two major airports, Kennedy International (JFK) and LaGuardia.

In 1985 over 800,000 passengers used MacArthur, Nassau and Suffolk's largest airport. Today the figure is more than one million passengers, and the passenger statistics continue to grow. "MacArthur is centrally located and much more convenient to Suffolk residents," said Alfred E. Werner, the airport manager. Major carriers such as American Airlines, Eastern Airlines, USAir, and United Express offer jet service to numerous cities, including the ones previously mentioned, plus Fort Lauderdale and Orlando, Florida, and Raleigh-Durham, North Carolina. Then there are the commuter airlines to Boston, Philadelphia, and

Baltimore, for a total of 88 MacArthur departures and arrivals per day.

A Ronkonkoma Transportation Hub is planned for the northern end of the airport. The LIRR has built a new Ronkonkoma railroad station, the LIE is only a block away, and construction of a hotel/office complex and a bus depot is under consideration.

Other Long Island airports include Republic Airport in East Farmingdale, which handled 165,000 planes coming and going in 1986. It is primarily a general aviation airport, as are Suffolk County Airport in Westhampton, Brookhaven Airport in Shirley, and East Hampton Airport in East Hampton.

Long Island is said to have more air traffic in its skies than anywhere else in the country. JFK, LaGuardia, and Newark airports, where Long Islanders can find flights to anywhere in the world, add to that statistic. The three airports handle nearly 80 million passengers per year.

By air, sea, or land, Long Islanders are on the move. However, a more efficient land transportation system continues to challenge business and government leaders. They've drawn together under the direction of the Long Island Association (LIA), forming organizations such as CLOUT, the Coalition of Leadership Organized to Upgrade Transportation. CLOUT lobbies for more state funds for the island's highways. With the formation of organizations such as CLOUT, it is apparent that Long Island's growing transportation needs are now a top priority for business and government officials.

What Long Islanders Have to Say About Transportation

Alfred E. Werner, manager, Long Island MacArthur Airport:

I've been at this airport for 35 years. I've seen it grow from a small general aviation airport with only one outside carrier, Island Air Ferries I think it was called, to what it is now. I think we can continue moderate growth. The residents who live around the airport were concerned with noise, so we came up with a noise abatement program, budgeting the amount of noise each airline could make. That's made the airlines fly quieter planes. Next I'd like to see the runway extended, a substantial addition to the terminal, and jetways added. Right now we're overtaxing everything."

Mitchell Pally, legislative and economic affairs director, LIA:

We have a 1990s economy running on a 1950s transportation system. They just don't mix.

Bruce McIver, president, Long Island Rail Road:

We want to be the best. The way you define the best is you keep getting better.

Facing page: "Go West, young man, but how?" may be the battle cry of these LIE morning commuters. Photo by Ken Spencer

Left: A jet lands at Long Island's MacArthur Airport. Photo by Ken Spencer

VIII
A Separate Identity

site, combining former Garden City and Ronkonkoma offices. Expansion has continued at *Newsday*. In 1985 it began printing *New York Newsday,* a city edition to rival the New York City-based newspapers. *New York Newsday* is not an entirely separate paper. "We're putting out one newspaper with two managing editors," said Schneider. "It's a challenge."

On Schneider's desk in Melville sits a beige telephone with "Hot Line" handwritten on masking tape attached to the receiver. The phone is a direct link to Manhattan and the managing editor of *New York Newsday,* James Toedtman.

"We talk several times a day," Schneider said. "There's a great deal of commonality. We share the same national desk, business desk, and others."

The expansion of *Newsday* into New York has not caused Long Island news to suffer, Schneider maintained. "It's made us reaffirm our commitment to Long Island and expand at the same time. We have more arts and entertainment, more Wall Street news, more television. The expansion made us a better newspaper."

It also brought about regionalization. In the last few years the paper has changed its local news format into regionalized editions—four in Suffolk, and four in Nassau. Local news pages are changed for the various editions. "Technology allows us to do more local reporting and give smaller advertisers an opportunity to come back into the paper," Johnson explained.

In keeping with the Long Island commitment, Schneider said, "We've put a safety net across the Island. Every Long Island community is covered by a reporter." The safety net includes 550 *Newsday* editorial staffers working on Long Island, and 200 more at *New York Newsday.*

With a total of 3,500 full-time employees and another 500 part-timers, *Newsday* "is not just a newspaper, it's a very big business," Johnson said. The paper is owned by the Times Mirror Corporation, "which operates on the philosophy of local autonomy," according to the publisher. Editorially, *Newsday* is allowed to go its separate way, he said, but in terms of infusion of dollars into the Long Island economy, Times Mirror plays an important part.

"Our first plant here in Melville cost $44 million," Johnson said. "Now with the expansion, by early 1990 Times Mirror will have spent $200 million to improve on its investment. It's put millions into the economy, and that's a big plus for the Island."

When the expansion of the Melville operation is completed in 1990, 10 presses will be in operation, and *Newsday,* on its 50th anniversary, Johnson said, "will have the single largest daily newspaper production facility in the country."

GET YOUR PAPERS

While *Newsday* is based on Long Island and considered Long Island's newspaper, the region is also serviced by New York City daily newspapers. The *New York Times* offers a Sunday Long Island weekly section. So does the *New York Daily News.*

Long Island's first newspaper, the *Long Island Herald,* started in Sag Harbor in 1791. In fact, that East End community was a focus of early journalism on the Island. It's said that Walt Whitman, when he was 12 years of age, served as an apprentice at the *Long Island Star* in Sag Harbor.

At the ripe old age of 19, Whitman founded Huntington's weekly newspaper, *The Long Islander.* The year was 1831. Whitman went on to become one of the nation's most prominent poets and one of the Island's most esteemed personages, and his newspaper, *The Long Islander,* went on too. It's still being published, joined today by more than 120 other local weeklies.

The Long Islander is now part of the Anton Community Newspaper Chain, one of the largest weekly newspaper operations in Nassau County. There are 21 Anton newspapers, each reporting the local news for communities such as Port Washington and Huntington.

Another weekly newspaper chain growing by leaps and bounds is the Record Newspapers of Port Jefferson. In 1987-1988 the Record chain went from two to nine newspapers—a circulation increase from 9,000 to 85,000. "And we're not finished yet," says publisher John Griffen. Record newspapers are located in mid-Suffolk.

Just about every Long Island village and town has its local weekly newspaper, and every local newspaper has its loyal following. From wedding announcements to high school sports, if you want to know what's happening to your neighbors or their children, the local weekly is where you'll find out.

The 1980s also witnessed the rise and influence of free distribution weeklies such as *Suffolk Life* and the weekly chain owned by Chanry Communications Ltd. With 74 editions and almost one million in circulation, Chanry's *Pennysaver* (some editions are called by different names) has become one of the largest free distribu-

Cablevision's Long Island cable system is the largest in the country. Photo by Bruce Bennett

tion newspapers in the U.S.

The print media on Long Island are rounded out by regional magazines, including *Long Island Nightlife, Long Island Monthly, Goodliving,* and *House in the Hamptons* and business weeklies and monthlies which include *Long Island Business News* and *Long Island Magazine,* which is published by the Long Island Association.

LONG ISLAND ON THE AIR

"We would like to be perceived as the home team," said Al Ittelson, president of "News 12 Long Island." "Whether you're winning or losing, people take pride in you."

Long Islanders do indeed take pride in "News 12 Long Island," the first local 24-hour television news channel in the United States. "News 12" was the brainchild of Charles F. Dolan, founder and chairman of the board of Cablevision Systems Corporation and the innovative cable entrepreneur who is credited with starting the first 24-hour cable movie channel, Home Box Office (HBO), and the first all-sports channels, Madison Square Garden and SportsChannel. Dolan is considered by many media experts as Long Island's answer to Ted Turner, the colorful originator of the Cable News Network (CNN).

Dolan's latest creation is "News 12." Long Island had long suffered in its search for identity from the lack of its own VHF (very high frequency, channels 2 to 13) television station. That point has been well publicized by the Long Island Coalition for Fair Broadcasting, a nonprofit group of local business, civic, and government leaders who are pushing for more television coverage for Long Island. While the coalition lobbied for Long Island's own VHF station and effectively hammered away at the New York City VHF television stations, demanding the Island receive more news coverage, Dolan saw a way of giving the Island video-news coverage outside the mainstream of commercial television.

"There's no question that Nassau and Suffolk have their own concerns and interests which separate them from the rest of the metropolitan area," Dolan said, "and cable is better able to service those interests than television since cable is municipally franchised. You have a communication system that's derived from smaller political units. You can network them together to provide a service to a specific geographic area.

"In television all the local VHF frequencies are assigned to this overwhelming metropolitan area, and each operator of a broadcast frequency has as his concern the entire area rather than just Nassau and Suffolk.

"Cable, however, can focus," Dolan said, "and it

also has the advantage of multiple channels so an entire channel can be concentrated on one area," which is exactly what "News 12 Long Island" does.

"News 12" began operations in December 1986 after Cablevision executives convinced the other Long Island cable operators to air the service on their channel 12s, thereby giving the local news channel the appearance of a hometown television station.

The channel broadcasts 24 hours of continuous news because, Dolan said, "There is a great deal of competition in the media and the public can't be expected to show up at 6 p.m. at a particular channel to see and hear what's there. The public must be catered to."

The "News 12" operation is impressive. A minimum of eight reporter-and-camera crews go out each day, at times utilizing a high-tech satellite news-gathering truck, an electronic news-gathering truck, eight tape-editing rooms, two satellites for national and international news sources, and a studio with production rooms that Dan Rather would feel at home in.

Just 11 months after going on the air, a week-long telephone survey showed that 89 percent of cable subscribers had watched "News 12." And the reporters and anchors of the news channel have all become Long Island celebrities. "I've had more recognition in nine months at News 12 then nine years as a Nassau County executive," said Francis T. Purcell, who joined "News 12" as a commentator after retiring from public office.

Ittelson said the success of "News 12" is due to that hometown feeling. "We're not reporting about them," he said, "We're reporting about us.

"In 1987 for the first time we did live coverage of the lighting of the Long Island Christmas tree at EAB Plaza," he recalled. "But we weren't in control of the presentation. Although we had three cameras and two live trucks, we couldn't control what they were doing, so it was like a guessing game . . . like doing a sporting event with no rules. And yet it came out a hometown happening. We had a tremendous response from it."

"News 12" is just one part of the Cablevision empire. Cablevision Systems Corporation, which is based in Woodbury, owns 14 cable systems throughout the country including the franchises for Chicago and Boston as well as most of Long Island. The Long Island cable system is the largest in the country by "number of subscribers, number of channels, and number of services purchased by subscribers" according to Dolan, who added that Cablevision will continue to expand on Long Island by purchasing other local cable systems.

"We think that cable television should correspond to print," he said. "It is better able to do that if there is a lot of commonality in the ownership, so we have tried to become as large as we can on Long Island. For any one medium to develop all the potential it can, the stronger the company pursuing that medium, the better."

Long Island cable has grown dramatically in the last decade. It's no longer just an antenna service. "Because of its affluence and its proximity to a major media market, Long Island is the beachhead for changes in cable," said Steve Tuttle, a vice president of the National Cable Television Association in Washington, D.C.

Approximately 60 percent of Long Islanders are hooked up to three cable companies operating on the Island, and besides a plethora of television stations to watch, the local cable systems offer innovative local programming and pay services, some of which originate on the Island.

"It's unbelievable that in 1975 . . . there was just one pay service and no satellite delivery or advertising support services. Today we have about 14 pay services and 35 satellite-delivery, advertising-supported services," Dolan said.

"This is absolutely unprecedented explosive development of programming sources," he continued. "I think history will view this period as a really remarkable transition in communications, and I think it's only started."

And much of it started on Long Island.

ROUNDING OUT THE AIR WAVES: TELEVISION

The Island does have television stations; they are UHF (ultra high frequency, channels 14 and up). Long Island's public broadcasting station, WLIW-TV/Channel 21, based in Plainview, and the Island's only commercial television station, WLIG-TV/Channel 55, broadcasting from eastern Suffolk, offer an interesting program mix, and both stations have their loyal followings.

As a public station WLIW gets much of its $3.4-million budget from the donations of viewers and corporations. The station's yearly fundraising auction—where items ranging from Islander hockey sticks to works of art are sold to the highest bidder—is a must-see on most Long Island television viewers' lists.

WLIW is seen in 24 counties in New York, New Jersey, and Connecticut. From nature programs to English sitcoms, rock-and-roll concerts to local call-in

LONG ISLAND

Above: Long Island radio stations continually surpass New York City stations in the ratings war for Long Island listeners. Photo by Jeff Greenberg

Right: Television has played an important role in Long Island's search for identity. "News 12, Long Island," WLIG/Channel 55, and the New York Institute of Technology all offer local television news programs. Photo by Bruce Bennett

A SEPARATE IDENTITY

shows, the diverse programming of WLIW makes it one of the most watched public television stations in the country.

The other UHF station on the Island is a commercial entity. WLIG-TV, also known as TV-55, went on the air in April 1985. The station offers what general manager Marvin Chauvin calls "all family entertainment." The format is popular on the Island, and the viewing audience and advertising sales continue to grow.

RADIO: LONG ISLAND'S SOUND

Another important element in Long Island's communications world is radio. "Long Island radio is hotter than ever," said Paul Fleishman, president of the Long Island Radio Broadcasters Association. Industry observers agree.

In recent years Patchogue radio stations, WALK-AM/FM, with a soft-rock format, and WBLI-FM, which plays top 40 songs, have led the ratings in Nassau and Suffolk counties, beating out the big-city competition. WBAB-FM, based in Babylon, is another industry leader.

With diverse programming—from the big-band sound of stations like WGSM-AM and WHLI-AM, to the hard- or soft-rock format of many others—all of Long Island's 23 radio stations have their share of listeners.

The Island radio stations vary as much in power as they do in programming. Station power ranges from 250 to 50,000 watts. The larger stations carry farther, but many communities are just as satisfied with their own, smaller stations.

Long Island's radio stations are interspersed throughout the two counties with a cluster of eight stations located on the East End. Come summertime, some of these East End stations have more listeners than their big city counterparts. A survey done in 1986 found that 63 percent of the East End audience listened to East End radio.

With the vast majority of Long Islanders now working on the Island, local radio has caught on in a big way. "Since we live and work on Long Island, we're more concerned about Long Island news, traffic information, and weather," Fleishman said.

And that desire to know more about the Island, to feel proud to be a Long Islander, bodes well for the continued success of Long Island media.

What Long Islanders Have to Say About The Media and Long Island Identity

Charles Dolan, chairman of the board, Cablevision Systems Corporation, on why "News 12" was so successful its first year:

The idea that somebody in Riverhead is not interested in what happens in Hempstead is pretty well laid to rest. People do have a feeling wherever they are, in Nassau and Suffolk, that they're part of Long Island, and they like going to a channel that tells them what happened.

The leadership of Long Island has become personified by "News 12." Instead of being in a one-dimensional news-and-photograph format [print media], they become personalities on the television screen.

Robert M. Johnson, publisher and president of Newsday, *about the paper's role on Long Island:*

Because this is one of the largest employers on Long Island and one of the few institutions on Long Island that actually combines all the Island together, we can't just sit back and report. That's what our news pages do and that's fine, but as an institution we have to do more. I believe the paper should be more proactive.

IX
Island at Play

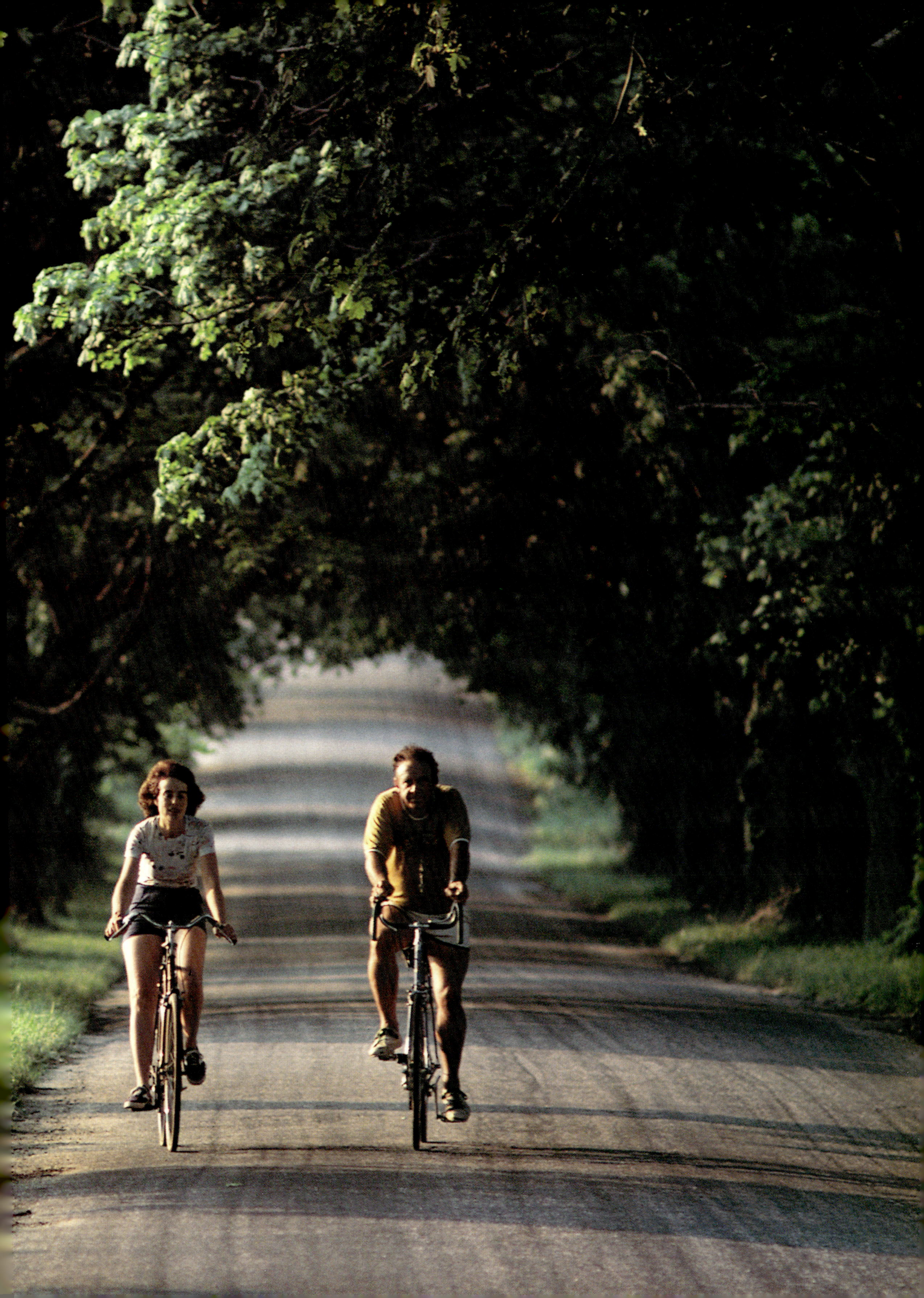

LONG ISLAND

Above: From the air, or on land, Long Island beaches are the place to be in the summertime. Photo by Ken Spencer

Previous page: Biking the byways of Long Island is a popular pastime. Photo by Ken Spencer

Forget the eye chart. For a Long Island child, the true test of good eyesight is how far away he or she can spot the Jones Beach Water Tower.

If yours was a Long Island childhood, chances are you remember being sandwiched in the back seat of the family car amid the towels, umbrella, blanket, beach toys, sand chairs, ice chest, and assorted changes of clothing. Traveling in the bumper-to-bumper traffic down Meadowbrook or Wantagh Parkway, you anxiously awaited that first glimpse of what some call "the needle" or "the pencil," but most simply refer to as "the tower."

The sooner you saw it, the sooner you would be there. Jones Beach, that magical place where you could make echo sounds in the tunnels, walk the boardwalk, and spend hours building castles or caves in the white sand. But most of all you had the ocean, the always cold ocean with its giant waves and knock-down surf that you'd race to escape but that always seemed to catch you. As a childhood memory Jones Beach was paradise. It still is.

While Jones Beach is a special world, a beach like no other, it's just one of many available to Long Island residents and visitors. With 1,180 miles of coastline, 400 of which are accessible to swimmers, Long Island is beach land. It's also boat land, and water-sports land.

If there's one thing an island has plenty of, it's water surrounding it. Long Island waters offer some of the best recreation in the world. Every type of boating is available and so is every type of water sport. In the summer the Island is truly a recreational paradise. That's why so many movie stars and millionaires choose Long Island for their summer home.

But it's not just the magnificent coastline that makes the region such a wonderful place to vacation or enjoy a day off. With its change of seasons and natural beauty away from the water, Long Island is the ideal outdoor place year-round.

At the many parks—797 of them on 55,000 acres—there are nature walks, picnic grounds, and bike paths, in addition to swimming and boating. In the winter the starkly beautiful landscape is a perfect backdrop for peaceful strolls. For the more athletic, there's sledding and cross-country skiing. "We have a diversity in our park system second to none," said John Sheridan, former Long Island regional director of the New York State Office of Parks.

ISLAND AT PLAY

And there's also diversity in sports and entertainment. From ice hockey to bocce ball, just about every sport can be played or watched on the Island. The local professional sports teams have all had their championship seasons, and the Island has been host to numerous outside athletic competitions such as the U.S. Open in golf, International Games for the Disabled, the United States Figure Skating Championships, and prestigious yachting events.

For animal lovers there's the Long Island Game Farm and the Animal Farm, both located in Manorville. And with entertainment centers such as the Nassau Veterans Memorial Coliseum, Westbury Music Fair, and the Jones Beach Theatre, top-name entertainment is always available.

BY THE SEA

Long Island's beaches are perhaps its best known recreational asset. The ocean, the Sound, the rivers, the bays, even a lake—Lake Ronkonkoma was one of the

Above left: With parkland preserved in every village and town, a quiet walk through a picturesque park is part of the Long Island life-style. Photo by Ken Spencer

Left: Frisbee players on Jones Beach take their game seriously. Photo by Ken Spencer

111

LONG ISLAND

Island's busiest resorts in the 1920s—offer swimmers, splashers, or sand-castle builders every type of waterside atmosphere.

There are private beaches, public beaches, federal, state, county, and local beaches, beaches with large boulders and pebbly bottoms and beaches with pure white sand, beaches with heavy surf and beaches where waves barely ripple, and beaches that are the favorites of families, singles, teenagers, gays, and nude sunbathers. The town of Huntington even has a beach for senior citizens only.

The most popular beaches are on the sandy oceanfront of the South Shore—the beaches of the Hamptons, the beaches of Fire Island, Long Beach with its three-mile boardwalk, and the granddaddy of them all, Jones Beach State Park.

JONES BEACH AND THE MOSES LEGACY

"If I had to pick one single asset that sets the tone of life on Long Island, it would be Jones Beach," said Lee Koppelman, Long Island's regional planning board director.

The year 1989 marks the 60th anniversary of the beach that Robert Moses built, six and one-half miles of clean, white sand bordering the Atlantic Ocean—"the most popular and best-known beach in the world," according to the Long Island Tourism and Convention Commission. Some call it Long Island's Disney World, but as Bob Nellen, Jones Beach's water safety director said, "This is better than Disney World—it's all natural."

Since it opened on August 4, 1929, Jones Beach has welcomed hundreds of millions of sun worshipers. Nearly 11 million people visit the beach in just one summer season, 267,000 per day.

For those growing up on the Island, Jones Beach is simply an accepted part of life. But look at it through the eyes of a child or a visitor from Des Moines and you realize how special it is. "There's such a majesty to the place, we do take it for granted," said Bob Lenti, captain of the lifeguards.

Jones Beach is named after Major Thomas Jones, an Irish soldier of fortune who in 1695 reportedly paid a barrel of cider to the Indians for thousands of acres of the oceanfront property.

But Jones Beach more accurately should be called Robert Moses Beach, after the man who created it and made it one of the world's most beautiful bathing beaches. (Some of that wrong was righted when the beach to the east became Robert Moses State Park.)

It's hard for most Long Islanders to comprehend the impact Robert Moses had on the recreational and leisure life of Long Island. As Levitt and his Levittown are synonymous with suburbia, Moses and his parks should be synonymous with recreation. When Robert Moses began building New York State parks in the 1920s, 29 states didn't have even a single state park, according to Robert A. Caro in *The Power Broker*. "Moses," Caro wrote, "was unquestionably America's most prolific creator. He was America's greatest builder." And much of that building took place on Long Island.

In the 1920s, it was Moses' contention that since Long Island was a dead end—you can only get off at the western end—it would never be a commercial community, therefore it should be a recreational community. He maintained that parks should be built all over the Island for New York City residents to play in. And he was able to convince the governor at the time, Alfred E. Smith, to let him do the building. In 1924 Smith appointed Moses president of the New York State Park Commission.

For the city folk to get to the Island, however, there had to be roads, attractive roads leading to the parks: parkways. Moses built the parkways and the parks. Jones Beach, Robert Moses, Bethpage, Captree, Hempstead Lakes, Sunken Meadow, Wildwood, Belmont Lake, Heckscher, Hither Hills, Orient Point—all were built by Robert Moses.

Long Island in the 1920s did not welcome outsiders. The roads to the water were closed and guarded. The wealthy of the Island cherished their privacy and considered the coastline their private playground. For example, when Moses tried to take over the Taylor estate in Islip to turn it into a state park, one wealthy Long Islander was reported to have asked, "Where can a poor millionaire go?" And when another millionaire objected to having the area overrun with "rabble," Governor Smith replied, "Rabble! Why that's me." The Taylor estate later became Heckscher State Park.

To make Jones Beach a reality, Robert Moses had to convince the townspeople of Babylon, Oyster Bay, and Hempstead to cede their Jones Beach property to the state—no easy feat—and then he had to devise a system to elevate the entire beach.

Since the main level of the barrier beach was only two feet above sea level and storm tides rose six to

The swimming pools and bathhouses of Jones Beach provide an alternative to ocean swimming. Photo by Robert Settles

eight feet, at times the beach was completely covered with water. Moses had to build up the beach and the bordering Ocean Parkway a total of 14 feet. The project was looked on as "Moses' Madness," but the feisty state official was able to do it. Eventually 40 million cubic yards of fill were brought up from the bay bottom north of the beach, leaving a vast dug-out area that became the State Boat Channel.

Everything about Jones Beach was first class. The water tower was hardly a nondescript tank on four poles. Moses built it to look like a Venetian bell tower. The bathhouses were made of Barbizon brick and Ohio sandstone.

Much has changed on the beach itself—gone are the popular calisthenic classes of the 1940s as well as the one-piece, chest-to-thigh bathing suits of the male lifeguards. And the lifeguards no longer check the parking fields with binoculars to make sure no one is disrobing there rather than in the bathhouses. But the buildings, the boardwalk, and the look of Jones Beach remain the same.

In the late 1980s, when the Long Island State Park and Recreation Commission gave Jones Beach a $30-million facelift, it became almost impossible to duplicate all that Moses had built. "We tried to keep everything as much like he built it as possible," said Sheridan, "but the Barbizon brick wasn't even made anymore and the original railing near the boardwalk was mahogany. There's just so much we could afford. We used aluminum."

Although the state park has expanded to 13 parking areas, each parking field at Jones Beach is a self-contained unit. The majority of visitors still like to go to the Central Mall area, parking fields 4 and 5, where you have to take the tunnels to get to the beach. At the Mall are the boardwalk, the softball field, Pitch and Putt, the archery range, and the Boardwalk Restaurant.

LIFEGUARDING

Bob Lenti, 40, of North Babylon, is captain of the lifeguards at the Central Mall area. Bob Nellen, 55, of Sea Cliff, is his supervisor, the water safety director for all of Jones Beach. The two men have spent most of their adult lives working at Jones Beach, and as they

LONG ISLAND

stood on the boardwalk overlooking the ocean on a crisp fall day, they talked of the thrill of lifeguarding at one of the country's most popular beaches.

"On a good Saturday in July it's so packed here you can't find the sand," said Nellen. It gets almost as packed in the water, which means busy times for Jones Beach lifeguards. "We keep a main stand and several wing stands open," Lenti said. "On the Fourth of July last year, we had 300 rescues."

Most of the lifeguards at Jones Beach are not teenagers or college students; they're much older. "It's a misconception that to be a good lifeguard you have to be young," Nellen said. "We use the three-person system here. The rescue is like a ballet, everyone playing a part."

"Experience can compensate for age," Lenti added. "You keep in excellent shape, you don't lose anything."

Being a Jones Beach lifeguard is a "great job," according to Lenti. "You have the surf, the outdoors, you're putting your body to work, and there's a great camaraderie among the people you work with. Where else can you get such satisfaction, doing something people consider heroic?"

The draw of the beach is part of that satisfaction. The lifeguards find themselves coming back weekend after weekend, long after the season is over. "In January this is a real special place," Lenti said.

FIRE ISLAND

Another special place is Fire Island. While the Hamptons offer some of the finest oceanfront in the world, public beaches there are kept to a minimum (Hither Hills State Park in Montauk is the exception). So it's to Fire Island that much of the ocean-loving crowd goes.

Fire Island, Long Island's major barrier island, is 32 miles long but only a half-mile wide. One hundred years ago the western end was marked by the Fire Island Lighthouse, but drifting sand built up the island for five miles to the west, allowing Robert Moses to build one more magnificent oceanfront park, this one named for him—the Robert Moses State Park. The state park is the western end of Fire Island. The eastern end is Smith Point County Park in Shirley.

In between is the Fire Island National Seashore; a combination of summer communities, each with a different life-style and view toward visitors; a wilderness area; town and federal beaches; marinas such as

ISLAND AT PLAY

Sailors Haven with its unusual Sunken Forest, a woodland protected by dunes growing below sea level; and Watch Hill.

The seashore, under the jurisdiction of the National Park Service, part of the U.S. Department of Interior, was set up by Congress in 1964 to help preserve the natural state of Fire Island. Western communities such as Ocean Beach were experiencing incredibly rapid development, and there was concern for the dunes, the fragile barrier of the island. Now development is no longer allowed in what is called the Dune District, and the eastern portion of the seashore has become a wilderness zone. The eight mile-long zone, established in 1980 as the first federal wilderness preserve in New York State, is an area left completely in its natural state.

Most of Fire Island is only accessible by ferries that run from Patchogue, Sayville, and Bay Shore. Car access is limited to the public beaches at either end. This inaccessibility makes Fire Island "the other type of beach," where you can walk and be alone with nature. Although the resort communities get quite busy and lively during the summer, there is always some part of the barrier island where it can be just you and a seagull.

ON THE SEA

"Any man who has to ask about the annual upkeep of a yacht can't afford one," said J.P. Morgan, probably as he stood on the deck of his own luxurious vessel, *The Corsair*, which he kept moored off his private island near Glen Cove.

If millionaire Morgan were alive today, he'd be astounded at the number of Long Islanders who own yachts—technically, any boat over 26 feet.

The Island has one of the largest concentrations of boats in the United States. There are 80,000 motor boats registered in the area. (Many more are registered out of state.) Speed boats and cabin cruisers abound. There are tens of thousands of sailboats as well. On a Sunday in July the State Boat Channel on the South Shore or any harbor on the North Shore can get as busy as the Long Island Expressway.

Boats are kept in the more than 430 marinas and yacht clubs on both sides of the Island. On the North Shore many boats are moored rather than docked, which means they're anchored away from shore, and boat owners have to take tenders or dinghies to reach them. On the South Shore, almost all boats are kept at docks.

From rowing in the smallest of rowboats to cruising in the largest of luxury yachts, just about every Long Islander gets on the water at one time or another. There are even some who kayak in the ocean. You can canoe on the rivers, paddle the Peconic, or sailboat race with the wind. "Race Week" is a yacht club tradition, and the Around Long Island Regatta for sailors grows in popularity each year.

Left: Vacation accommodations on Long Island take many forms. Camping on Fire Island near the Watch Hill Marina is one of the most economical. Photo by Ken Spencer

Facing page: Jones Beach lifeguards appreciate the day's end. Photo by Ken Spencer

LONG ISLAND

Above: You don't need a boat to fish the waters of Long Island. Some try their luck at this dock near Point Lookout. Photo by Ken Spencer

Above right: The Manhasset Bay Yacht Club is one of the many Long Island clubs which sailors call their home-away-from-home on the weekends. Photo by Ken Spencer

Right: At sunrise a sailboat awaits the wind on Long Island Sound. Photo by Ken Spencer

ISLAND AT PLAY

Fishing is one of the recreational activities people like to do while out boating. Long Island waters offer some of the best fishing on the East Coast. Migrating fish heading north along the coast come to a dead-end at an area of water called the New York Bight and therefore have to turn east, right into Long Island waters. With the continental shelf just off the Island and the gulf stream touching the shores every now and then, the Island offers almost every water condition for fish. That's why 80 world fishing records have been set in the area since 1980.

There's no license required for salt-water fishing, but there is a minimum size on fluke— "throw back the shorts," they'll tell you—and striped bass are limited to one a day. Fresh-water fishing—usually for trout—is available at several parks. There are seasons, and licenses are required.

You can fish with your rod and reel in the surf of a public beach, a pier, a dock, or a boat. If you don't have your own boat, you may rent a small one from a local marina. You can also charter a fishing boat or take an open "party boat," which requires no advance reservations. There are about 200 charter boats operating out of 30 ports around the Island. The major fishing ports are Freeport, which bills itself as the boating capital of the East Coast; Montauk, where they go for the big ones; Greenport; and Captree.

And what can you catch? Bluefish from the baby snapper size to the whopping big ones; striped bass and weakfish are fun to catch and good to eat. Many people, however, prefer bottom fishing—putting a sinker on the line and bouncing the hook along the bottom hoping for a flounder or a fluke (a summer flounder), a blackfish, or a porgy.

Or you can go out in the ocean and try for the biggies— blue marlin, tuna, or shark.

TEE TIME

For those who prefer terra firma for their recreation, there's golf, one of the most popular of Long Island sports. Just how popular is golfing on Long Island? Golfers at Bethpage State Park have been timed in an effort to speed up play and get more golfers on the course. "Fairway to Golf Play" was an experimental program that allocated four and one-half hours for 18 holes of golf. "The main complaint we get from golfers is that people are playing too slow," said Jim Evans, Bethpage State Park superintendent. That's why for a few weeks golfers had to fill out timed "report cards" and park rangers were out in force to speed them along.

"It worked, it definitely made people play faster," said Sheridan, former Office of Parks regional director. Even though there are 113 private and public courses in Nassau and Suffolk, tee-off times are still at a premium.

Bethpage Park's five golf courses, color-named, are considered some of the best 18-hole courses in the country. More than 1,500 rounds are played there each day. "It's the largest public golf facility in America," said Sheridan. The black course, which is long and hilly with tricky sand traps and narrow fairways, is considered so difficult that in 1939 Sam Snead reportedly walked off cursing it.

Another well-known Long Island course is the Shinnecock Hills Golf Club in the town of Southampton. The golf course there was created in 1891, making it the first on the Island and one of the first in the country. Tens of thousands of golfing enthusiasts from all over the world came to Shinnecock Hills in 1986 when it was the site of the U.S. Open.

LET'S GO IS—LAN—DERS

Long Islanders love to watch professional athletes in ac-

117

LONG ISLAND

tion, and the Island's championship hockey team, the New York Islanders, is a major source of pride.

The hockey pucks were hitting the seats like acorns off an oak tree, but with a lot more speed and power. The New York Islanders were finishing up a practice session at Nassau Coliseum, and half the team was lined up at the blue line shooting pucks at goalie Billy Smith. As Smith blocked most of the shots, the pucks came flying over the glass partition, making visitors do some serious ducking.

In between dodging, Greg Bouris, public relations official for the team, was explaining what Long Island means to its most successful professional sports team.

"The majority of these hockey players are Canadian," said Bouris. "Most of the guys have never seen the ocean or Manhattan until they come to play for the Islanders. This is such an attractive area and it's so close to the City. They love it here. The weather is a major consideration. Summers are beautiful and the winters are mild. This is a place players want to be. Not like Winnipeg for example, where it gets to 40 degrees below zero.

I've heard most of the fans there take intermission time to go outside and charge up their car batteries."

Another reason New York Islanders enjoy being Islanders is the team's record. The Islanders' first season was 1972-1973. By 1980 they had won the Stanley Cup. Then they won three more in a row—four Stanley Cups in four consecutive years by a team that had only been in existence for 10 years. It's quite a record, and just one shy of the NHL record for consecutive titles held by the Montreal Canadians.

"When Montreal won their five consecutive cups there were only six NHL teams," Bouris said. "When the Islanders won their four, there were 21 teams. That meant a lot more playoff games had to be won." And win they did. The Islanders hold the NHL record of 19 consecutive playoff series wins. They've had 13 consecutive winning seasons. That's been a boon to the local economy. Everybody loves a winner and the Islanders have been selling out for years. Local businesses feel the ripple effect.

Many of the hockey players choose to live on

Long Island year-round. Canadian Brian Trottier, an NHL superstar, is one of them. The New York Islanders is the only team Trottier, a native of Saskatchewan, has ever played for, and he's owned a home on the Island for 12 years.

During the off-season, "I do absolutely nothing," Trottier said. "I just relax with my family. My wife and I are real homebodies."

"That's what's so nice about Long Island. Long Island provides everything. You're close to the city, and there are different types of recreation. I used to own a boat, but now we belong to a country club so we swim there."

About three-fourths of the Islanders team have become Long Islanders, Bouris said. They've bought homes and started businesses. They're active in local charitable organizations. Most settle in the Huntington/Northport area. "It's become a tradition," Bouris said.

The New York Islanders have become Long Island's celebrities: Trottier; Mike Bossy, with his record of nine consecutive years of 50-goal seasons; goalie Billy Smith, an original Islander; and Denis Potvin, a leading defenseman who played his last season of hockey in 1987-1988, are among the players who have won Long Islanders' hearts over the years.

Although many Long Island hockey fans remain loyal to the New York Rangers, a hockey team with a much longer history, it's the Islanders who are exciting the youth of Long Island. And the team itself is becoming more youthful.

"You're seeing a changing of the guard," said Bouris, "a transformation from an older team." The names of the new young players may not be famous right now, but "we could be looking at the future superstars of hockey," Bouris predicted.

THE METS, THE JETS, EVEN THE NETS

Shea Stadium is just over the border from Nassau County, and physically it's on the Island, so Long Islanders consider the teams that play at Shea their own. That means the former world champions, the New York Mets baseball team, has many a fan in Nassau and Suffolk. Many of the Mets live on the Island during the season. The Port Washington/Manhasset area is a favorite spot.

For many years the Jets, the former Super Bowl

Facing page: The New York Islanders receive a tremendous amount of local support. Photo by Bruce Bennett

Below: A Mets game at Shea Stadium is a popular spring and summer outing. Photo by Bruce Bennett

champions, played at Shea Stadium. Even though they now call the Meadowlands home, Long Islanders still root for the Jets. Their coach, Joe Walton, lives in Suffolk County, and the Jets return each year to Long Island to their training camp at Hofstra University. The football players are usually quite willing to sign autographs or have their picture taken with a fan.

Over the years there have been other professional teams to woo the attention of the Long Island fan. The New Jersey Nets basketball team did their first dribbling and shooting at the Nassau Coliseum when they were called the New York Nets. There have been professional soccer teams, another hockey team, and even a tennis team.

THE OTHER SPORTS AND RECREATION

Long Islanders love tennis (witness the popularity of the U.S. Open held in nearby Flushing Meadows), running (there's the Long Island Marathon race down Wantagh Parkway to Jones Beach), racquetball, softball, soccer, walking, hiking (the Greenbelt Trails in Nassau and Suffolk offer wonderful hikes through secluded woodlands), and camping.

Bowling is a favorite Long Island hobby, and the Island has hosted national professional bowling championships at some of its fine alleys. Several bowling alleys are completely computerized. You get a strike at one of those facilities and the video screen makes you feel like you've just scored a touchdown for the Jets.

Another popular Long Island sport, rich in heritage, is bicycling. In the late 1800s, with the advent of the safety bike—two wheels of equal size—bike mania took over the Island. There was a 15-mile toll road from Patchogue to Port Jefferson exclusively for bicycles.

In 1898 the LIRR carried 176,000 bikes on its trains, mostly to Patchogue, the biking capital of the Island. A century run—100 miles of biking—was a popular weekend recreation for New York City residents, and since Patchogue was 50 miles from the City line, it became the biking destination.

From Mile-a-Minute Murphy, a bicyclist who raced a Long Island railroad train, to today's Long Islander who does a little Sunday bike touring, Long Islanders' love of bicycling has continued.

Another sport that had some of its earliest days on Long Island is auto racing. In the early 1900s the region was the auto racing capital of the country. William K. Vanderbilt, Jr., "Willie K" as his friends called him, was an auto racing aficionado. He created the Vanderbilt Cup, an auto race run through the public streets of Lake Success and Jericho. In 1908, he opened the Vanderbilt Motor Parkway, which ran from Flushing to Ronkonkoma. It was the first paved highway in the country. Used almost solely for racing in the early 1900s, at its peak Motor Parkway held 150,000 race cars a year.

HORSES, HORSES

Long Island is the original home of horse racing in this country. The first race track in America was constructed on the Hempstead Plains in 1664. The Island's early settlers loved horse racing and held many unusual contests. One favorite stipulated that the winning horse was the one that could cover the most amount of ground without dropping dead. Another race had owners riding each other's horses—the one who stayed on the longest won. They even had cross-country horse races 100 miles long.

Long Island became the capital of horse racing in colonial America. Competition that pitted the best horses in the North against the South brought crowds to the Hempstead Plains of up to 70,000 people, more than double the entire population of Suffolk at the time.

Long Island's love for horses and racing has continued. Belmont Park Race Track in Elmont, which was named for local philanthropist August Belmont, is not far from the Hempstead Plains. The track is host each year to the Belmont Stakes—"the test of champions." That race, the Kentucky Derby, and the Preakness make up the Triple Crown.

While Belmont Park and Aqueduct Racetrack in Queens are for Thoroughbreds and what is called flat racing, Roosevelt Raceway in Westbury has been the home of Standardbreds, or trotters, and harness racing. Trotters are bred on Long Island, so if you go to Roosevelt Raceway, chances are you will see Long Island horses run.

Many Long Islanders own horses and ride them on private property or specially marked trails. Some horse lovers even play polo. Often considered the sport of the rich, on Long Island polo can be viewed by everyone since matches are played every Sunday afternoon in the late summer and early fall at Bethpage State Park. "It's sort of like soccer on horses," one novice observer was heard to say about the sport that may be the fastest game played on land.

Animals, birds, and fish play important parts in the Island's recreational scene. The Smithtown Hunt Club still holds fox hunts, and duck hunting is a popular

ISLAND AT PLAY

sport. For those on the other side of the fence, bird watching is popular, and so is whale watching, a recreation unavailable in many parts of the country. There are horse shows, dog shows, cat shows, and rabbit shows. Long Island is even home to an annual guppy show. Guppies are flown in from all over the country to vie for "best guppy" in the prestigious Long Island guppy extravaganza.

LET ME ENTERTAIN YOU . . .

The Nassau Veterans Memorial Coliseum has been host to almost all of the Island's professional sports teams. For the New York Islanders' games, 16,270 fans pack the Uniondale arena. "The sightlines are great for the fans and the ice surface is good for the players," said Bouris of the Islanders.

But it's not just sports that lure Long Islanders to the coliseum. Besides the trade shows and the circus, just about every popular entertainer has performed there, from Frank Sinatra to the rock group Whitesnake. Coliseum management has even installed a "quiet room" for parents who drive their children to and from the rock concerts but prefer to pass the time in-between a little more serenely.

Other popular entertainment centers include The Westbury Music Fair, a theater in the round, and the outdoor Jones Beach Theatre, which in the 1950s offered Broadway musical productions. In recent years the Jones Marine Theater has been a success with pop entertainers such as Diana Ross and the Beach Boys.

Nassau and Suffolk counties and local towns also have entertainment theaters. Nassau County's Chapin Lakeside Theatre in Eisenhower Park holds 16,000. The facility was named after the late Harry Chapin, one of Long Island's most popular balladeers.

The Bald Hill Cultural Center in Farmingville, when completed, will be home to an 18,000-seat amphitheater. The arena, on one of the highest elevations of the Island, will be the largest permanent outdoor facility in Suffolk.

For a night out on the town, vacations, weekends, or just a day of playing hookey, Long Island is the place to be, and that's year-round. So whether you're reading this on a sunny summer day with the ocean breezes flipping the pages, or as the snow begins to fall on a brisk winter day, think about going out to play, the Long Island way.

What Long Islanders Have to Say About Recreation and Sports on the Island

John Sheridan, former regional director, Long Island region, New York State Office of Parks:

We don't have any of the carnival atmosphere in our parks. We don't have the Florida water slides—those types of amusements that are basically of the Hula-Hoop variety—here today, gone tomorrow.

I must have had 50 inquiries from people interested in taking a room at Jones Beach and setting up Pac Man or some type of video game. We don't have any of that. Yet we still draw a full house on Saturdays and Sundays. The people have told us loud and clear, they want the parks to stay the way they are.

It all goes back to Moses. He set the standards. We're just carrying the baton."

Greg Bouris, public relations official, New York Islanders:

A lot of the players are buying houses or condos on the Island. Long Island is such a prime market for real estate they figure even if they have to leave in two or three years they can turn over the house and make a profit.

Brian Trottier, professional hockey player, New York Islanders, on talking to other players about Long Island:

We don't talk up Long Island or try to put it on a pedestal. It's really nice, so we don't want zillions of people flocking here.

**Facing page: Golfers in East Hampton enjoy the beauty of the Long Island greens.
Photo by Ken Spencer**

X

Culturally Speaking

122

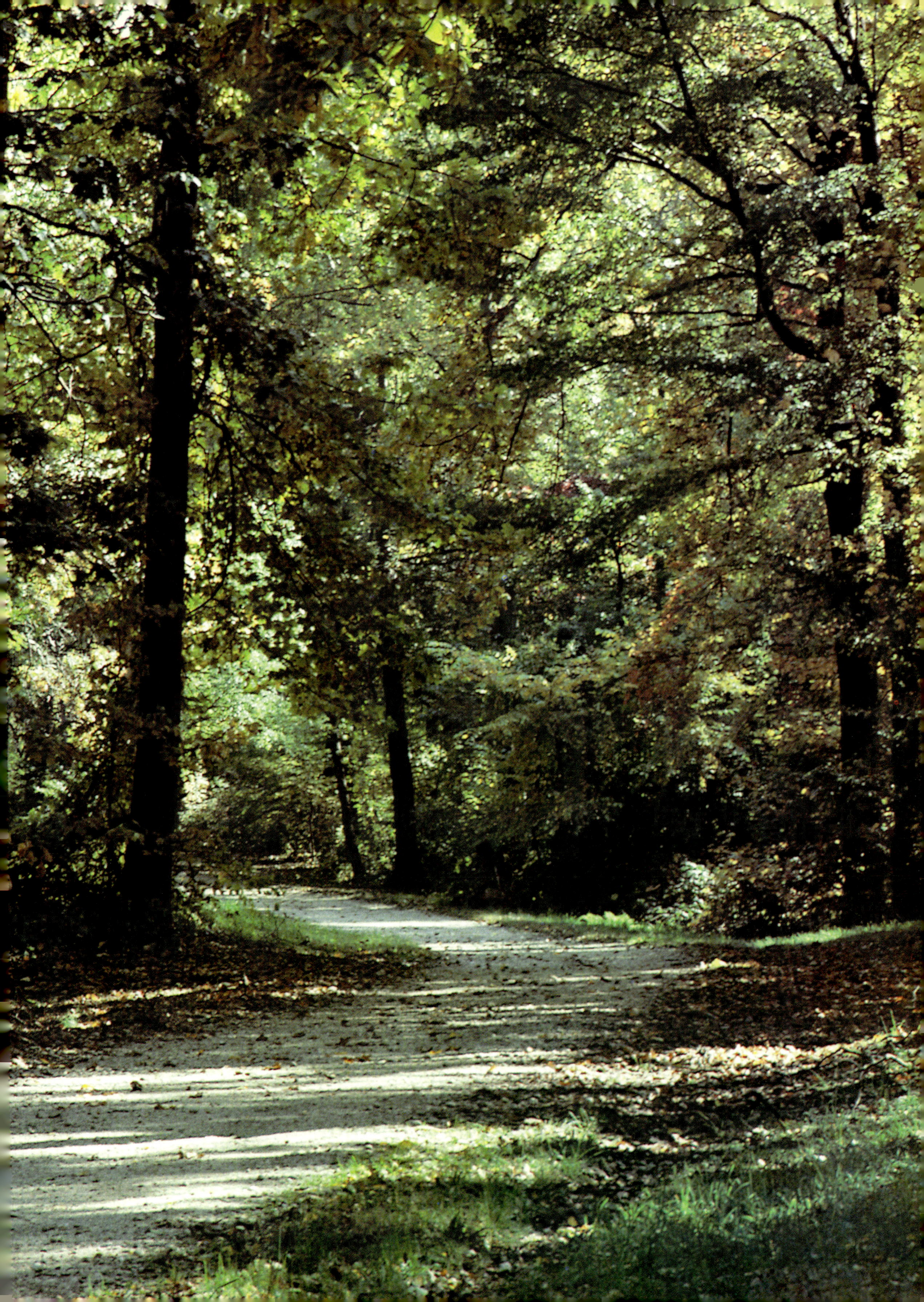

LONG ISLAND

Above: The lighthouses of Long Island are as popular with photographers and painters as they are with boaters. Photo by Ken Spencer

Previous page: This infrequently traveled path in Caumsett State Park, Lloyd Neck, offers visitors a chance to get away from it all. Photo by Colin Photographics

Facing page: Shafts of light lend a pastoral glow to a historic cemetery in East Hampton. Photo by Ken Spencer

Courtney Brady, a mouse from Great Neck, watches from the sidelines, as the Sugar Plum Fairy leaps across the expansive Tilles Center stage.

"Next year I hope to be a sugar plum," whispers 15-year-old Brady, who, in her third production of *The Nutcracker* ballet, has already moved up to portraying a mouse from previous stints as a soldier. Brady is one of many young Long Island dancers who join the local Eglevsky Ballet company for the annual Christmas production of *The Nutcracker*.

The Eglevksy *Nutcracker*, one of several versions of the popular holiday ballet presented on Long Island, is performed in the ultramodern Tilles Center on the grounds of the C.W. Post campus in Brookville. A few weeks earlier the angelic voices of the Vienna Boys Choir had wafted through the air at Tilles.

The Boys Choir is Long Island's annual Christmas gift from the Friends of the Arts, a nonprofit group founded 16 years ago "to address the lack of cultural enrichment" on the Island, according to its executive director, Theodora "Teddy" Bookman.

"When we began there was only a smattering of arts on the Island, small regional groups, nothing of significance," Bookman recalled. "There was only the City. But life-styles change. As more and more people made their lives here, worked here, grew up here, the City became a farther-away place. Now people look for alternatives in entertainment. People say 'let's try it at home.' There is no reason that Long Island, with its population base, can't support its own arts."

And Long Island is beginning to do just that. In addition to the popularity of cultural traditions, such as the Eglevsky *Nutcracker*, Island cultural events are more and more the choice for those who don't want to travel into the City.

Such illustrious performers as Itzhak Perlman, the Chicago Symphony Orchestra, and the Dance Theatre of Harlem have graced Long Island concert halls, thanks to the sponsorship of the 1,300 members of Friends of the Arts. And the Tilles Center, one of the Island's premier concert halls, offers its own extensive agenda of international and national artists. These guest performances supplement the many fine Island-based orchestras, dance groups, and theater troupes. The history and art museums of Long Island add to the area's cultural world.

Long Islanders are proud of their culture, both present and past. "If you lose your heritage, you lose your soul," said John C. Bierwirth, former chairman of the board of the Grumman Corporation. Long Islanders give of both their time and money to make sure that doesn't happen.

SAVING HISTORY

It stands as a sentry on watch, a solitary figure on the easternmost bluffs of Long Island. The brown and white octagonal lighthouse was commissioned by President George Washington in 1795, making it one of the oldest lighthouses in the country. Today the Montauk Point Lighthouse is one of the most recognizable structures in the world.

Although the Montauk lighthouse may be Long Island's most famous historic landmark, it is by no means the oldest, nor is it the only lighthouse that has stirred the emotions of Island preservationists. The Fire Island Lighthouse was recently restored through Long Islanders' efforts, and the 15 other lighthouses on Long Island all have their loyal followings. So do thousands of historical homes, buildings, and even windmills.

More than 60 historical societies operate in the two counties, and with groups such as the Society for the Preservation of Long Island Antiquities and the 2,800-member Friends for Long Island's Heritage, preserving the Island's history has become a top priority.

With 350 years of history Long Island has no short supply of historic buildings. From Sagtikos Manor in West Islip, where George Washington slept, to Sagamore Hill in Oyster Bay, where President Theodore Roosevelt not only slept but raised his family, historic landmarks are as common to the Long Island scenery as are pitch pine trees.

Drive down the main streets of any of the older

LONG ISLAND

Right: Time stands still on this street in the Old Bethpage Village Restoration. Photo by Ken Spencer

Facing page: Rural life of the 1800s is displayed in Old Bethpage. Photo by Ken Spencer

Below: Autumn is pumpkin time on Long Island. Jack-o-lantern lovers make their selections at the annual Long Island Fair. Photo by Ken Spencer

communities—Huntington, Roslyn, Amityville, Stony Brook, Southold, East Hampton, or Southampton, to name just a few—and you'll find numerous examples of preservation. Markers pointing out the site where some important historic event occurred or plaques in front of historic houses and buildings are an integral part of the Island's landscape.

And then there are the historic museums. From the whaling museums in Cold Spring Harbor and Sag Harbor to the maritime museum in West Sayville, to the Afro-American Museum in Hempstead, which traces the history of Long Island's black population, Long Island history is preserved and on display in just about every community.

The Museums at Stony Brook, a group of several museums, offer a collection of nineteenth-century history and art, most notably paintings by William Sidney Mount, Long Island's most prominent colonial artist and a native of Stony Brook. And the recently opened Carriage Museum there offers one of the finest collections of horse-drawn carriages in the world.

The Stony Brook museums, which started with the collection of philanthropist Ward Melville, another Stony Brook native, continue to grow. So does Long Island's most popular look at the past, the Old Bethpage Village Restoration in Old Bethpage.

126

CULTURALLY SPEAKING

OLD BETHPAGE VILLAGE

"You're supposed to lick it," explained four-year-old Jesse Kirdahy-Scalia of Farmingdale as he took the first lick of his very first candy apple.

"He's been bugging me for weeks to have a candy apple," said his mother, Donna Kirdahy. "I know he shouldn't have sweets, but, well, this is special."

And special it was. As Jesse proudly displayed his apple, even allowing his 21-month-old sister Mikki to take a lick, the Kirdahy-Scalia family continued their tour of the Long Island Fair, an old-fashioned agricultural fair held each fall on the grounds of the Old Bethpage Village Restoration in Old Bethpage. A tribute to Long Island's farming heritage, the Long Island Fair is educational and entertaining at the same time.

Just about every type of livestock, vegetable, dessert, and hand-sewn product is on display or in competition. While Long Islanders of today compete over who grows the best string beans, sews the finest quilt, bakes the best apple pie, or has the cockiest rooster, the atmosphere of the fair is geared to the past. Employees of Old Bethpage are dressed in nineteenth-century garb and fiddlers fiddle while magicians offer tricks as old as the era they're portraying.

Numerous yearly festivals and parades celebrate the Island's diverse heritage. Events range from Indian pow-wows to the Oyster Festival in Oyster Bay, sponsored by the Oyster Bay Chamber of Commerce. The Oyster Festival draws tens of thousands of spectators who commemorate Long Island's golden days of oystering by feasting on every type of oyster dish and watching oyster-eating and shucking contests.

But on any day a visit to Old Bethpage Village means time to turn back the clock, slow down, and enjoy. There are no amusement rides. This is a quiet look at Long Island's past. Costumed villagers welcome you to antique-furnished homes and shops. The restoration village, set on 200 acres of Nassau countryside, is a living museum of Long Island in the 1800s—a working farm community. While dressed in nineteenth-century costumes, the Nassau County employees actually farm the land, take care of the animals, make candles, and serve as blacksmiths. Old Bethpage Village is considered one of the major outdoor restorations in the United States.

While other areas of the Northeast may offer a history as old as Long Island's and have similarly preserved eighteenth-century and nineteenth-century buildings, no area of the country can match Long Island's combination of historic eras.

Long Island's history and therefore its museums encompass the Indian days, the colonial days, the whaling days, the Gold Coast mansion days, and the space age.

One of the more fascinating periods of Long Island culture was the early 1900s and the birth of Long Island's mansion era. "The Gold Coast days," they call it, and it took place on the Island's North Shore.

MANSION REMEMBRANCES

"Remember in the film *Love Story*, when Ali McGraw and Ryan O'Neal were driving up this long driveway and finally seeing this incredible house, she turns to him and says, 'You live there?'"

"Well there is here," said Eleanor Simpson of the Long Island Tourism and Convention Commission. She finished her story just as she and a visitor completed the drive up the same long driveway that the *Love Story* lovers drove up years back.

The mansion that caught the attention of Ali McGraw and impressed thousands of others since is the Westbury House at Old Westbury Gardens. Old Westbury Gardens, where the movie *North by Northwest* was also filmed, is the former estate of the John S. Phipps family. Visitors who tour the lovely mansion or stroll the grounds, the site of some of the most

127

LONG ISLAND

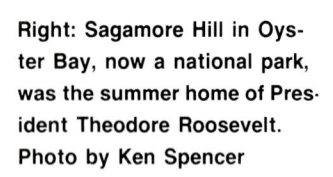

Right: Sagamore Hill in Oyster Bay, now a national park, was the summer home of President Theodore Roosevelt. Photo by Ken Spencer

Below: Theodore Roosevelt slept in this bed on display at Sagamore Hill. Photo by Audrey Gibson

exquisite gardens on Long Island, might just run into a Phipps, since Peggy Phipps Boegner has spent her entire life on the estate.

Boegner currently lives in a smaller house just a few hundred feet from the mansion. "I come up to the house often when visitors are here, I just don't say who I am," the 80-year-old Boegner said.

She recalled how the mansion became a museum. "We wanted to keep the house so we could keep mother's gardens," she said. "We had sold off the polo fields and the nine-hole golf course."

So the museum/estate includes the formal gardens and the manor home, which is furnished as it was when the Phipps family lived there. "It's 99 and one-half percent the way it was when I was a child," Boegner said, adding, "I refer to it as a stately home; it's too bad it sounds so snobbish."

Other North Shore mansions are now museums, such as Falaise, the former Guggenheim estate, part of The Sands Point Preserve museum complex in Port Washington. And several preserved mansions with their lavish landscapes have become arboretums. Planting Fields and Bayard Cutting are two.

The Vanderbilt Museum and Planetarium in Centerport is the former estate of William K. Vanderbilt Jr., great grandson of Cornelius "Commodore" Vanderbilt, founder of the New York Central Railroad and builder of the Staten Island Ferry. The Vanderbilts loved Long Island, and their family mansions dot the region. The one called Idle Hour in Oakdale is now the site of Dowling College.

The Centerport mansion Vanderbilt called Eagles Nest sits on 43 acres overlooking Northport Harbor and Long Island Sound. The mansion's 24 rooms are kept as they were in the early 1900s when "Willie K" called the place home. Besides tours of the mansion, visitors can enjoy the Sky Theater in the planetarium, and an observatory where you can look at the moon, the stars, or the sun.

SPACE AGE MEMORIES

The sky is also the focus of the Cradle of Aviation Museum, located at Mitchel Field in Uniondale. Since Long Island was the site of some of the nation's earliest air travel, and airplane building has been a major Island industry, an aviation museum was a natural for the region. The museum, started 11 years ago, features a collection of restored aircraft.

Planes on display include Charles Lindbergh's first plane, his 1918 *Jenny*; locally built fighter and bomber planes from World War II; and one of the four remaining Lunar modules built by Grumman.

There are plans to build a theater and expand the aircraft and space collection, according to Gerald Kessler, president of Friends for Long Island Heritage. The expansion would give Long Island its own version of the Smithsonian's Air and Space Museum.

ON STAGE

While Long Island museums house Long Island's past culture, its modern-day culture can be viewed at several impressive auditoriums. The Island lacks a giant cultural center, a type of Lincoln Center where various art forms congregate under one roof, but the Tilles Center on the C.W. Post Campus of Long Island University is used for many cultural events. So are the facilities at Hofstra University and other area colleges and universities.

Guild Hall, with its John Drew Theatre in East Hampton, has been called "Long Island's mini-Lincoln Center," since it offers diverse entertainment, especially during the summer season, and also houses excellent art exhibits.

Theater on the Island ranges from local and regional groups to the Long Island Stage, a professional equity company. Long Island Stage performs its elaborately staged productions in an

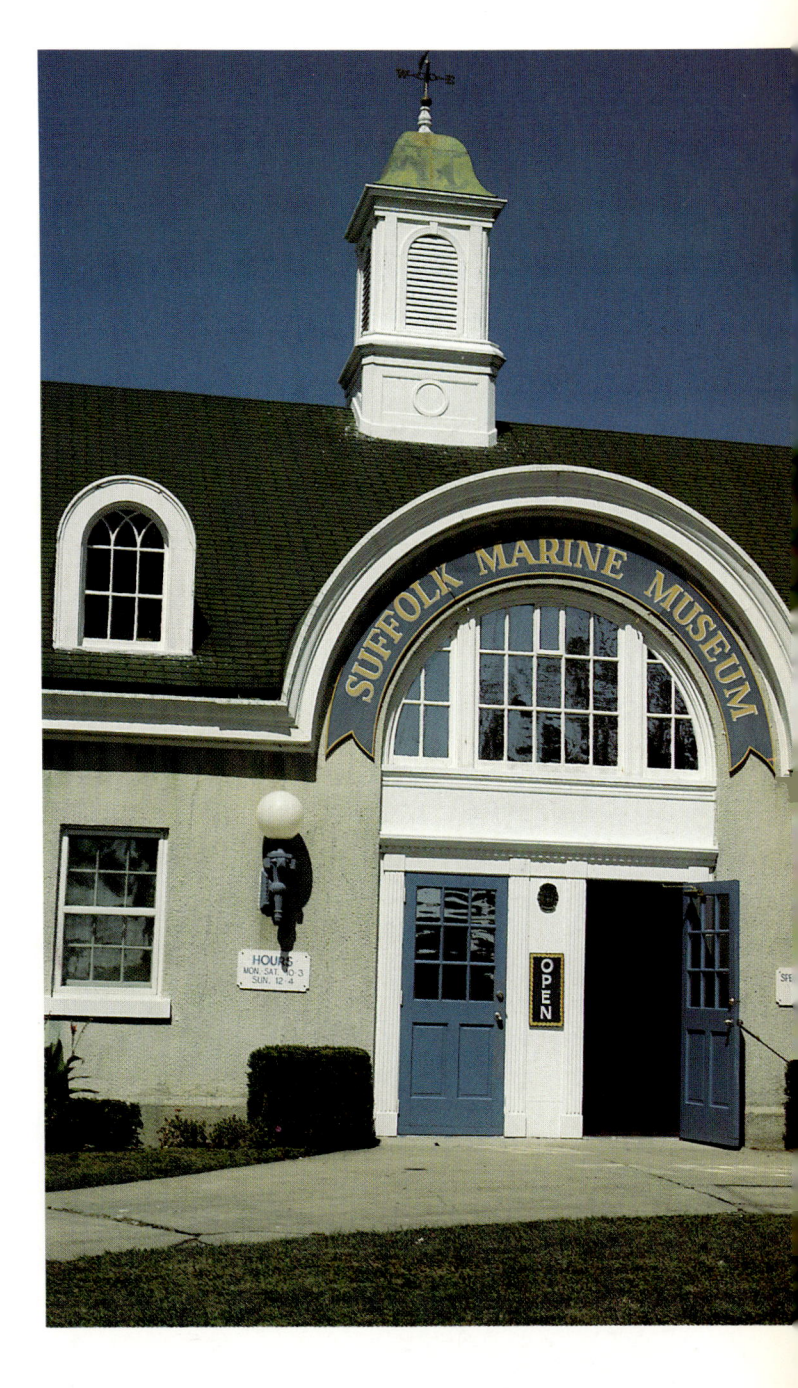

The Suffolk Marine Museum offers a look at the history of oystering on the Great South Bay. Photo by Bjorne M. Keith

Above: The Tilles Center for Performing Arts, located on the C.W. Post campus, is one of the most popular Island performance halls. Photo By Ken Spencer

Right: The music room of the William Sidney Mount home is on display at the Museums of Stony Brook. Photo by Ken Spencer

CULTURALLY SPEAKING

attractive theater at Molloy College in Rockville Centre.

Long Islanders can see the best in acting, dancing, and singing, and they also have the opportunity to listen to the finest music. "It's important for a community to have its own resident orchestra," said Katherine Wichterman, general manager of the Long Island Philharmonic. "We have a commitment to serve the Long Island community," she added.

Long Island's philharmonic, which performs at the Tilles Center and Hauppauge High School, offers mostly American music, Wichterman said. "We perform the music of our time." A special treat for Long Islanders is the annual outdoor evening performance the orchestra gives for free every summer at Heckscher State Park in East Islip.

The Nassau Symphony Orchestra, which turned professional six years ago, performs at Hofstra University, and Long Island even has a Senior Pops Orchestra made up primarily of senior citizens.

Art is also an important part of the Long Island cultural scene. The Heckscher Museum in Huntington offers a permanent collection of American and European paintings from the sixteenth to twentieth centuries, and changing exhibitions throughout the year.

Nassau County has its Museum of Fine Art, there's the Fine Arts Museum of Long Island (F.A.M.L.I.) in Hempstead, and there's the Parrish Art Museum in Southampton. Southampton and East Hampton are home to many of the Island's and the country's most prominent modern artists. The beauty of the East End has drawn artists to the area for decades, making the region Long Island's artist colony.

Art, music, dance, theater, and preserving the Island's past—Long Island's cultural world is alive and well. And, many add, the best is yet to come.

What Long Islanders Have to Say About Culture

Theodora "Teddy" Bookman, executive director, Friends of the Arts, about developing a summer arts festival:

Nothing can compare to Long Island in the summertime. You can go to the City for good food and good entertainment, but combine good food and entertainment with summer on Long Island, and I don't think anyone can compete with that.

That's why we're working to bring Long Island a summer festival, our own Tanglewood or Saratoga. We're looking for just the right site.

Gerald S. Kessler, president, Friends for Long Island's Heritage, about the health of Long Island's cultural scene:

It's very healthy. It's also insatiable. A simple restoration of an historic home can cost $250,000. And we're not running out of any historic homes to restore.

Donna Kirdahy of Farmingdale, mother of Jesse, 4, and Mikki, 21 months, on enjoying the Long Island Fair at Old Bethpage village:

I was thinking of taking my kids to Disney World when I realized the Long Island Fair was this weekend. We came here instead. They're having a great time, and it's a lot cheaper.

Above left: Age is not a factor when reliving Long Island's rich historical past. Photo by Bruce Bennett

131

XI
Shores of Challenge

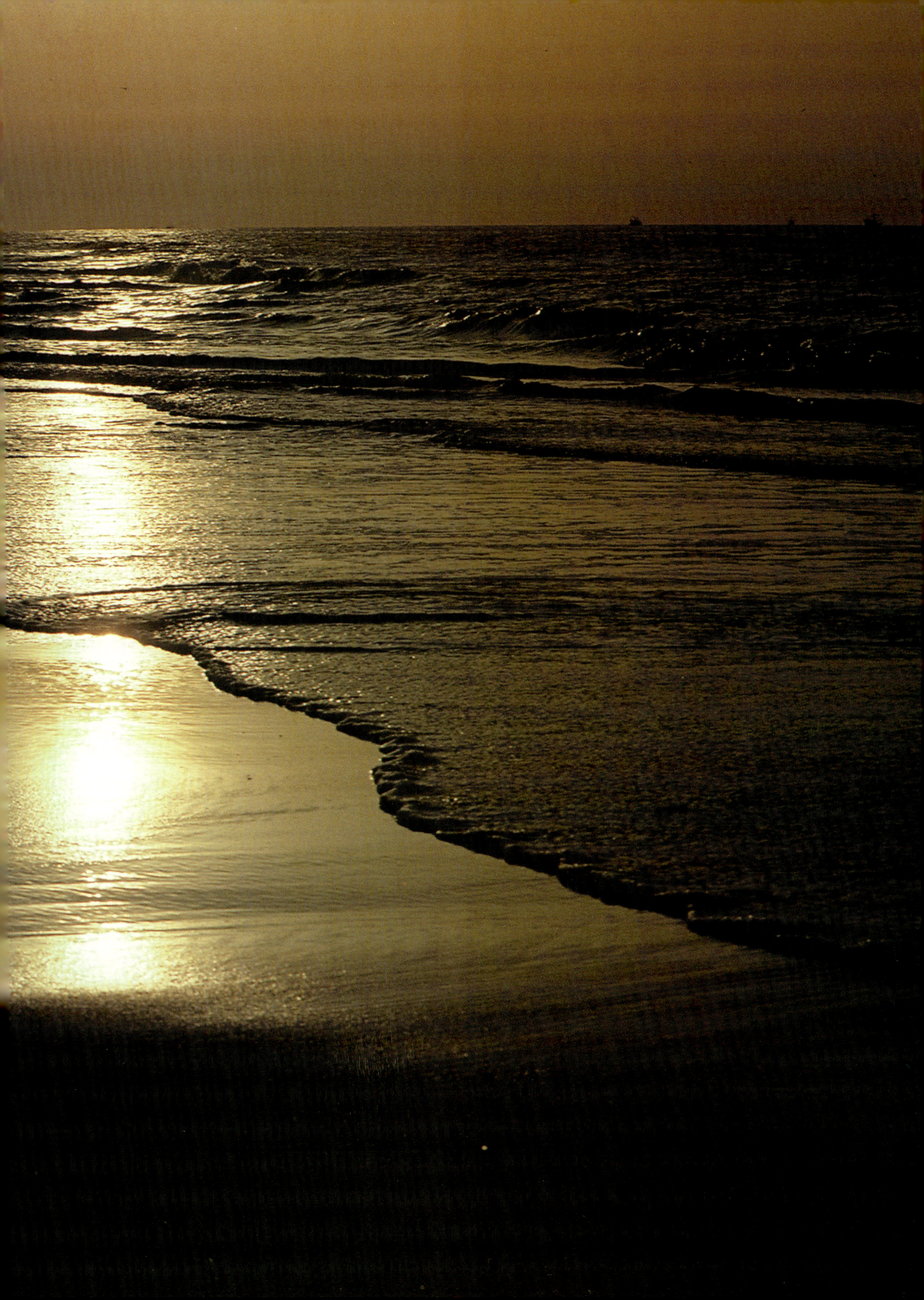

LONG ISLAND

Above: Tulips are indicative of springtime on Long Island. Photo by Bruce Bennett

Previous page: The sun sets over the ocean at Hither Hills State Park in Montauk. Photo by George Michell

Facing page: Another Long Island office building nears completion in Westbury. Photo by Ken Spencer

In 1949 the *New York Times* ran a series of articles about an incredible phenomenon that was taking place to the east of New York City. "An economic and sociological shift on a scale and at a tempo such as this country has seldom seen since the closing of its western frontier, is now taking place on Long Island," wrote reporter Frederick Graham.

Graham also reported on the incredible population explosion Long Island was experiencing and what that meant for the future of the region. The infrastructure was being overtaxed, Graham pointed out, and a debate was beginning to surface about whether or not light industry should be welcomed on Long Island. Some residents, content to keep Long Island residential, said bringing industry in would change the character of the Island.

Others believed diversified industry (defense plants were the major employers on the Island at the time) would bring great wealth to the area and offer jobs to thousands of Long Islanders. The industry proponents won out, and in the following decades Long Island was not only settled by hundreds of thousands of new homeowners but by thousands of new businesses as well.

The decision in favor of growth was important. It allowed Long Island to become a separate economic region, and the surge of development brought great prosperity to the area. But throughout the 1950s, 1960s, and 1970s, Long Island's motto appeared to be "Growth First, Infrastructure Second."

Now, 40 years later, Long Island is again on the threshold of a decision. The population infusion has subsided, and as Long Islanders prepare for the twenty-first century, they are taking stock of their past as they carefully plan their future. The 1990s must be a time of change, many say. It's time to balance growth with a rebuilding of the infrastructure and protection of the environment.

"We've been like a photographic negative that is developing," said Howard Schneider, managing editor of *Newsday*. "We're still developing but we're starting to get into focus. We're beginning to see what Long Island is going to be like, what kind of place this will be. For many years everything was changing at such a rapid pace, but we're not that fluid anymore."

Long Island's future will be shaped by nature's challenges today. Long Islanders are concerned about preserving their fragile Island environment while coping with the questions that face Americans in all parts of the country—how to dispose of garbage, how to produce enough energy, how to ease traffic congestion, how to keep the water pure, how to build affordable housing for the young and old.

"The challenge Long Islanders face is how to sustain the appropriate level of economic growth while not endangering the high quality of life that exists," said Jim Larocca, president of the Long Island Association. "It's always been easy to push eastward. Too little land? Too little water? Go east. Well, now we can see the borders. We're approaching the physical limits, and the challenge is how to accommodate those physical limitations with an economy that must continue to grow."

To find the solutions, Nassau and Suffolk county government, business, civic, academic, and labor officials, coordinated by the LIA, have joined together and formed Long Island Project 2000, a regional attempt to define and solve major problems facing Long Island. The two county governments are also working on master plans and mutual cooperation.

Government and business leaders agree that transportation, garbage disposal, affordable housing, protecting Long Island's drinking water, and meeting energy demands will be the major challenges to face the region in the next few decades.

The New York State Department of Commerce projects a 23 percent increase in car and truck traffic on Long Island by the year 2000. To ease congestion Long Islanders would like to see a fourth lane added to the LIE and service roads completed, the complete expansion of Sunrise Highway, and construction of an interchange at Meadowbrook and Northern State parkways.

Solving Long Island's transportation needs "is not a planning problem. It's a money problem," said Lee Koppelman, executive director of the Long Island Regional Planning Board. "Long Island has to be willing to tax itself. We've done that for open space. There seems to be no problem getting public support when you talk about parks, but when you talk about self-taxation for transportation, then everybody cries bloody murder."

Robert Johnson, publisher of *Newsday*, predicted that "eventually you're going to have to develop some form of transportation authority that will overcome the NIMBY [not in my backyard] mentality."

Affordable housing on Long Island is becoming "a critical issue," according to Larocca. "The real tragedy would be if the Long Island dream—moving out from the crowded city and raising a family in a home of your own—turns out to be a one-generation phenomenon. We want to retain our younger generation, those who were raised here, but with the high cost of housing, young people aren't always able to stay."

While the median income on Long Island is about

$41,000, the median price of a house in 1988 was $186,000. That's a sizable investment for a young couple just starting out.

"The only way we're going to have affordable housing is if the government intervenes," Koppelman said. "We need 50,000 units. We could revitalize the downtowns by putting in a variety of housing, over-the-store apartments, two- to four-family units, and condominiums."

Long Islanders have joined together to work on this challenge too. The Long Island Housing Partnership, a coalition of businesses, educational institutions, and the Roman Catholic Diocese of Rockville Centre, was formed by the LIA in 1987 to develop housing for those who earn between $25,000 and $50,000 a year. The partnership hopes to build 2,000 single family homes in the $70,000 to $110,000 price range on publicly owned land in the next two

This sailfish must wait for another day's breeze, as another splendid Long Island summer day draws to a close. Photo by Ken Spencer

years. Long Island's housing partnership is reported to be the first in the country to focus on the housing needs of a suburban area.

Protection of the area's water supply means handling growth and development by planning. One-hundred trillion gallons of water are said to flow under the ground of Long Island, and government officials are working to make sure that water remains pure. And in Suffolk, preserving the Pine Barrens, which stand atop Long Island's aquifers, the sole source of water, is a top priority.

Energy needs for the Island have also been the focus of Long Island officials and business leaders. Arguments about the controversial Shoreham Nuclear Power Plant went on for two decades. In 1987 the Long Island Power Authority was formed to discuss alternate jurisdiction over Long Island's energy supply.

As an alternative to nuclear power, local leaders have been pushing for the completion of the Marcy South transmission line, which will bring less expensive hydropower from Canada and upstate to the downstate area. A vital link to this energy source will be the installation of a transmission cable under Long Island Sound, which will connect Long Island with the end of the Marcy South line in Westchester.

Long Island is also facing the challenge to dispose of solid waste. As landfills become full, Long Islanders are turning more and more to recycling and resource recovery plants. For many years the disposal of solid waste was looked on as an issue solely for local towns; today it is a regional concern.

And to help those less fortunate on affluent Long Island, the area has an extraordinary volunteer network. From the larger organizations such as United Way, Catholic Charities, and United Jewish Appeal, to the smaller neighborhood walk-in centers, caring about others has become a Long Island tradition.

While the challenges facing Long Island in the decades ahead will require the continued commitment of government and business, optimism abounds for the future of this island region. Long Island offers something for everyone. Located next to the world's most exciting city, this resort island with its parks, beaches, and booming economy is also home to millions of the most educated and dynamic people in the world.

Long Island's shores are truly the shores of plenty.

What Long Islanders Have to Say About the Challenges of Ensuing Decades

Robert M. Johnson, publisher and president of Newsday, *about Nassau, Suffolk, and the different government bodies splitting the Long Island identity:*

The identity of Long Island is somewhat schizophrenic. I don't know a single opinion leader outside of politics who doesn't believe that the single greatest challenge of the Island is to eliminate some of the artifical political boundaries.

From mansions to condos, just about every Long Island homeowner has a garden. Photo by Bruce Bennett

PART II

Partners in Progress

Photo by R. Settles

XII

Networks

Long Island's energy, communication, and transportation providers keep products, information, and power circulating inside and outside the area.

The Long Island Lighting Company, 142

AT&T, 146

The Long Island Rail Road, 147

Photo by R. Settles

LONG ISLAND

THE LONG ISLAND LIGHTING COMPANY

Electric and gas utilities often have reputations as depersonalized organizations. Long Island Lighting Company (LILCO) has worked hard to make sure that description doesn't fit its operations by developing a company-wide sensitivity to meeting the needs of customers in an individual, caring way.

When Arthur Van Riper, a LILCO customer service representative, as an example, received notification from a field representative that an elderly Sea Cliff customer was not answering the door, he set out on a routine investigation. Van Riper works with customers whose health or financial problems make it difficult for them to pay their utility bills.

He failed to make contact with the customer on his first visit and followed up a few days later. Van Riper had caught a glimpse of an elderly woman inside the house on his first call and was now concerned because it was an extremely hot day, and all the windows and doors were closed. "I figured it must have been about 110 degrees in there," he recalls.

Alarmed, Van Riper returned to

Senior customers receive special services through the Golden Link Program.

his office and contacted the Nassau County Department of Social Services. The elderly woman was contacted by a medical team and taken to a local hospital for treatment. She is awaiting placement in a nursing home.

"My job at times is frustrating because sometimes people don't want help. But, it is satisfying when things work out well and you can really help someone. This incident happened on a Friday afternoon. I couldn't wait to get to work on Monday to find out what

LILCO's Gatekeeper Program trains employees to watch for the special needs of older customers.

had happened. I know you shouldn't bring your work home with you, but this case was different," says Van Riper.

While this case is indeed special, for LILCO's 6,000 employees, helping people is part of their daily routine. LILCO's array of programs to service its one million customers range from the only 24-hour customer-assistance telephone service operated by a New York utility to special outreach activities for senior citizens and other groups.

The elderly Sea Cliff woman was brought to Van Riper's attention by a field representative involved in LILCO's Gatekeeper Program, which trains employees to identify vulnerable senior citizens and to help them obtain the social services they may need.

"We recognize that as Long Island's population matures, its needs are changing," says Cathy Tautel, consumer affairs specialist, who initiated the program. "Gatekeeper gives us a chance to perform a valuable service for a growing part of our customer base while adding to our employees' job satisfaction."

LILCO employees echo Tautel's assessment of the program. "I used to feel frustrated that I couldn't do any-

NETWORKS

LILCO is the first New York utility to offer 24-hour, seven-day phone service for customers to conduct business.

thing to help," says Ann Alexander, a meter reader and Gatekeeper participant, "but now I have an outlet and can contribute."

Among the utility's other services is the Golden Link Program, which offers a quarterly newsletter and a toll-free hot line providing information on subjects and programs of interest to customers 62 years of age and older.

LILCO offices are equipped with special devices that can receive typewritten messages from customers with hearing and speech difficulties. Customers dependent on dialysis, oxygen support, and other equipment of this type can notify a customer relations office so that a LILCO representative can contact them to determine if special assistance is needed during a power outage. In addition, through LILCO's Peace of Mind program customers who are hospitalized can receive an extension on their bills or can arrange for a deferred payment plan if financial circumstances do not permit timely payment.

Tautel reports that LILCO's outreach programs have uncovered a great lack of awareness among special-needs customers of social services available to help them. Consequently, the company has added several human services professionals to its staff to assist with the more difficult cases.

Another LILCO program, the 24-hour, seven-day telephone service, has proved widely successful, averaging 3,000 calls per week, about one-third of them received between the hours of 8 p.m. and 8 a.m. "Let's face it, we don't live in a nine-to-five world anymore," says Steve Maslak, manager of customer relations. "Life-styles today demand the flexibility of continuous service."

Consumer education is a critical part of LILCO's customer service efforts because a knowledgeable customer saves energy and money. The 55 members of LILCO's speakers' bureau are kept busy informing community groups about services, conservation, safety, and other related matters. "When members of my audience tell me 'Thanks. I really learned something' or 'You answered my question,' I get a real sense of satisfaction," says Jean Hersey.

Schoolchildren receive special attention from LILCO educators, not only because they are the future energy users, but also because children are often more vulnerable to energy-related accidents. In addition to its year-round program of school safety demonstrations, LILCO sponsors an Electric Safety Day each spring.

"Electric Safety Day is our way of getting children interested in safety.

A wide range of safety programs are available to schools.

143

LONG ISLAND

LILCO's Energy Works Center is a store filled with energy-saving items for consumers.

Our linemen demonstrate the use of protective equipment to kids. We have the electric safety presentation we give at the schools, and we have a kite-flying demonstration," explains Mary Castellana, community relations specialist. "It takes about two months of coordination and organization, but it's well worth it. I had a great time doing it, and I can't wait for next year."

The Energy Works Center, located in Massapequa's Sunrise Mall, and its accompanying mobile unit that tours the island, contain displays, exhibits, and high-efficiency home-lighting equipment, appliances, air conditioners, and water and space heaters. The center's employees also staff LILCO's Energy Hot Line, a toll-free telephone service that provides advice on a wide range of energy conservation matters.

"The hot line is very popular," says Jim Madsen, program coordinator for the center. "In fact, in the first quarter of 1988 we set a new record by responding to more than 5,000 customers."

Free home energy audits are provided for both new and existing customers. LILCO also offers low- and no-interest loans and grants to eligible customers who install conservation measures recommended during the audit. As a particular service to senior citizens, energy audits are performed by fellow seniors. "It makes senior customers feel more comfortable since they're able to relate better to fellow seniors. It provides work for retired professionals on fixed incomes. And it helps us deliver specific messages about the many programs geared strictly to senior citizens," explains program coordinator Bob DeLorenzo.

Commercial and industrial customers also benefit from free energy analyses, as well as from rebate programs for installation of energy-saving equipment and energy management courses for their employees who are responsible for energy use.

LILCO's aggressive energy conservation program is recognized as an industry leader. "These programs have now become an important part of the company's overall plan to help solve Long Island's energy crisis. In implementing them, we hope to reduce electric use significantly during the peak summer period," explains Tony Ricca, manager, energy management. "With all these programs, we are working in advance to help prevent power shortages. And, equally important, we are helping our customers better understand their electric use and lower energy costs."

Keeping LILCO's five major power stations, 40 smaller plants, 325,000 utility poles, 50,000 miles of electric wires, 160,000 transformers, and 10,000 miles of gas mains in top working order and providing uninterrupted service are the most critical components of the utility's customer service program.

In 1988 LILCO spent $15 million and dedicated 150,000 man-hours to power plant maintenance alone. "The results of the plant maintenance program are quite evident. Our equipment availability is high, our unit availability is high, and our capacity factor is higher. That's all related to mainte-

LILCO energy experts make free house calls to provide customized energy-saving advice for homes and businesses.

144

NETWORKS

nance," explains chief engineer Joe Short.

For many LILCO employees, however, helping Long Islanders doesn't stop when they leave the work place. "There is something about the atmosphere in the company. Perhaps it's because our people realize the vital service LILCO provides to their families and neighbors. LILCO employees have a great loyalty to the company and to the community," says vice-president Joseph McDonnell, who notes that during times of emergency the firm's retirees are among the first to report to work.

In 1987 LILCO employees formed a community service group called the Lamplighters, a name chosen because it represents the community spirit of gas lamplighters who also served as neighborhood watchmen. The group's purpose is to consolidate all the various activities in which LILCO personnel already participate, and to create a volunteer network that can be tapped by employees and community members alike.

LILCO Lamplighters have organized food drives, Toys for Tots collections, holiday visits to nursing homes and other institutions, fund-raising campaigns for numerous charities, and a recruitment drive for literacy volunteers to help adults learn to read.

The utility's employees were well represented in the 1988 March of Dimes 25-kilometer annual Walk America fund-raising effort. "March of Dimes holds a personal spot in my heart because my brother is handicapped and I have multiple sclerosis," says Jen Shedrick, a customer service representative who helped staff a refreshment table along the walk route. "Because I couldn't walk, I felt I should do anything I could to be a part of the event," she adds, displaying LILCO employees' traditional commitment to cooperation and good will on and off the job.

LEFT: Maintaining LILCO's electric system of 325,000 poles and 50,000 miles of wire is the most important part of LILCO's consumer program.

BELOW: LILCO's power plant team operated the company's generators at peak productivity to meet record consumer electric demand.

LONG ISLAND

AT&T

AT&T has long been a part of Long Island and New York. In fact, it has been headquartered in the state since Alexander Graham Bell, AT&T's founder, incorporated the company there in March 1885.

For more than a century the company provided local telephone service, equipment, and long-distance lines that connected Long Island with the rest of the country and the world.

AT&T remains an integral part of the community, though local telephone service is no longer a part of its business. The corporation has more than 1,400 employees at 25 locations, including a satellite earth station in Coram. The people of AT&T serve homes and businesses with a complete range of telephones, computers, typewriters, FAX machines, and long-distance services.

In today's Information Age, AT&T is working diligently to supply advanced technology and electronic networks that provide the best voice, data, and video communications.

On Long Island, AT&T long-distance operators help people with special needs to make calls, whether it's a person-to-person call or assistance to disabled persons. The conference operator center in Huntington is one of four such AT&T centers in the country. The 125 conference operators handle customers from Maine to Virginia and east to Ohio.

The firm has 10 Phone Center stores on Long Island—the largest number serving any one geographic area. Phone Centers provide AT&T products ranging from residential telephones and accessories to electronic typewriters, FAX machines, and small business systems.

AT&T marketing people serve both large and small businesses, from Grumman Aviation and Avis to retail shops and professional offices.

A tradition of customer service is basic to every AT&T employee's work ethic. The AT&T people on Long Island are committed to seeing that the right equipment is installed quickly and correctly—from traditional home telephones to complex information and data systems.

Sales professionals work with their customers to design systems and networks that meet special business needs. For example, the Long Island Savings Bank in Melville has the largest AT&T System 85 in the area. The System 85, with 1,000 stations and 230 trunks, uses fiber-optic cable and controls a network connecting 110 outside lines to other bank branches.

The technicians who install equipment and maintain AT&T's sophisticated long-distance network are among the most experienced anywhere. Living in the communities in which they work, these men and women have responded to the needs of their neighbors and have often proven their remarkable skill by quickly restoring telephone service after floods and storms.

The company also has a long tradition of community service, helping neighbors and organizations through volunteerism and financial support. Both active and retired AT&T employees volunteer countless hours through projects sponsored by the Telephone Pioneers of America.

AT&T is looking forward to meeting the needs of its Long Island customers with leading-edge telecommunication products and services, new technologies, and global communications as it faces a new decade and a new century.

AT&T operators in the Conference Center in Huntington.

The AT&T Phone Center in Jericho has a complete line of telecommunications equipment for sale or lease.

THE LONG ISLAND RAIL ROAD

As Long Island's economic base expands, more and more local residents are making their living on the island. But this does not diminish the Long Island Rail Road's importance to the region's economy or the vital role it plays in meeting the island's transportation needs.

Each weekday more than 700 LIRR trains transport nearly 250,000 passengers to and from the 134 stations that extend from the easternmost points of Greenport and Montauk to three terminals in New York City. The LIRR, founded in 1834, is the nation's busiest and most densely configured commuter railroad, and it is the oldest U.S. railroad operating under its original name.

Today—as part of the Metropolitan Transportation Authority, which includes the Metro-North Commuter Railroad, the New York City Transit Authority, and the Staten Island Rapid Transit Operating Authority—LIRR is in the midst of a $2.1-billion capital improvement program aimed at preparing it to meet the area's future transportation needs.

The capital program, which spans the period 1982 to 1991, includes purchase or refurbishing of train cars; major upgrading of maintenance shops, some of which are little changed since early this century; improvement or expansion of tracks, bridges, switches, signals, and power systems; modernization of Penn Station, the destination of 80 percent of the LIRR's passengers, and improvements to terminals at Flatbush Avenue in Brooklyn and Hunterspoint Avenue in Queens.

Completion of the $196-million Caemmerer West Side Yard facilities just west of Penn Station and electrification of the Main Line from Hicksville to Ronkonkoma represent major accomplishments of the capital program. The Caemmerer Yard eliminates the need to shuttle trains back east for storage, and has maintenance and cleaning shops and a fully computerized control tower. Electrification has reduced the time of the trip from Ronkonkoma to Manhattan to about an hour.

Complete renovation of Jamaica Station, the capital program's centerpiece, is just now under way and will continue through the late 1990s. All but one of the railroad's nine lines converge at Jamaica en route to New York City, creating a difficult situation for moving trains efficiently, particularly during rush hours. The plan calls for rebuilding switches and signals, constructing a modern control tower, and adding a second pedestrian overpass.

While upgrading the railroad's physical plant will have the greatest impact on the LIRR's future performance, improved management systems that encourage teamwork among the organization's 7,000 employees also will make a difference.

The LIRR is looking to the future. Dual-mode locomotives that can operate on electric and nonelectric tracks and pull bi-level cars that can accommodate 50 percent more passengers than present cars are being tested. Reverse signals are being installed between Penn Station and Jamaica and elsewhere to accommodate traffic in either direction on electrified track. New market studies are under way to help predict commuting patterns into the 1990s.

The Long Island Rail Road is modernizing both its physical and management infrastructure as it prepares to meet Long Island's twenty-first-century transportation needs.

More than 700 Long Island Rail Road trains carry some 250,000 passengers each weekday from outlying points on Long Island to three westernmost terminals in Manhattan, Brooklyn, and Queens. Here, an electric train glides into Huntington Station to pick up midday passengers.

A feature of the new John D. Caemmerer West Side Yard in Manhattan is an entirely modern control tower with a computerized operations system that actually anticipates train movements according to the schedule of empty trains into the yard, selects routes from a "notepad" of up to 24 choices out of 282 possibilities, and in milliseconds sends the approaching trains to the first open route.

XIII

Manufacturing

Producing goods for individuals and industry, manufacturing firms provide employment for many Long Island area residents.

148

Lumex, Inc., 150

Sedco, A Raytheon Company, 152

Quantronix Corporation, 154

Pall Corporation, 156

Altana Inc., 158

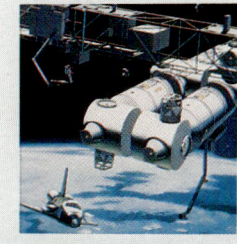

Grumman Corporation, 160

Photo by R. Settles

LONG ISLAND

LUMEX, INC.

Consider an average person's typical morning routine. Most people turn off the alarm, stumble into the shower, dress, eat, and leave for work. Sounds simple. Now, imagine doing all these things when your legs are paralyzed or you are suffering from a slipped disk. It's not so simple anymore. However, thanks to the wide array of products manufactured and distributed by Lumex, Inc., of Bay Shore, functionally impaired people and those recovering from injuries are leading more comfortable and independent lives.

Since its founding in 1947 by Charles Murcott, Lumex and its divisions have become world leaders in designing, manufacturing, and marketing institutional and home health care equipment, and physical rehabilitation, exercise, and performance testing systems. Lumex exports reach all corners of the globe, including Australia and the People's Republic of China.

The company's stock is publicly traded on the American Stock Exchange. Lumex is divided into two divisions: The Lumex Division and the Cybex Division. In 1987 sales for both divisions totaled $75 million.

The Tub Guard™ Bathtub Safety Rail by Lumex.

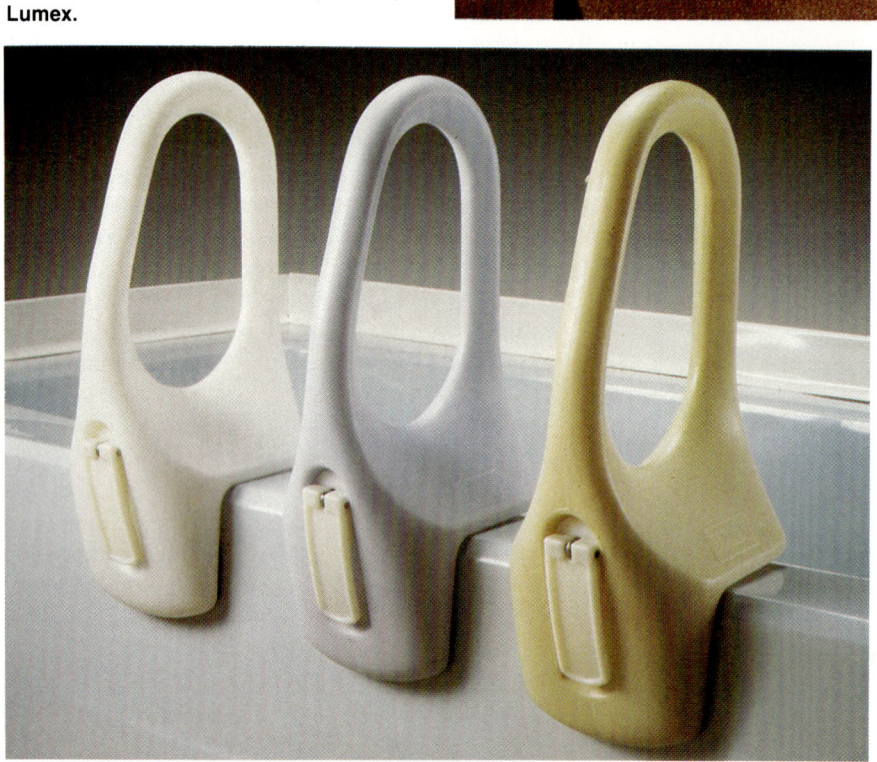

The Preferred-Care™ Recliner by Lumex.

The Lumex Division, based in newly expanded quarters in Bay Shore, offers a diverse line of innovative products dedicated to improving lives.

Bathroom safety equipment is instrumental in assuring safety in the most accident-prone room in the house. It is made for younger and older people alike, but children and those with arthritis or injuries find it most helpful. Walkers, crutches, commodes, and a line of tools for independent living have also helped earn the Lumex Division a sparkling reputation in home care. The Lumex Division offers specialty health care chairs and recliners and a patented mattress system that helps prevent and manage pressure sores. Lumex products are

MANUFACTURING

The Rotary Torso by Cybex Eagle Fitness Systems. Photo by Barry Axelrod

considered the finest in the industry.

Lumex innovation is credited with creating the transfer tub seat, telescoping bed side rails, and geriatric chairs, and for building the market for specialty recliners in hospital and nursing home settings. Such products have helped improve the quality of life for many people.

The Cybex 340 Extremity Testing and Rehabilitation System.

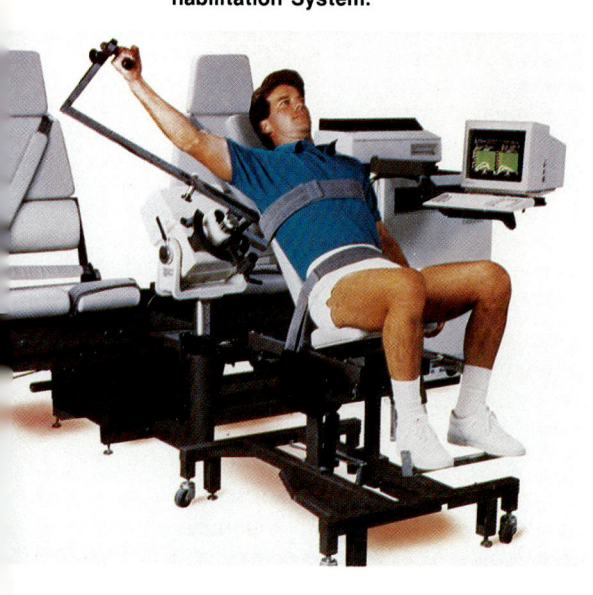

The Cybex Division, headquartered in Ronkonkoma, is the world's leading manufacturer of sophisticated rehabilitation, performance testing, and fitness equipment. Its systems, which are based on the principle of isokinetics, objectively measure, quantify, and rehabilitate the muscle capability of every major joint, including the back. Isokinetics enables injured patients to exercise at functional speeds, providing safe and efficient rehabilitation for daily activities. "Before Cybex isokinetic equipment was available, the delivery of physical therapy was subjective. Now, you can objectively measure a patient's level of disability or successful rehabilitation," says David Hillery, president of the Cybex Division.

According to Hillery, his division's products helped to pioneer the development of sports medicine. "We can take a great deal of credit for helping this field grow because we gave orthopedic surgeons, physical therapists, and athletic trainers the tools they needed," he says.

Athletic trainers are able to formulate individualized muscular and cardiovascular training programs for rehabilitation, strength training, and injury prevention after evaluating their players on a Cybex system. Frequently used side by side with its rehabilitation equipment, Cybex Eagle Fitness Systems (22 variable-resistance machines) exercise every major muscle group. Because of the systems' quality engineering, biomechanically-correct positioning, and smooth feel, they are considered the Rolls-Royce of the fitness field.

"Product users are our most valuable source of suggestions," says Lumex Division president Kenneth Coviello. "They're responsible for many of the equipment ideas. Our field representatives come back and work with our engineers and designers. We then send the equipment out to the field for testing and refinement," he explains, adding, "If we are going to help people, we have to listen to them."

Lumex is not content to just provide equipment that will help the disabled. It also wants to make more meaningful contributions to improving their lives. The firm maintains an active veterans' employment program and has received numerous commendations for its work on behalf of the Veterans' Administration Olympics held annually for disabled veterans. Company representatives speak nationwide to groups for the disabled, health care professionals, senior citizens, and journalists who write for them.

As life expectancy increases and home health care moves into wider use, and as more people undertake serious fitness programs, the market for Lumex products grows. Murcott reports that the firm is currently developing products and personnel that will keep it in its leadership position.

Lawrence Cohen, chairman and chief executive officer of Lumex, Inc., says he is proud that he and his employees have been able to help those in need. "We often get letters from people telling us how our equipment has helped them live better. I can't think of anything more satisfying."

151

LONG ISLAND

SEDCO, A RAYTHEON COMPANY

Thanks to the engineers, technicians, and production workers of a Melville-based firm, Sedco, a Raytheon Company, U.S. military planes contain the most sophisticated radar-jamming equipment available to give them the advantage they may need to protect them from offensive weapon systems.

Since its founding in Hicksville in 1963, Sedco has been a leader in designing electronic countermeasure (ECM) systems for military use. It was the first company to develop and produce an airborne-phased array ECM system—a highly effective, electronically scanned directional antenna system—for U.S. Air Force operational aircraft.

Sedco led the industry in the development and large-quantity production of ferrite ECM antenna switches that were high powered, broadband, and operated in submicro seconds. The firm developed antenna ECM array systems, as well as numerous components of modern radar-jamming systems, such as ferrite phase shifters and drivers, antenna feeds and radiators, and electronic-beam-control digital processors and microprocessors.

One of the best-known achievements is the application of an ECM-phased array system for the B-1B bomber. Working as a member of the Eaton Corporation's AIL Division team, Sedco designed and built the phased array transmit antenna and multibeam direction-finding system, critical components of the aircraft's defensive electronics system. This subcontract was awarded on the basis of the excellent work Sedco already had performed on earlier development models of the electronic defense systems for the B-1B and B52 bombers.

The firm's manufacturing facilities include modern, efficient assembly lines, automated production equipment, a computer-controlled machine shop, model shop, and highly trained, skilled operators, assemblers, and supervisors. Every product component is carefully tested, using either standard test equipment or devices especially designed by Sedco.

Support engineers review designs to ensure maintainability. They recom-

A subs and mains assembly station with a skilled operator.

BELOW: Printed circuit board assembly using semiautomated component-insertion equipment.

BOTTOM: Computer-controlled machining.

Automatic circuit testing using a DITMCO circuit analyzer.

LEFT: An automatic printed circuit card assembly fault finder.

ABOVE: Temperature chambers in the on-site environmental test facility.

BELOW: Production inspection using state-of-the-art measuring equipment.

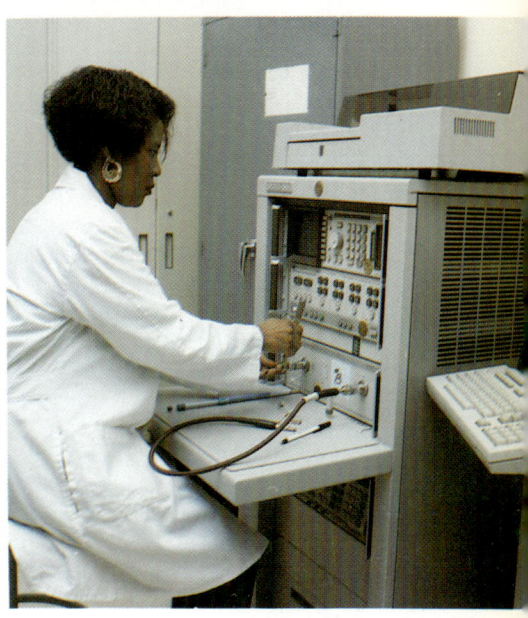

mend proper mechanical packaging, component selection, and accessibility so that routine maintenance can be performed easily. Finally, all products are tested in the environmental test facility on site. There is a wide variety of sophisticated systems and equipment that simulate the environmental conditions in which military and space hardware must operate, such as temperature, altitude, humidity, and atmospheric contaminants.

The firm has a long, illustrious history of working for the military. One of its first contracts was to build a phase shifter for the Army Signal Corps in 1963. By the following year the staff had grown to about 20 to accommodate the larger workload, and a move to larger quarters in Plainview was necessary. In 1967 the company moved to East Farmingdale, where it remained for some 10 years and grew to a staff of approximately 100. At this stage Sedco was building complete antenna systems, not just components, and was also under contract to the Air Force and the Navy.

"Dealing with the government is difficult at times, but it has very definite advantages," explains Murray Simpson, Sedco founder, former president, and now a consultant. "There is a very formal process for evaluating proposals. If the program is within the capability of a company and has excellent technical merit, it has a reasonably good chance of winning."

In 1979, when Raytheon acquired the firm, Sedco was a leader in its field, but still concentrated primarily on research and development. With Raytheon's guidance, Sedco moved wholeheartedly into manufacturing, expanding from a one- to three-building complex in the Melville area.

At present, Sedco is a major supplier of military electronics and an important element of the U.S. industrial base for defensive systems. According to Neil Hansen, president of Sedco, "We are in the process of broadening our business base to take advantage of the engineering talent and matured manufacturing capability that we have developed."

Sedco's focus for the future will remain in the electronic countermeasure systems field, working toward building smarter, smaller, and less costly equipment.

R.F. component testing using automated test equipment.

LONG ISLAND

QUANTRONIX CORPORATION

Quantronix' new 85,000-square-foot corporate headquarters and manufacturing plant in the Hauppauge Industrial Park.

Since its founding in 1967, this Smithtown firm has become a leader in the laser system industry, developing innovative tools for medicine, pure science research, and the semiconductor industry, among other fields. In 1987 Quantronix Corporation moved its 180 employees into a specially designed and modern 85,000-square-foot corporate headquarters and manufacturing facility on Wireless Boulevard.

Approximately 20 percent of its nearly $20 million in annual sales are to foreign countries. Quantronix maintains an office in West Germany, and also has offices in California and Texas. In 1987 it acquired an Oxnard, California, firm, The Optical Corporation—manufacturer of precision optical components and subassemblies for the aerospace and defense markets—thereby opening up new areas of endeavor.

The word "laser" is derived from the term Light Amplification by Stimulated Emission of Radiation. A laser emits a beam of light that is essentially of a single wavelength and uniform direction. This permits laser beams to be focused on extremely small areas with exceptionally concentrated power and energy. As a result, a laser may be used with microscopic precision for numerous procedures, including to cut, weld, heat, and anneal a wide range of materials such as metals, semiconductors, diamonds, and human tissue.

With nearly 20 years of experience in the design and manufacture of equipment to inspect and repair masks used in printing semiconductor microcircuits, Quantronix is considered the industry leader. A mask is the detailed master used in a photolithographic process to create the circuit on a semiconductor chip. The Quantronix Defect Repair System (DRS) utilizes the laser's ability to focus on a spot smaller than one micron (1/25 of 1,000th of an inch) to locate, classify, and repair any defects that may occur on the mask.

The yield of a defective mask is greatly reduced, so that the ability of the DRS to enhance productivity is a boon to semiconductor manufacturers. "We are told that these machines, which each cost about $500,000, pay for themselves in six to 12 months," says Vincent Mooney, treasurer and chief financial officer, who adds that among the firms that use the DRS are IBM, Hewlett-Packard, Intel, and DuPont-Tau.

The firm now offers a second-generation DRS capable of repairing defects with submicron resolution, in response to the industry's move to more sophisticated production methods. Quantronix also is the exclusive North American and European distributor of Focused Ion Beam Mask Repair Systems manufactured by Seiko Instruments.

Lasers are now used in a wide range of manufacturing equipment. Quantronix provides laser units and accessories to original-equipment manufacturers primarily in the electronics, graphic arts, and automotive industries. Laser-based industrial systems are used in trimming resistors, producing thin-film capacitors, micromachining, and product-marking systems, to name a few applications. The plates from which *The New York Times* is printed each day are engraved with

MANUFACTURING

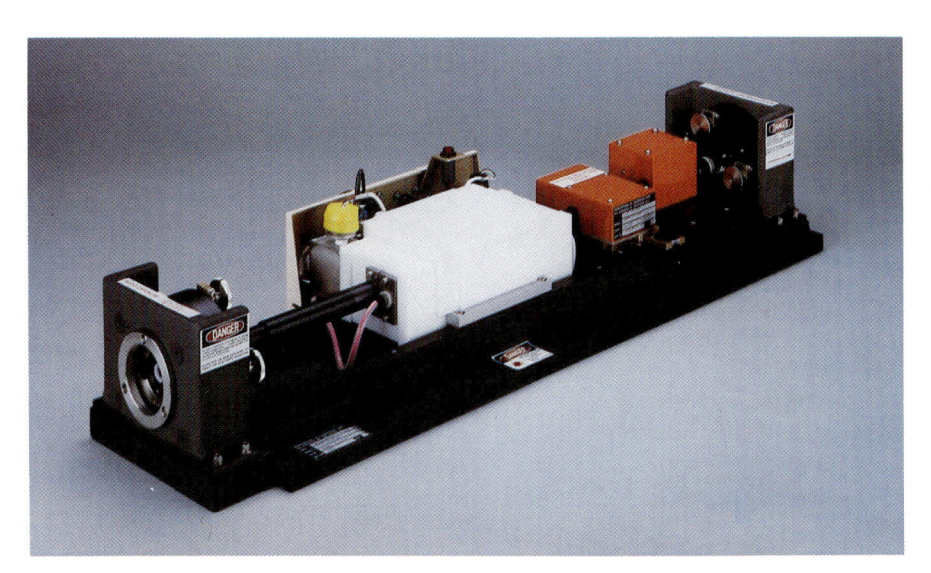

The DRS II, a state-of-the-art laser-based system used by the semiconductor industry in the repair of both opaque and clear defects in photomasks and reticles.

equipment utilizing a Quantronix Corporation laser. The crystal of almost any quartz watch bought today is trimmed with a Quantronix laser.

In the field of science, lasers have revolutionized research techniques. They can produce pulses of light in the range of one picosecond, which is one-trillionth of a second. These pulses act as strobe lights and permit scientists to study physical processes that occur in these brief time spans. For example, biologists are studying photosynthesis by illuminating and probing plants or algae with short optical pulses. Quantronix scientific laser systems are in use at such prestigious institutions as AT&T Bell Laboratories, Lawrence Livermore National Laboratory, Tokyo University, and British Telecom Research Lab.

In the past decade the use of lasers in medicine has grown by leaps and bounds. Quantronix designed and is testing a cardiac surgical system to treat blocked arteries, which, when it is released in the 1990s, may prove a viable alternative to open-heart surgery.

Dr. Richard Daly, the firm's chairman, and his two partners were motivated to establish Quantronix when the company for which they were working was acquired, and they believed the new management was not sensitive enough to the needs of its employees. For this reason, maintaining good employee relations always has been a high priority at Quantronix. In recent years the organization has undertaken an extensive management-training program, and has adopted a formal manufacturing and inventory-control program.

Quantronix also places great value on research and development, employing 13 engineers and scientists with advanced degrees. Presently approximately 16 percent of net revenue is dedicated to that field, twice the traditional rate of between 7 percent and 9 percent.

"When you're small and entrepreneurial, you can develop and bring to market a product in a much smaller time frame than a bigger organization with many levels of bureaucracy," says Mooney. "In this field you have to move quickly because advances happen so fast. We're putting our resources into developing products of the future."

BELOW: System 1500 medical device for laser balloon angioplasty.

BOTTOM: Series 100 industrial laser used by OEM customers to provide laser power in the systems they market.

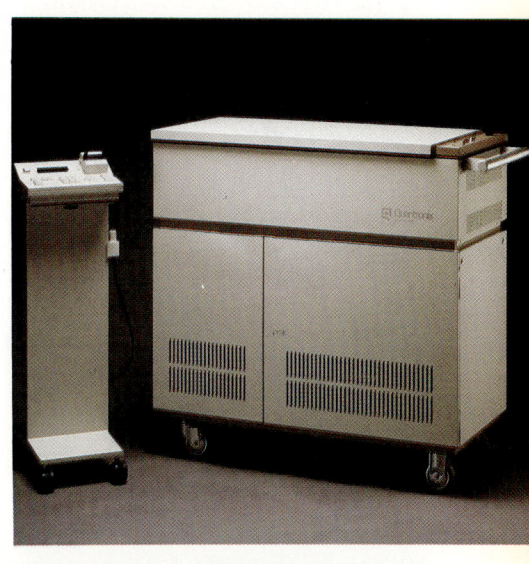

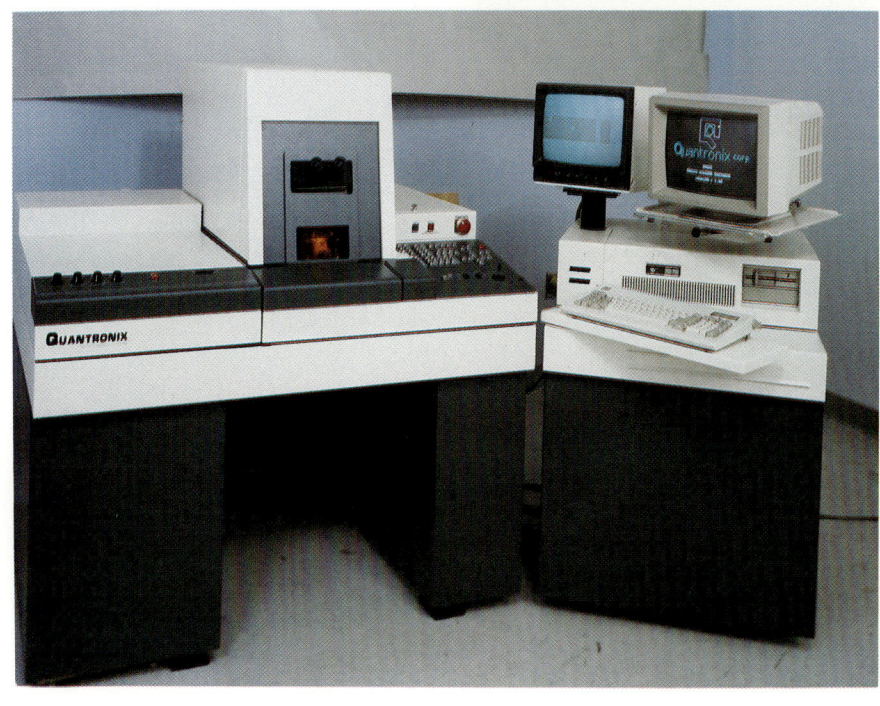

155

LONG ISLAND

PALL CORPORATION

When those responsible for cleaning up after the accident at Pennsylvania's Three Mile Island nuclear power plant needed a special filtering system to remove contaminants from wastewater and other liquids, they contacted Glen Cove-based Pall Corporation, the world's leader in fluid clarification. The firm designed and built special filters that proved critical to the cleanup process, and that were then adopted by the nuclear industry for general use.

Heightened concern over the safety of blood transfusions led Pall researchers to develop new blood filters that remove white blood cells called leukocytes from donated blood. These cells may carry viruses for such diseases as CMV, HIV, or hepatitis or may cause a patient to reject new blood. The removal of these leukocytes represents a major breakthrough in the delivery of quality health care worldwide.

These examples of Pall filter applications, while dramatic, are only the tip of the iceberg. The company's filters, air cleaners, and oil purifiers are used to remove microscopic solid, liquid, or gaseous contaminants from liquids and gases in a very broad range of applications and markets in the health care, aeropower, and fluid processing fields.

Pall filters purify fluids used to manufacture pharmaceuticals, microelectronics, automobile and appliance surface finishes, magnetic tape and photographic film coatings, and even wine, beer, and water, to name only a few uses. In many systems the firm's products are also used to collect or recirculate useful particles such as catalysts, and in others to collect a product such as fumed silica or penicillin.

Military and commercial aircraft, naval vessels, combat vehicles, and industrial and mobile equipment use Pall filters to protect vital oil, fuel, and air systems from contamination. The firm's innovative CENTRISEP air cleaners are designed specifically to protect helicopters from ingesting dirt and other particles, and will be installed in U.S. military helicopters un-

Pall Corporation's 307,000-square-foot administrative offices and manufacturing facility in East Hills.

U.S. Navy attack aircraft use Pall hydraulic filter modules to remove contaminants from its flight control systems. Photo by Peter J. Kaplan

MANUFACTURING

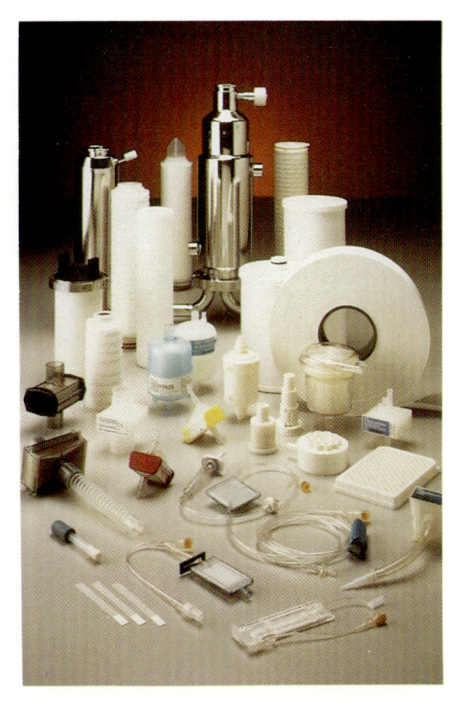

The stringent purity requirements of the patient protection, immunodiagnostics, pharmaceutical, and food and beverage processing markets are met through the utilization of reusable and disposable filter cartridges, plastic filters, and devices incorporating Pall proprietary filter membranes.

dergoing refurbishing.

The company's fastest-growing sector is health care. Pall developed a filter used during open-heart surgery to remove air emboli and particulate debris from blood that circulates outside the body during the operation. Its intravenous fluid filters are the only ones on the market rated for 96-hour protection, as compared to the industry standard of between 24 and 48 hours. Breathing filters are used to purify inhaled and exhaled gases in respiratory therapy and anesthesia administration.

Pall, which is an active supporter of several important Long Island charities, was founded in 1946 to market to existing filter companies a porous stainless-steel material invented by the firm's chairman and founder, Dr. David Pall. Lack of acceptance led to the development and sale of laboratory devices and ultimately to the process filter business. Today Pall continues to advance the state of the art in metal filter technology and applies its

Manufacturers of the leading video cassettes use Pall filters to remove impurities from solutions that coat video recording tape. Photo by Peter J. Kaplan

expertise to the development and manufacture of a variety of reusable metal filters and disposable filters made of paper and synthetic materials. Dr. Pall remains the company's driving research and development force.

Shortly after its founding in Brooklyn, Pall, which today operates in 38 countries, moved to Glen Cove. Approximately 800 of the firm's 5,500 employees worldwide work at Pall's three Long Island facilities. The organization's corporate offices, research and development laboratories, and scientific and laboratory services operations are housed in its headquarter building in Glen Cove; corporate training and health care sales, marketing, research, and management offices are located in the former F.W. Woolworth mansion, also in Glen Cove; and manufacturing and various sales, marketing, and administrative services groups are located at the 307,000-square-foot plant in East Hills. Pall Corporation generates some $500 million in sales annually, approximately half of which is outside the United States.

Pall Corporation executives (left to right): Henry Petronis, executive vice-president; Maurice G. Hardy, president and chief operating officer; Dr. David B. Pall, chairman; and Abraham Krasnoff, vice-chairman and chief executive officer.

LONG ISLAND

ALTANA INC.

It is safe to say that almost every hospital in the United States uses products manufactured on Long Island by the pharmaceutical divisions of Altana Inc.

The E. Fougera & Co. division is one of the nation's oldest pharmaceutical companies. Founded in Brooklyn in 1849, it is currently a leading supplier of topical products to institutions in the United States. Fougera pioneered the field of unit-of-use packaging for ointments and cream with its Foilpacs®; 164 million of these individual doses were used in hospitals, clinics, and nursing homes in 1988. Fougera continues to utilize its expertise to create unique packaging to accommodate the needs of its customers—the medical professionals in every community.

Fougera also enjoys the position of being one of the nation's largest suppliers of sterile ophthalmic ointments. In fact, 50 percent of the infants born in U.S. hospital delivery rooms are treated prophylactically with Fougera's Erythromycin to prevent the disease that can lead to blindness.

The Savage Laboratories division markets its brand-name products to dermatologists, allergists, obstetricians, and gynecologists in the United States. Savage is expecting a substantial future growth by introducing several new unique patented products to the medical profession in the next few years.

The Pharmaderm division sells, via wholesalers, dermatological and veterinary products to pharmacies and drugstores nationwide.

All pharmaceutical manufacturing is done at the Long Island facilities located in Hicksville and Melville. Each plant adheres to stringent procedures to guarantee the integrity of the pharmaceuticals it produces. All employees are highly skilled in the performance of their respective duties, and all new

A stainless-steel pharmaceutical compounding kettle.

sumers of its products. To ensure quality and safety of its products is the principal goal of the company and its 350 employees working in the manufacturing plants on Long Island.

In addition to the pharmaceutical divisions, Altana Inc. also includes the Milupa division, manufacturing baby foods in Wisconsin, and the Byk Chemie division, manufacturing paint and plastic additives as well as technical instruments in Connecticut.

With all its divisions, Altana Inc. is part of an international group, Altana-Byk Gulden-Milupa, which is headquartered in West Germany. As its American representative, Altana Inc., with its corporate offices in Melville, Long Island, expects to introduce new products and expand its services.

ABOVE: A high-speed automated tube filling line.
BELOW: Here foil laminate enters high-speed Foilpac® filling equipment.
BOTTOM: Altana Inc. corporate headquarters in Melville, Long Island.

A liquid pharmaceutical filling apparatus.

personnel must attend training programs to ensure compliance with corporate and governmental requirements. These facilities are models of efficiency, utilizing state-of-the-art equipment and systems to best serve Altana customers and the ultimate con-

LONG ISLAND

GRUMMAN CORPORATION

If any one company can be said to have put Long Island on the map, the most likely candidate must be the Grumman Corporation. To the millions of people worldwide who lived through World War II, the heroic deeds of U.S. pilots flying Grumman Avengers, Wildcats, and Hellcats are familiar stories.

Grumman continues to build military aircraft, but today its 30,000 workers in nine divisions are employed in a wide range of fields, including electronics, information systems, space, boats, and specialty vehicles. The firm has grown and diversified in ways Roy Grumman, Jake Swirbul, and their four associates could not have imagined when they opened their aircraft repair business in a rented garage in Baldwin on January 2, 1930.

The firm has long held the position as the island's largest employer, engaging some 20,000 workers locally. From the modern, architecturally striking headquarters in Bethpage, Grumman managers oversee activities in approximately 130 manufacturing plants, field sites, and offices nationwide and around the world. The company ranks among the top 200 firms on the *Fortune* 500 list.

Much of the aircraft production continues to be done on Long Island at the firm's Bethpage and Calverton facilities. In 1987 Grumman began delivering to the Navy the F-14A(PLUS), an updated version of the F-14 Tomcat. Work is in progress on an even newer model, F-14D, which will contain highly sophisticated electronics. The Navy's E-2C Hawkeye and EA-6B Prowler also are being upgraded, and production of C-2A Greyhounds will continue through 1989.

Grumman does a brisk business as a supplier of aircraft parts to other manufacturers. For example, the 14,000-pound wings of the space shuttle are designed and built by Grumman, as are the center wing section of the Boeing 767 airliner and major components of that company's 757 aircraft. Other major products include nacelles and thrust reversers for commercial transports and business jets. Nacelles muffle an aircraft's engines, while thrust reversers assist in braking.

While airplanes have not changed radically in their outer design, computers and electronics have revolutionized what they contain inside. Grumman has led the way in this electronic revolution.

The company, from its Bethpage, Bohemia, Melville, and Great River facilities, among others in the United States, develops and integrates electronic systems into its own aircraft and those of other manufacturers. It also provides systems for automatic test equipment, space programs, surveillance, missiles, and display and trainer products.

Among the most important electronic systems being developed are the Air Force/Army Joint Surveillance Target Attack Radar System and the Army's Intermediate Forward Test Equipment, which will detect faulty components in the electronics of weapons systems.

The F-14D avionics development laboratory opened in mid-1987. From the outside the F-14D looks much like its predecessors, but electronically it is a completely new plane. In the lab 180 software and electronics engineers and technicians develop the computer code for the F-14D's electronics systems.

MANUFACTURING

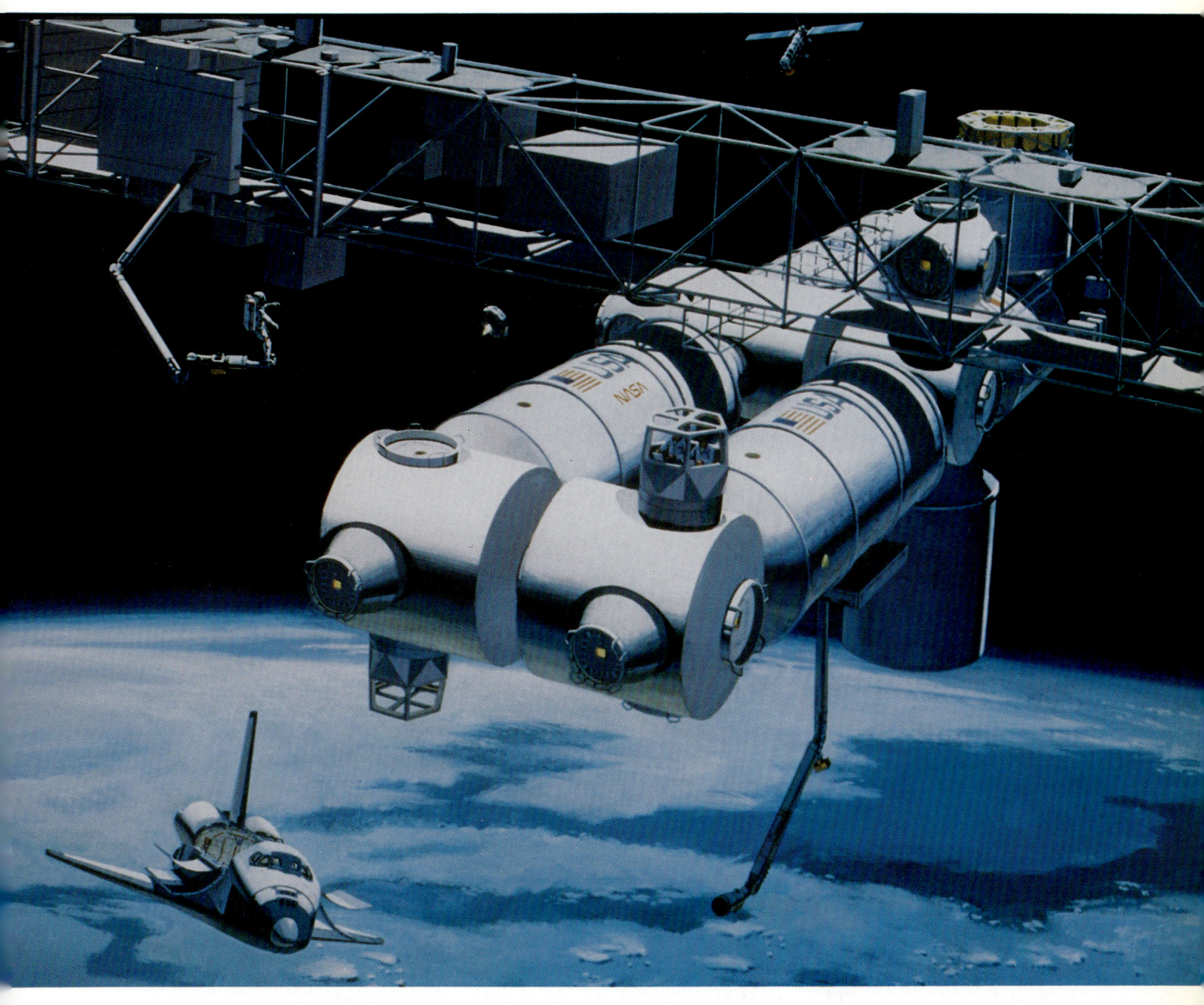

Grumman's computer systems business was initially established to provide in-house expertise on aircraft and space projects. The operation today has more clients outside of the firm than within it, and is a thriving profit center for its parent. From major facilities in Woodbury and Holtsville, Grumman designs, develops, installs, operates, and supports computer systems for technical and management information.

For example, Grumman Data Systems designed a test instrumentation system for the U.S. Air Force's Arnold Engineering Development Center in Tullahoma, Tennessee. The engineering analysis and data system at NASA's Marshall Space Flight Center in Huntsville, Alabama, was designed and installed by Grumman, and since 1982 the firm has been meeting the demanding management information needs of the New York State Department of Social Services.

Recently the Air Force awarded Grumman a contract for a computer-management information and operations system called Depot Maintenance Management Information System (DMMIS). DMMIS will enable Air Force Logistics Center Depot managers to better plan and manage aircraft and weapons systems.

With its rich history in U.S. aviation, it's no wonder that Grumman was

The Space Station Program Support Contract is the largest systems integration job any company has ever received. Grumman will assist NASA with program control and management, and help to integrate the four work packages.

LONG ISLAND

In October 1987 the Egyptian Air Force accepted delivery of three Grumman E-2Cs, completing its fleet of five Hawkeyes. More than 200 members of the Egyptian Air Force came to Long Island for extensive training on the E-2C.

chosen to help lead the march into space. The company developed several scientific research satellites that gathered information critical to the space program's ultimate success. It also developed the Apollo program's lunar module, the *Eagle,* which in 1969 brought Neil Armstrong down on the moon's Sea of Tranquility, an event of historic importance.

Today Grumman is teamed with other companies in numerous space-related projects. The firm is working on space surveillance for the Department of Defense and is a member of the team developing NASA's manned space station. It is concentrating on the station's central radiation system, developing the extravehicular activity systems, and outfitting the living quarters.

Grumman began building special-purpose vehicles after World War II, when aircraft orders became lean, Grumman aluminum truck bodies proved so practical and durable that the firm remains the largest manufacturer of this product. Grumman will be supplying the U.S. Postal Service with trucks through the early 1990s, and is a major contractor for the United Parcel Service. The company also produces and refurbishes fire-fighting vehicles, and builds aluminum boats and canoes.

Stories abound about the camaraderie that existed among Grumman workers during wartime production. While circumstances have changed, much of this spirit of cooperation continues today. Many Grumman employees serve their communities individually through volunteer work, and the company as a whole has an impressive community service program.

Unlike other corporate donors, Grumman's charitable contributions are the responsibility of a 12-member council of employees who serve without pay. The council reviews some 4,000 funding requests annually, and generally awards Long Island projects about one-half of the one-million-dollar budget. Grants are awarded to universities, hospitals, youth groups, and health service and arts organizations, among others.

With its commitment to quality products and its loyal work force, for the Grumman Corporation, the famous words spoken in 1942 by Vice Admiral John S. McCain ring true today: "The name Grumman on a plane has the same meaning to the Navy as sterling on silver."

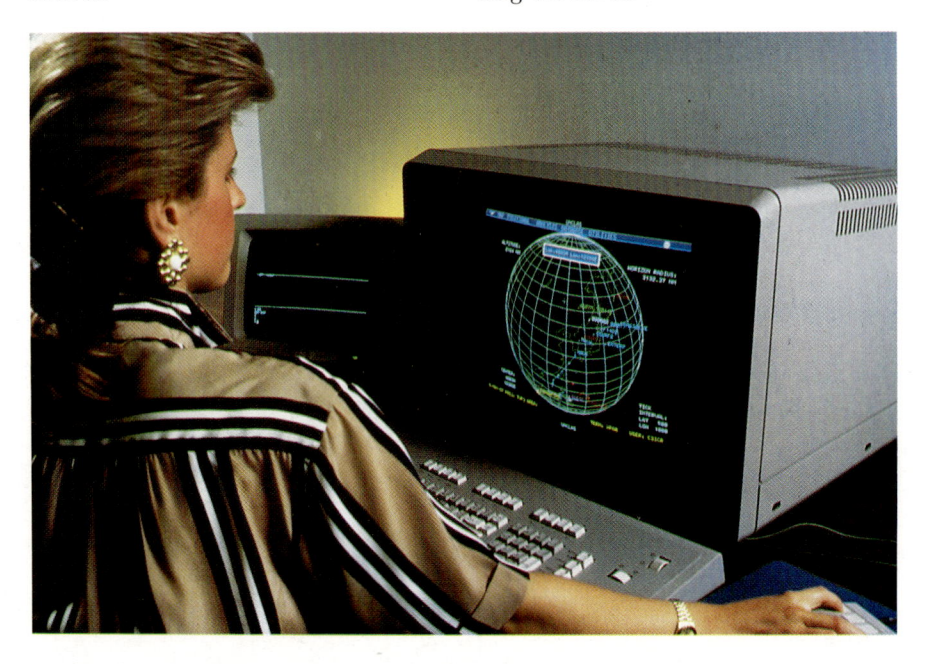

A command, control, communication, and intelligence system gives decision makers real-time information to assess the status of friendly and hostile forces, and then lets them communicate their decisions. Grumman has developed this workstation as a stand-alone product and as a tool for developing larger systems.

Photo by George Michell

XIV

Business

Building on the past while planning for the future, Long Island's business community moves into the forefront of technological innovation and financial leadership.

Long Island Association, Inc., 166

Halbro Control Industries, Inc., 167

Florence Building Materials, 168

Dale Carnegie & Associates, Inc., 170

Allstate Insurance Company, 172

Fairfield Properties, 174

Photo by R. Settles

LONG ISLAND

LONG ISLAND ASSOCIATION, INC.

Without effective public dialogue and debate, Long Island's leaders will be unable to achieve viable solutions to the myriad of challenges that rapid and successful development have brought to the region. It is fortunate, then, that the Long Island Association (LIA), the region's largest and most influential business and civic organization, provides members of the business, civic, health care, education, and labor communities with a forum for tackling the diverse issues affecting Long Island.

Involvement in the public policy process is a major component of the tion funding, world trade, and small business concerns.

LIA played a critical role in New York State's decision to allocate more dollars to improve Long Island highways, and it also was instrumental in forming the Long Island Housing Partnership, Inc., a public/private corporation that is building affordable housing.

Long Island Project 2000, initiated by the association, is the first regional planning effort since 1970. It will play an important role in the next few years. "Project 2000 has been well received because there has not been a joint reflection on where the region is headed for a long time. People realize that we need to plan our future," says LIA president James L. Larocca.

Providing services to its thousands of member firms is equally important to LIA. The organization offers members low-cost group insurance, reasonably priced education programs, a business help hotline for advice on any business problem, and a business referral service. Monthly networking social functions are popular and effective. LIA annually participates in the largest nonpartisan gathering of elected and appointed officials on Long Island, and its awards dinner dance is among the area's most prestigious social events on the Long Island calendar.

Nearly 90 percent of Long Island businesses employ fewer than 100 workers, so LIA's Small Business Council is an important voice for this sector. In addition to supporting legislation of interest to small business, the council holds frequent seminars and workshops, and works closely with the White House Conference on Small Business.

Promoting the region and keeping members informed is the goal of LIA's communications program. LIA publishes the island's only monthly business magazine, *Long Island,* and produces the area's only weekly business television program, "Long Island Talks Business." It also publishes *Business Directory and Buyers Guide of Long Island* and *Long Island Guide to Public Officials.*

The Long Island Association's ability to bring together the diverse elements that make up Long Island is a valuable regional resource. "We're filling a vacuum. Long Island is dispersed politically, geographically, economically, and socially. Because we cross all those lines, LIA helps bring it all together," concludes Larocca.

Pictured here is a view of the televised public debate on Long Island Project 2000, a bi-county effort coordinated by the Long Island Association to define regional goals and create an action agenda for the year 2000 and beyond.

James L. Larocca, president of the Long Island Association.

LIA's efforts to protect and enhance the economic health and quality of life in the community. Members, who serve on committees voluntarily, work with the organization's full-time professional staff, and participate in activities aimed at addressing such critical issues as water quality, solid-waste management, affordable housing, future energy needs, tax policy, transporta-

166

HALBRO CONTROL INDUSTRIES, INC.

A company's customers are influenced by the overall appearance of its business. A clean image reflects success, which is why executives in the know turn to Halbro Control Industries, Inc., for their general, as well as unusual, cleaning needs. Halbro's reputation as Long Island's Clean Image Builder and Maintenance Problem Solver is well deserved.

Founded in 1946 by two brothers, Sol and Sam Halpern, Halbro Control Industries has had many years of experience in solving everyday and tough cleaning problems. In fact, Halbro's success at designing and implementing tailor-made cleaning programs has earned it a reputation as Long Island's finest maintenance supply company.

Halbro is now being managed by their sons, Stanton Halpern, chief executive officer, and Chuck Halpern, president. Halbro began as a distributor of institutional cleaning products. It remains a major player in this business, distributing some 2,000 janitorial supplies, maintenance equipment, and paper supplies to thousands of clients in the Northeast.

Building on its reputation, Halbro currently develops in its own laboratory more than 250 specialty maintenance chemicals at its Farmingdale facility. The product line ranges from the unusual, such as deodorants to combat odors at solid-waste-treatment plants and antigraffiti coatings to protect surfaces against vandalism, to products to tackle common cleaning tasks.

"It's a fascinating business because of the diversity of assignments. We've developed products to be used in cleaning everything from cages at a zoo to the ceramic walls of a tunnel. We pride ourselves through our chemical lab's technical know-how in analyzing the toughest problems," explains Stan Halpern.

Halbro also offers numerous training courses, both for its clients and its own employees. "Whether we're servicing our customers or educating our staff, it's important that we teach them not only which product to use, but, more important, the correct cleaning techniques. We also teach basic chemistry so they understand how and why products work, and how to use them safely and effectively," says Halpern.

This emphasis on education stems from Halbro's philosophy that custodians are proud professionals and need to have their maintenance techniques updated on a regular basis. Recently Halbro organized a full-scale maintenance fair complete with vendor booths, equipment demonstrations, and product-use seminars because the firm believes its customers deserve professional image upgrading, too.

As for the future, Halbro Control Industries, Inc., hopes to open several retail outlets where businesses and home owners can conveniently visit for advice on their cleaning problems. Chuck Halpern, president, adds, "Even in the days when my father and uncle started this business, our maintenance consultants were always ready to assist customers with their cleaning needs. Today our continued success at creating effective cleaning programs and upgrading maintenance standards for our valued customers is considered a Halbro tradition within our company."

Chief executive officer Stan Halpern (standing) introduces a unique specialty chemical line to Halbro's management team. Seated (counterclockwise) are Richard Appel, chemist; Linda Cohen, purchasing; Chuck Halpern, president; Frank Pitti, operations manager; Shannon Baltzersen, office manager; Joe Carbone, vice-president/sales; and Marion Linder, vice-president/finance.

Halbro's chemist, Richard Appel (left), reviews a new cleaning concept in the laboratory with customer Charles Tallman, a LILCO maintenance supervisor.

LONG ISLAND

FLORENCE BUILDING MATERIALS

Richard Droesch, president and the company's sole owner since 1980, with a memorial plaque of his father-in-law, Arthur Florence, who started the business that bears his name in 1946.

When the builders of the elegant Garden City Hotel and the striking Marriott Hotel in Uniondale wanted windows for these projects, they did what hundreds of contractors across Long Island do. They called Florence Building Materials.

Arthur Florence opened his exterior building supply business in Garden City in 1946, just as the post-World War II building boom was getting under way. The company continues to specialize in roofing, siding, windows, doors, and skylights, but has expanded its distribution network to serve all areas of the island. It also has enhanced its materials-handling capability and, for example, can deliver roofing to the actual roof of a structure by means of state-of-the-art conveyor belts, a timesaver for contractors.

Warehouses are located in Jericho, Huntington, Medford, and East Quogue, and the firm now has 34 trucks and employs 144 workers. "We pride ourselves on maintaining a total inventory so that a builder can call at the last minute and get what he needs. The key to distribution is to locate the product within 10 miles of the user," explains Richard Droesch, the founder's son-in-law and sole owner of the organization since 1980.

The desire to meet the demand for exterior building products by developers in the fast-growing town of Brookhaven led Florence to open its Medford facility in May 1987. The firm received a low-cost $1.3-million loan from the Town of Brookhaven Industrial Development Agency, and built a warehouse on the 3.5-acre site.

Florence provides quality products and a high level of service, Droesch says, but, more important, it keeps abreast of changes in the construction industry and anticipates builders' requirements. Droesch speaks proudly of his staff's efforts to learn about the newest developments so they can help clients using products for the first time or save them money by suggesting more efficient materials.

This commitment is nothing new. When aluminum siding first came into popular use in the early 1950s, Florence was the first supply house on Long Island to carry it. So, when architects on the East End began using unusually shaped windows and skylights in the area's luxury homes, the corporation set up a factory at the Medford site to provide these items, as well as steel-insulated entry doors. Glass for these popular geometric-shaped openings and standard vinyl replacement windows are produced in New York City by Cordo Window Company, a firm affiliated with Florence.

The supplier has benefited from the building boom that has spurred a 20-percent growth for Florence in each of the past seven years. Florence was ranked among Long Island's top 50 private companies in 1987 by *Long Island Business News*.

However, should interest rates climb and construction slow down, Florence will still have a healthy remodeling business to serve. "Whether it's a big office building or an extension to a small house, we're happy to service them," Droesch says, demonstrating the dedication to service that has kept customers coming back year after year. He notes that in many cases Florence supplied the original materials for a project, and 30 years later provided sup-

Florence vice-president Jon Bieselin with operations manager Greg Barnych (right) and architectural sales manager Bill Marzuk (left).

BUSINESS

plies for its renovation. "We really enjoy this special relationship with a building," he adds.

With its combination of inventory and service, the future looks bright for Florence Building Materials. Any home owner will agree with Droesch when he says: "A house is a permanent customer."

LEFT: The company's 3.5-acre Medford warehouse was constructed in 1987 to help meet the increasing demand for exterior building products by developers in the rapidly growing town of Brookhaven. Priding itself on maintaining a complete inventory, Florence operates additional warehouses in Jericho, Huntington, and East Quogue. In all, the firm has 34 trucks and employs 144 people.

BELOW: Since its inception more than 40 years ago, Florence Building Materials has had a policy of keeping abreast of the latest developments in the construction industry to ensure superior customer service and availability of the newest and highest-quality products. When steel-insulated entry doors were introduced, the firm quickly began manufacturing its own at its Medford facility (above), where it also produces windows.

LONG ISLAND

DALE CARNEGIE & ASSOCIATES, INC.

What do 400 of the 500 companies on the *Fortune* 500 list have in common? They all are or have been clients of Dale Carnegie & Associates, Inc., a leader in the adult continuing-training field.

Today, in any bookstore or on the best-seller list, one will find books on managing everything from employees to stress, and on developing everything from self-esteem to listening techniques. While trends in self-improvement come and go, the Garden City-based empire that grew from the most famous of all self-help books, Dale Carnegie's *How to Win Friends and Influence People*, remains as vigorous as ever.

Carnegie's book celebrated its 50th anniversary in 1986. More than 30 million copies have been sold in hardcover and paperback, and it is available in 30 languages. "It's a phenomenon. Normally, a nonfiction book doesn't have this longevity," says J. Oliver Crom, Dale Carnegie president.

The company's success is no less impressive. Dale Carnegie & Associates offers eight human relations courses in 18 languages. It has 12 company-owned institutes in the United States and 133 licensed sponsors nationally and in 68 foreign countries, employing some 4,000 instructors. Annual enrollments exceed 150,000—and graduates, which include such well-known figures as Chrysler Corporation chairman Lee Iacocca and actress Linda Gray, number more than 3 million.

On Long Island the firm employs some 100 workers at its Garden City headquarters and its Hauppauge distribution center. "From Hauppauge, our class kits literally go around the world," explains executive vice-president Stuart R. Levine.

How did this all come about? Born in 1888 and raised on a struggling Missouri farm, Carnegie left a brief, but successful, sales career after college to study drama in New York City. When things didn't work out as planned, Carnegie decided to concentrate his talents on writing, but still had to find a way to support himself until he could break into print.

Drawing on his experience as a member of the college debating team, Carnegie convinced the manager of the 125th Street YMCA in Manhattan to let him teach a public-speaking course in 1912. His teaching techniques were extremely well-received, and by 1920 he was in business for himself.

A keen observer of human behavior, Carnegie began to believe that teaching his students to speak better

Dale Carnegie, founder of Dale Carnegie & Associates, Inc., and author of *How to Win Friends and Influence People*. Carnegie's book, still a best-seller, recently celebrated its 50th anniversary.

would not benefit them if they also didn't know how to get along with others. When a search for literature on interpersonal relations uncovered nothing, Carnegie wrote his own book. The message was straightforward: People want to be treated like the important individuals they believe they are.

This simple, yet powerful, principle is the base upon which all Dale Carnegie courses are built. In addition to the original course, The Dale Carnegie Course™ in Effective Speaking and Human Relations, seven business-related offerings are available: The Sales Course, the Management Seminar, the Customer Relations Course, the Employee Development Course, the Executive Image Program, the Dale Carnegie™ Professional Development Series, and the Strategic Presentations Workshop.

Corporate training today accounts for a large share of the organization's business. "When companies become committed to quality, they come to Dale Carnegie because they realize the most important asset they have is their people," explains Levine.

"We are not an off-the-shelf product," adds Crom. "We look at a company's particular needs and apply the Dale Carnegie principles in a way that will meet them best." The firm works with large and small companies and also customizes specific programs for various industries.

Indeed, ensuring that courses meet student needs is a high priority. "Each year we take a program and see what needs to be done. When we revise a course nothing is sacred. We review suggestions from all our instructors. The educational objectives don't change. What changes are the methodology and the techniques," says Crom.

Each revised course is then test marketed at one or more of the firm's institutes. These regional facilities also serve as training sites for instructors, who undergo a rigorous selection process. "Our standards have to be very high. After all, we are the first proprietary training organization to have courses approved for college credit by the American Council on Education," says Levine. The institutes also serve as a link between regional licensees and the corporation.

Crom and Levine are well known on Long Island for their community involvement, each having served as president of public television station WLIW, among numerous other activities. The company itself is active through Junior Achievement. Between 2,000 and 3,000 high school students each year are awarded scholarships for Dale Carnegie courses.

"Young people in this age group are at an important stage in their lives," says Crom. "If we can help them move in the right direction and can have a positive effect on them, then we can contribute to the course of our nation."

J. Oliver Crom, current president of Dale Carnegie & Associates, Inc.

LONG ISLAND

ALLSTATE INSURANCE COMPANY

Innovative management systems that encourage employee teamwork and leading-edge technology that reduces paperwork, delays, and errors are the secrets of Allstate Insurance Company's success.

In 1983 the firm embarked on a new direction entitled The New Perspective, which aimed to enhance growth, visibility, employee development, participative management, and, most important, customer service. Today it is reaping the rewards.

On Long Island the organization has 193 sales locations, 10 claims-processing offices, and 2,300 employees—approximately 900 of whom work at the regional headquarters in Farmingville. The impressive Farmingville complex contains sales, underwriting, human resources, and claims departments.

Reasoning that well-informed, capable employees are the most important ingredient to improving customer service, Allstate launched The New Perspective program by training all managers in the participative management system. Employee quality circles, called improvement teams, were formed to identify and resolve local problems—an approach that has been very successful for employees, customers, and the firm.

In reviewing its sales approach Allstate determined that its system of large offices with six to eight representatives was not convenient enough for customers and also did not allow agents to focus on the particular needs of a geographic area.

The company has now decentralized, opening more one- and two-agent offices in which the representatives have greater authority in deciding how to meet their particular customers' needs. Market research also has played a large role in determining how local offices operate. Customer and employee focus groups are used to gauge product and service satisfaction and provide Allstate with vital information that helps it solve problems quickly and serve clients better.

Allstate's Operations Center, located here at Allstate Drive in Farmingville, provides employee and customer service and related data processing for all of the three regions of Allstate coverage in New York State.

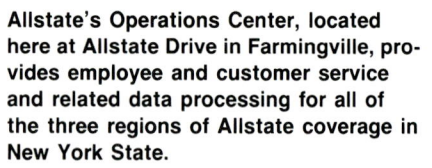

William Lehnertz of Aurora, Illinois, purchased the first Allstate policy to insure his 1930 Studebaker. The restored automobile is on display at the Allstate Historical Exhibit at the home office.

BUSINESS

The regional management staff of Allstate are (from left) Susan L. Farrell (seated), territorial sales manager, Queens; Louis J. Varisano, territorial sales manager, Suffolk; Julio A. Portalatin, underwriting manager; Albert L. Rook, territorial sales manager, Nassau; V.J. DeLuca (seated, center), regional vice-president; Richard C. Crist, Jr., human resource manager; Steve Petti, controller; Christine A. Sullivan, territorial claim manager; and Margaret G. Palermo (seated), territorial claim manager.

One of the most impressive aspects of Allstate's service improvement efforts is its companywide automation. For example, in the area of claims processing, the firm is an industry leader. Through its coast-to-coast computer network, any Allstate agent can access information on clients within seconds. This is of particular importance to vacationers or business travelers who may need assistance outside their home state.

The network allows automobile damage estimates to be prepared quickly and accurately, as the system contains up-to-date parts prices, and provides the property owner and repair facility with a legible, error-free estimate almost immediately.

Allstate clients who need estimates on home-owner structural damage repair also benefit from the expanded information system. A claims representative can input the size of a room and the number and size of windows and doors to determine in seconds how much paint is required or the amount of wallpaper needed, with waste extracted for matching or nonmatching paper.

Sales personnel, through the new computer system, can accurately quote prices, compute and analyze life insurance values and relative savings, and keep track of customers. This allows sales representatives more time to work with the client on a personal level.

Computerization has greatly improved Allstate's underwriting process, as much of the traditional processing was routine and lent itself easily to automation. The underwriting staff does not have to spend so much time on routine tasks, and now can work more closely with agents and can perform greater business analyses in order to make more knowledgeable decisions that result in cost savings to Allstate and its customers.

Employee commitment and state-of-the-art information processing have allowed Allstate Insurance Company to retain its prominent position in the insurance industry on Long Island and nationwide.

General Robert E. Wood, the founder of Allstate, and William A. Lehnertz, the first policyholder, stand beside an Allstate tire—the source of the company's name.

173

LONG ISLAND

FAIRFIELD PROPERTIES

Finding ways to provide affordable housing is one of Long Island's priorities for the 1990s, and the region is fortunate that private real estate partnerships such as Fairfield Properties are hard at work trying to find solutions.

Fairfield entered the real estate arena in 1974, when it purchased a 256-unit rental complex in Commack. Today the firm owns and manages some 3,000 rental units and has converted 1,100 units to cooperative ownership in Suffolk County. It also developed and operates three office buildings that combined have some quarter-million square feet of space.

"Fairfield is primarily in rental and co-op housing. We're trying to provide affordable housing, and, most important, we're doing it without government participation," says partner Mark Broxmeyer. "Any type of affordable housing that has been done traditionally has been with government sponsorship. We are doing it alone, and I think that's impressive," he adds proudly.

Broxmeyer explains that Fairfield can offer cooperative apartments at reasonable prices because it buys existing buildings, thus saving on development and land acquisition costs. Buildings are gutted, and the apartments are rebuilt. "The buyer essentially gets a new apartment. Very often the profit on a resale by the original owner is larger than the one we made at the initial offering," says Broxmeyer.

Fairfield-on-the-Water, a 248-unit middle-income cooperative conversion in Patchogue, is a good example

Providing affordable rental and co-op housing on Long Island is the goal of Fairfield Properties, whose corporate offices are located in Commack.

Pinecrest Gardens, at 1750 West Main Street in Calverton, is the farthest east of Fairfield Properties' estates.

of how Fairfield can help buyers and their community. "When we purchased the property, it was in deplorable condition. It was an eyesore in the community.

"We've kept only the brick exterior and have completely redone the inside. We're giving people a chance to buy something with a modest amount of cash down, and we're giving the Village of Patchogue a property it can be proud of," Broxmeyer says. The real estate executive also notes that Fairfield uses Suffolk County suppliers for its projects, further contributing to the recycling of dollars into the area's economy.

A change of attitude by Long Island's people and planners is what will make affordable housing possible in the future, according to Broxmeyer. "The communities have to cooperate and revise zoning to allow more building of affordable housing. That is the most efficient way to bring housing costs down," he says. "I think in Suffolk County in particular it will be possible to accomplish the goal of affordable housing."

Photo by Ken Spencer

XV

Professions

Long Island's professional community brings a wealth of service, ability, and insight to the area.

Henderson and Bodwell, 178

TSI, 180

The Law Offices of Andrew D. Presberg, 182

Marine Midland Bank, N.A., 183

The Bank of New York, 184

National Westminster Bank USA, 186

Chase Manhattan Bank, N.A., Long Island Region, 188

EAB, 190

Citibank, N.A., 192

Farrell, Fritz, Caemmerer, Cleary, Barnosky & Armentano, P.C., 194

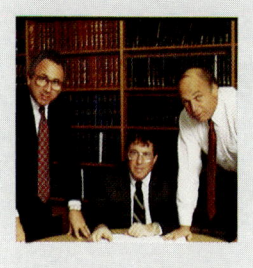

Meltzer, Lippe, Goldstein & Wolf, P.C., 196

Cushman & Wakefield of Long Island, Inc., 198

Photo by R. Settles

LONG ISLAND

HENDERSON AND BODWELL

The Henderson and Bodwell management team (from left) are James R. DeLand, Jr., W. Hall Clarke, managing partner Russell S. Bodwell, John J. Price, and Steven L. Samet.

Engineers working closely together on a hotel site plan design.

Henderson and Bodwell, a full-service engineering consulting firm, was established in 1975 when the partners of Henderson and Casey, P.C., joined with Russell S. Bodwell, then senior vice-president of the major home builder Levitt and Sons. From 22 employees headquartered in Plainview, the firm has grown to more than 100 workers and four branch offices in Ohio, Illinois, New Jersey, and Florida.

The firm's main emphasis is providing civil engineering and land planning services to private developers. Henderson and Bodwell performs feasibility studies; site engineering; storm drainage, sewage disposal, and water supply planning and design; construction management; environmental control approval processing; and miscellaneous services such as landscape architecture.

State-of-the-art computer programs help the firm meet the diverse needs of its clients. Henderson and Bodwell has been in the forefront of computer-aided design use and has developed software packages for various disciplines, including hydraulics, water supply distribution, flood routing, and sewage collection.

Managing partner Russell Bodwell explains that because each project has its own particular set of challenges, civil engineering is more creative than most people think. Bodwell, who was a serious trumpet student, says that for this reason he often seeks engineers with some artistic background. "I have a high respect for the combination of a good musician and a good engineer. Music teaches you something about accuracy and dedication. This allows you to develop the creativity you need as an engineer," he says. Bodwell's interest in the arts prompted him to lead an $8-million fund-raising drive for the Maine Center for the Arts on the campus of his alma mater, the University of Maine.

Henderson and Bodwell has been finding creative solutions to difficult problems for developers all across the country, including the Prudential Insurance Co. and six of the nation's top home builders. On Long Island, the firm has some 20 clients and has provided consulting engineering services for an impressive list of projects, including the Grant Mall, a one-million-square-foot shopping complex on the William Floyd Parkway. The company also has been involved in large-scale

178

PROFESSIONS

A computer-aided design and drafting workstation is being used to design a sanitary sewage pumping station.

residential developments in the towns of Smithtown, Brookhaven, and Islip, and in the development of waterfront condominiums in the Hamptons and office buildings in Westbury and Huntington.

Henderson and Bodwell supports the activities of such professional organizations as the Urban Land Institute, believing that proper planning is critical to good land management. Russell Bodwell has been a panelist for several institute discussions and participated in the group's 50th anniversary infrastructure solutions program in May 1986. The firm is active in the Long Island Chapter of the National Association of Home Builders.

Over the course of history, civil engineering has made great contributions to society by devising improved sanitary systems that reduce disease and safeguard the environment. Henderson and Bodwell has developed expertise in designing sewer and water systems in environmentally sensitive areas, such as New Jersey's Pine Barrens, and has worked with numerous Long Island water districts to improve their supply and distribution systems.

Bodwell believes that Long Island will be able to handle its tremendous growth and protect its natural resources if all parties remain open minded. "People shouldn't abandon their goals, but they need to make intelligent compromises," he advises.

The outlook for the construction and development industry on Long Island is favorable, Bodwell says. "There is a greater recognition and understanding now of the need for moderately priced housing to provide homes for recent college graduates and beginning workers. This will become an important issue in the years to come and will be good for our business.

"It is my belief that the Long Island development community that we serve will prove to be creative enough to develop housing and industrial facilities that will make this region competitive within the Northeast," he concludes.

The finished product—an office development in a park-like setting.

LONG ISLAND

TSI

Can two hardworking and talented engineers find self-fulfillment and financial success on Long Island? For Mario Maltese and Garani Srinivasan, chief executive officer and president, respectively, of TSI, the answer is, "absolutely."

The two men set up shop in Maltese's Williston Park home in 1979 to provide audiovisual and sound system products and services, such as those used in boardrooms and training facilities. They had met while working for a firm that at that time was the industry leader. A change of ownership and management direction spurred Maltese and Srinivasan to branch out on their own. "We wanted the opportunity to do some fine work for ourselves. TSI is now about three times as large as the firm we used to work for," says Maltese proudly.

When a company does good work, word gets around. Within a year TSI had outgrown Maltese's basement, and the neighbors who weren't already on the payroll began to complain about the trucks delivering materials and equipment. TSI moved to a 4,000-square-foot building in New Hyde Park. Shortly thereafter, success again caused it to move—this time to the 22,000-square-foot facility the firm and its 55 employees presently occupy in Mineola.

Gone are the days when a communications system consisted of a public address system. Today's boardroom or training facility may have a system that includes teleconferencing capacity, video projection for computer displays and videotape playback, high-level surround sound, and speech reinforcement. All these functions, as well as controls for lighting, draperies, and screens, for example, may be operated from a custom-designed command center located at a lectern, consolette, or both.

TSI will work directly with a client or with an architect or other consultant to review carefully a customer's needs and design a communications system that meets those requirements precisely—even if it means having to design and build some of the equipment. The firm's project management system identifies specific targets to be reached during the course of the project, and clients receive weekly status reports. Once assembled, the entire system is subjected to extensive testing. After the system is installed the client receives a certificate defining the equipment's performance level, which is guaranteed by TSI, and the company's personnel are fully trained to operate the system.

TSI's computer-aided design capabilities, its sophisticated testing facilities, and its years of experience contribute—but are not the key—to meeting the corporate mission of designing systems, products, and services "that exceed the expectations of our clients." Its in-house training program is TSI's secret weapon.

"We grow our people," explains Maltese. "Because today's systems are so sophisticated, our people have to be trained in many areas, and we find it best to do it ourselves." He estimates that employees spend about 20 days per year in training programs. Finding qualified workers on Long Island has been no problem, he says. "The human resources in the Mineola area are excellent. We have no trouble finding people in our community who are ambitious, bright, energetic, and willing to accept challenges and grow."

Design engineers at work using the latest CAD (Computer Automated Drafting) equipment.

Mario Maltese, chief executive officer of TSI.

Garani Srinivasan, president of TSI.

PROFESSIONS

Rear Projection Booth for the American Express boardroom, New York.

This dedication to quality and service has earned TSI the respect of its peers and a client roster that reads like the *Fortune* 500 listing. In 1987 the firm completed a $2.5-million communications system for American Express' new headquarters at the World Financial Center in New York City. Audio and visual systems were installed on the trading floors, conference facilities, and meeting rooms.

AT&T has been a TSI client from the very beginning. TSI provides all the communications systems used for the firm's annual stockholder meeting. Its innovative use of special telephone-type equipment to allow stockholders to speak directly with AT&T board members at the 1985 meeting earned TSI a standing ovation from the 15,000 attendees.

TSI also designed and installed a million-dollar, state-of-the-art audio and visual system for the new headquarters of an international advertising giant, Saatchi & Saatchi Advertising.

ABOVE: Policy Committee Room at Chemical Bank, New York.

RIGHT: Equipment in Rear Projection Booth at Philip Morris, New York.

Despite this success TSI does not forget its community. The firm has a standing policy of lending communications equipment to worthy organizations. For example, it provided a speech reinforcement and videotape system for the Village of Mineola's ceremonies commemorating the bicentennial of the U.S. Constitution.

For Maltese and Srinivasan, their dream has come true. They are doing work they love and having fun at the same time. "There's really a 'homey' feeling here because we have such great people working for us," says Maltese. "This makes it fun to work here, and the work we do is a lot of fun, too."

181

LONG ISLAND

THE LAW OFFICES OF ANDREW D. PRESBERG

Buying land, constructing a new commercial or industrial facility, finding the money to finance it, and dealing with all the legal issues associated with these items, including the day-to-day legal problems associated with one's business, all can intimidate even the most experienced business owner. The Law Offices of Andrew D. Presberg have successfully assisted with eliminating those problems for many New York and Long Island executives.

The firm provides top-quality professional and legal services, advising and assisting clients on all aspects of a proposed transaction, from advice on negotiating or structuring a new real estate or expansion project to finding the best financial package available, be it specialized government financing or conventional financing. "We analyze what will be good for the client," explains Presberg, whose firm specializes in corporate and commercial law, as well as complex commercial and industrial real estate matters.

Presberg and his associates have extensive experience in specialized financing programs for business growth, expansion, and relocation, including industrial revenue bond financing, New York State Job Development Authority loans, and U.S. Small Business Administration lending programs—as well as in traditional bank loans. Indeed, banks are a large source of client referrals for the firm. "It's a very good feeling when a major commercial bank has a client constructing a multimillion-dollar facility and recommends our firm to do the legal work. They know that we have the familiarity with the sophisticated type of programs they are offering their customers, and, as a result, there will be fewer problems down the line.

This high level of professional success and recognition is even more impressive when you consider that Presberg himself has been out of law school less than 10 years. "Some people initially have reservations about working with someone without grey hair," Presberg admits. "But I consider myself an expert in the fields I specialize in, and soon enough people realize this, respect our work, and then stop worrying. We try to present ourselves as having the skills and ability equal to a large, prominent, New York City firm, but without the large, prominent fees or the lack of personal service associated with such firms."

Presberg also does a brisk business representing real estate developers and contractors. As a matter of fact, he recently purchased the firm's tastefully appointed, modern office condominium at the new Islandia Corporate Plaza, after assisting the developer in putting together the entire project from land acquisition to financing and through his actual preparation and filing of the condominium offering plan.

The firm also advises clients on limited partnerships, syndications, private placement offerings, as well as all aspects of general business, corporate, and contract matters. The move to Islandia was the firm's third in the five years it has been in existence. "Our client list just keeps growing. We had to double our space and double our staff," says the young attorney, who now heads a team of law associates and paralegals.

The new site of the Law Offices of Andrew D. Presberg at Islandia Corporate Plaza Condominium, 100 Corporate Plaza, Islandia, New York, for which the firm handled all legal work and condominium filings.

Andrew D. Presberg, with members of the firm's professional and support personnel at a regular staff meeting.

Presberg's success is, in large manner, due to the fact that many clients who may have initially come to the firm for a one-shot deal, such as a real estate transaction, want his firm to then handle all their corporate legal affairs as well. "In most instances, we've kept clients as a result of our achievements for them," he says. "I give my personal attention to clients and have people working for us who have the qualifications to service all the typical needs of a regular corporate or business client."

Long Island, and Suffolk County in particular, according to Presberg, are overcoming their image of a small-town, rural community. "There is a lot happening here, he says. "I'm an entrepreneurial kind of person, and I enjoy working with business professionals who have a similar outlook. This is certainly evident from the growth of the Long Island business community, which has repeatedly defied logic, what with Lilco costs, transportation limitations, and the like. I love real estate and business law, and it's exciting to work in a place where I can participate in so many diverse projects and watch the growth of our clients and friends."

PROFESSIONS

MARINE MIDLAND BANK, N.A.

Marine Midland Bank's Long Island headquarters at 534 Broad Hollow Road, Melville.

Long Island, with its thriving businesses and upscale population, is a prime market for banks. While most financial institutions are seeking to expand through the acquisition of smaller banks, Marine Midland Bank, with 32 branches and more than one billion dollars in deposits on Long Island, is building new branches to ensure that they are convenient to customers and that they provide the services customers need.

"The focus going forward is to meet the needs of our customers by providing them with the products and services they feel are appropriate, not just by giving them what we already have," says Robert D. Davis, region executive. He notes that deregulation in the next few years will allow banks to directly offer many more services than they can now, such as brokerage services, insurance, and financial planning.

Consequently, Marine's new branches, to be located in select Long Island communities, are physically larger than most bank branches to accommodate these new services when they arrive. In a related move to improve existing services, Marine established a central customer service center at its Melville headquarters to handle telephone inquiries, an added convenience that has been well received by customers.

David Lebens and Lorraine Delaney accept an award on behalf of Marine Midland Bank from March of Dimes Youth Ambassadors Meghan Coutieri and Cheryl LaFalce.

Founded in Buffalo, New York, in 1850 to finance the thriving Great Lakes shipping trade, Marine Midland continues to serve the small- and middle-market business community. "Long Island's businesses are growing and Marine Midland Bank has been active in helping them expand by providing lines of credit, real estate transactions, and a series of innovative commercial transaction and investment-based products. Through its parent, the Hongkong Shanghai Banking Corporation, Marine also can provide a variety of services worldwide for its business customers.

In addition to providing standard consumer banking services and special products such as home equity, car loans, and credit cards, Marine is moving to make banking as easy as possible for its customers. Under an agreement with Suffolk County, Marine handles the direct deposit of paychecks for about one-third of the county's 12,000-member work force. This move saves the county approximately one million dollars annually in reduced paperwork and loss of employee work time for personal banking. "We've had such success that we are hoping to expand this program in the public and private sectors," says Davis.

Helping to improve the quality of life in communities in which Marine customers live and work is important, too. "Marine Midland is committed to working with both the public and private sectors in reaching workable solutions to major issues affecting Long Island's future," says Davis, citing as an example the bank's work with the Town of Brookhaven, Community Development Agency, to develop affordable homes. In addition to helping the town develop the project, Marine foregoes fees and other customary charges to keep project costs as low as possible.

Whether working to promote affordable housing or sponsoring local events such as the March of Dimes TeamWalk, a Long Island Philharmonic concert or the Walt Whitman Poetry Contest for Students; Marine takes seriously its responsibility as a corporate citizen.

Marine's commitment is to deliver professional service to individual businesses and the community. This commitment is reflected daily by Marine's willingness and ability to meet the needs of the vibrant Long Island market.

LONG ISLAND

THE BANK OF NEW YORK

The Bank of New York has neither missed a dividend payment nor been merged into another financial institution since its founding in 1784, a tribute to its sound financial practices. This adherence to conservative fiscal management does not mean the bank has not been innovative and aggressive in its chosen markets. On the contrary, The Bank of New York, founded by a group of New York's leading citizens—including the nation's first Secretary of the Treasury, Alexander Hamilton—has many firsts to its credit.

The Bank of New York was the first lender to the fledgling United States of America. The institution lent the new government $200,000 in 1789, evidenced by a series of warrants, the first of which the bank still owns and displays in the museum at its Wall Street headquarters. It established the first bank trust department in 1830 to serve its portfolio management clients, was the first in the 1920s to begin investing in stocks on behalf of its customers, and was the first bank allowed to reopen after President Franklin D. Roosevelt declared a bank holiday in 1933. The Bank of New York also was the first to own a computer. A new chapter in the bank's history was written in October 1988 when an agreement was signed to acquire Irving Bank Corporation, creating one of the nation's largest bank holding companies.

With its characteristic ability to recognize and seize a good opportunity, the institution entered the Long Island market in 1972 through the purchase of Valley National Bank. Today there are 79 branches from Maspeth to Montauk, providing a wide selection of services and more than one billion dollars in outstanding loans to Long Island businesses and individuals. Through its subsidiary, the Bank of New York Mortgage Co., the bank is an active mortgage lender in the area.

"If you're going to succeed on Long Island, you have to gear your products to the growing, entrepreneurial client base," explains vice-president Owen Brady. Indeed, the institution's business product line is impressive. Cash-management services for small and medium-size businesses include Quest, an electronic account information system providing 24-hour access to business accounts from a personal computer, and Check Invest, an exclusive product that automatically invests idle account balances.

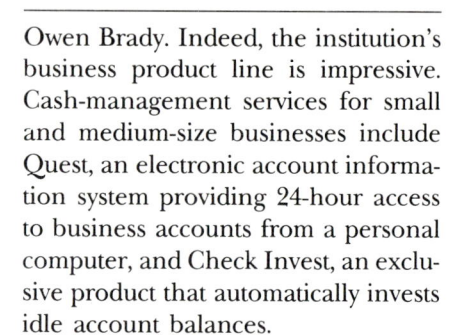

The institution's Capital Markets Group assists business owners in obtaining much-needed capital through such innovative techniques as leasing and asset-based financing, and firms interested in undertaking foreign trade programs will find a helpful, experienced hand at the bank. In keeping with its founding purpose—to finance trade between Europe and the colonies—The Bank of New York always has been active in the international arena, and in 1984 created a team of import-export finance specialists to serve Long Island exclusively.

Business lending centers are maintained in Maspeth, Great Neck, Garden City, Plainview, Melville, Hauppauge, and Lakeland Bohemia to give

The South Farmingdale office is one of many branches in the Nassau County area.

The Long Island division headquarters of The Bank of New York at 1401 Franklin Avenue in Garden City.

PROFESSIONS

The Greenport office, located in Suffolk County, is housed in the oldest building in the town of Greenport. The Bank of New York has many branches throughout Suffolk County—in the Hamptons and on the North Fork.

Long Island business customers easy access to the bank's people and services. "We have made these sophisticated products available to everyone. You don't have to be someone with sales of $100 million before we'll do business with you," says Brady in explaining the bank's success in the region.

The Bank of New York's business sector growth has not been at the expense of its individual clients. A trust and investment center operates at the institution's divisional headquarters in Garden City. With nearly 160 years of trust department experience, the bank still controls a major share of this market. It is among the top three custodian banks in the United States.

Service to the community also is a high priority. The Bank of New York is the largest lender to municipalities on Long Island, and serves as finan-

Automated banking is available all over Long Island. Pictured here is a special 24-hour action banking drive-up in Hicksville.

cial adviser to some 40 local government entities. "We're mindful of our responsibility to support the communities where we are present," says senior vice-president Paul Leyden. "Our people become involved."

The bank's If I Were Mayor contest, sponsored in Garden City in 1987, bears this out. Garden City residents were asked to propose minor improvement projects they would undertake if they were mayor. The bank awarded $1,000 to the person with the best suggestion and contributed $10,000 to making the project a reality.

The Bank of New York's impressive ability to balance fiscal prudence with innovative product development places it in a prime position to help Long Island grow. Says Leyden, "Long Island is not our birthplace, but it is our home."

LONG ISLAND

NATIONAL WESTMINSTER BANK USA

Most major banks arrived on Long Island in pursuit of the thousands of New York City residents who migrated east after World War II. However, the bank that today is named National Westminster Bank USA was born and bred on the island.

NatWest USA traces its origins to the 1905 charter of The First National Bank of Freeport, under which it operates today. The institution's growth began in 1949, when it merged with First National Bank of Merrick to form the Meadow Brook National Bank. During the next decade Meadow Brook continued to grow and in 1960 acquired two New York City banks, thereby becoming the first Long Island bank to establish a Manhattan base.

In 1967 Meadow Brook merged with the Bank of North America to form National Bank of North America (NBNA). In 1979 NBNA was purchased by National Westminster Bank PLC of London and four years later changed its name to National Westminster Bank USA.

Today the institution strives to become a superregional operation. On February 1, 1988, National Westminster Bank USA and First Jersey National Corporation merged under National Westminster Bancorp Inc., a newly formed holding company based in New York. With this merger, NatWest USA, which at year-end 1987 had $11.5 billion in assets, 133 branches, and 4,600 employees, combined its strengths with First Jersey, the fourth-largest bank in New Jersey, with 4,000 employees, 110 branches, and $4.8 billion in assets. The holding company is headed by chairman and chief executive officer William T. Knowles, also NatWest USA's chairman and chief executive officer.

NatWest USA has always maintained a very strong presence on Long Island. Currently 3,000 of its employees and 75 of its 133 branches are located there, along with commercial lending headquarters in Jericho, an administrative center in West Hempstead, and a major computer and operations center in Huntington.

In consumer banking, the institution tailors its branch network to suit the needs of its client base. For example, the explosive commercial development in the industrial parks of Hauppauge and the area around MacArthur Airport spurred it in early 1988 to establish business-banking centers in those locations.

"In opening the Hauppauge office, we consolidated two nearby branches into a larger facility, enabling us to provide better service for businesses and consumers. It's new, it's beautiful, and it's efficient," says William Laraia, senior vice-president/branch banking.

The bank's computerized Personal Banker Program is another example of how NatWest tailors services to customer requirements, enabling customer service representatives at any branch to serve customers immediately, regardless of where the customers' primary branch is.

"At NatWest USA, a top priority is giving high-quality service to consumers through our wide branch network," says L. Douglas O'Brien, executive vice-president/Community Banking Group.

In targeting middle-market customers (with $10 million to $250 million in annual sales), NatWest USA offers a broad selection of services, including cash management, trust, and trade financing and commercial real estate. Typical of its innovative approach is Trade Beam, a system that allows customers to initiate letters of credit on their own business computer terminals and transmit them directly to the bank's computers.

Senior vice-president Morris Danon, who oversees the bank's middle-market activities on Long Island, points out that NatWest's streamlined loan-approval process makes life simpler for mid-size companies. "We have a higher degree of autonomy than many of our competitors in terms of how much money we can

---

NatWest USA serves mid-size firms in Nassau and Suffolk counties from its regional headquarters in Jericho. The bank also has specialties in cash management, trade finance, trust, and commercial real estate—located there as well as a branch office.

PROFESSIONS

NatWest USA established a business banking center in Hauppauge in 1988 to better serve commercial firms in a fast-growing industrial area. The company tailors its branch network to suit the specific needs of its client base and has a total of 73 branches on Long Island.

allocate to a transaction. If someone needs an answer fast, we can often get one the same day. Our customers certainly appreciate that," he says.

Businesses with annual sales volume below $10 million also find an open door at NatWest. "This is a very important market. In the metropolitan area, about 80 percent of all companies are under $15 million in sales. When you help somebody start out, it is gratifying to see them grow, and generally you get rewarded as they get bigger and stronger," says Arthur Thompson, senior vice-president.

Automated teller machines (ATMs) have now become a way of life, and NatWest has ATMs, named Teller Beam, in key Long Island locations. Customers are also served from ATMs at stand-alone kiosks and at corporate locations, such as Fortunoff and North Shore Hospital. The bank is part of the NYCE and CIRRUS ATM networks, giving its customers access to their accounts at more than 18,000 machines nationwide.

NatWest USA is proud that its ATM network regularly registers more than 97 percent availability for any given month, ranking among the industry's leaders.

ATM availability is one example of the bank's effort to be a leader in quality services. All of its 4,600 employees have participated in quality training programs, and incentives rewarding quality performance have created pride in serving the customer in the best possible way.

The bank's Statement of Values, Mission, and Commitment to Quality stresses commitment to the communities it serves. Not only is the institution active in community service and a leader in support of United Way, but its officers take a leadership role in many cultural, service, and civic organizations. Executive vice-president Paul Kreuch, for example, serves both as a board member and head of the Transportation Committee for Long Island Association, Inc.

On Long Island and throughout the New York area NatWest USA supports a broad range of cultural events through its Arts in the Community program, including outdoor concerts, music for children and for the elderly, performances by local theater groups, radio broadcasts, and telecasts on PBS.

"We have made a commitment to the community that goes beyond mere compliance with the Community Reinvestment Act," says William Knowles. "It is our responsibility as a good corporate citizen to help keep the community vigorous and attractive, and to contribute to the quality of life."

National Westminster Bank USA's exceptional support of the arts has earned it a Presidential Citation as part of the White House Program on Private Sector Initiatives.

NatWest USA installed its first automated teller machine (ATM) in 1980 in Hicksville. Since then the bank has increased its total number of ATMs to more than 106, of which 55 are located on Long Island. The institution regularly registers better than 97-percent ATM availability in any given month, placing it among the industry's leaders.

187

LONG ISLAND

CHASE MANHATTAN BANK, N.A., LONG ISLAND REGION

Long Island boasts not only one of the nation's leading per-household income levels, but a growing and competitive business and industry arena as well. Individuals are concerned with turning hard-earned assets into high-quality life-styles. They turn to Chase Manhattan Bank, N.A., Long Island Region, to maximize and protect personal assets. Similarly, Long Island companies have come to depend on

Chase Manhattan Bank, N.A., Long Island Region, has established community ties with individuals and businesses on the island. The bank places particular emphasis on community, commercial, and personal financial services to provide high-quality, comprehensive counsel and assistance. Standing in the top photo is Edgar F. Braun, personal financial services executive. In the bottom photo is Julian Simone, vice-president. Photos by Bob Klien

188

PROFESSIONS

Chase for support through a growth phase for optimum investments and utilization of corporate equity.

Chase Long Island Region executive William H. Hoefling emphasizes the bank's strength as an outgrowth of its established community ties. "When I think of Chase services, I think of quality and support for the community in which our clients live and conduct business. Tapping a global network of banking professionals, our experienced relationship managers and branch personnel can respond to the specific needs of area consumers, businesses, and local communities.

"We take a very personal approach," continues Hoefling. "Every senior officer in the Chase Long Island Region sits on the board of at least one organization. Looking at the area town by town, Chase can point to specific contributions it has made to community success and spirit."

Chase's community service record is impressive. In 1988 the bank allocated $86,500 in grants on Long Island for projects ranging from cultural events to the support of senior citizens and youth groups. Through direct grants or board activity it also participated in programs of some 275 not-for-profit organizations. "Chase is very much a hands-on participant, whether sponsoring a soccer game for special children or promoting a showing of area artists," says Hoefling.

As a commercial bank, Chase offers extensive services to businesses. Teams of trained commercial lending officers provide expert advice, tailored to meet a company's individual needs. In addition, the merchant banking and trade development team stands ready to help clients who need assistance with foreign trade transactions, mergers and acquisitions, capital evaluation studies, and other important services. The bank's real estate team provides assistance with various building and property transactions.

Chase offers a variety of business support and investment banking products such as commercial mortgages, capital expansion, loans, and global and regional cash management. Employee stock-ownership plans can also be arranged.

In addition to meeting corporate banking requirements, Chase Manhattan Bank, N.A., Long Island Region, now has more than 50 specialists to assist with an individual's banking needs. Pictured here is Chase Long Island Region executive William H. Hoefling.

"Our customer is a Long Island customer, to whom we bring our vast financial resources," explains commercial banking executive John Lopinto. "Chase has the capacity to meet commercial needs here and abroad. For the entrepreneur, we can deliver personal services, as well as trust and estate planning," he says.

"Chase places particular emphasis on cross-servicing, or utilizing the strengths of each banking area—community, commercial, and personal financial services—to provide high-quality, comprehensive counsel and assistance. Our clients gain considerably from this single-source banking service."

A longtime provider of private banking services primarily through its Trust Department, Chase has widened the scope to reach today's larger market. "The individual who owns or runs a company has needs that transcend his corporate role. In addition to meeting corporation banking requirements, we now have more than 50 specialists to assist with an individual's personal banking needs. Chase relationship managers make a commitment to work on a personal level, consulting with clients at their home or business, displaying the extra effort that is the cornerstone of professional service and, ultimately, customer benefit and success," explains Edgar F. Braun, personal financial services executive. Investment, financial planning, mutual funds, and loan programs, such as home equity loans and mortgages exceeding $250,000, are available for individuals with household incomes exceeding $75,000.

At the core of Chase's Long Island operation is its 30 branches that serve the needs of both individual and business customers. According to Julian R. Simone, community banking executive, "Providing transactional support to the bank's different teams, Chase branch managers and personnel go beyond the traditional realm of service. While offering versatile products at competitive rates, we also make every effort to focus on each of Long Island's diverse communities. Our branch managers are active within their marketplaces, reaching out both to meet with customers, as well as serve on local boards."

Simone stresses the importance of personal involvement on the part of branch managers and their staffs. "We build relationships with our banking customers, creating the quality service tradition to support Chase's distinctive product offerings. To achieve this, we are consistently working with our people, instituting new training programs, reviewing our policies, and renovating branch facilities—all toward achieving the highest level of customer service."

All teams and support staff are located on Long Island, primarily at the bank's Melville regional headquarters. The bank currently employs 3,400 individuals on the island.

Chase people concentrate on individual priorities as a means to best serve area interests. "Our mission is to be the best in our chosen field," says Hoefling, adding, "We are continuing to build our relationship with the Long Island community, and are enjoying professional and personal achievements."

LONG ISLAND

EAB

To EAB, Long Island is home. That thought is best expressed in the bank's advertising, with its simple yet powerful message: "EAB—the bank for Long Islanders—where you belong."

EAB's predecessor, Franklin National Bank, was considered to be one of the most influential forces in the development of Long Island after World War II. Established in Franklin Square in 1926, Franklin National—under the visionary leadership of Arthur Roth—lent money to the home builders, gave mortgages to the new buyers, and then provided banking services for their families and businesses. By the 1950s Franklin National had approximately 65 percent of the market share.

"If there is any place in the United States that a bank dominated, it was Franklin National on Long Island," says EAB chairman and president Raymond J. Dempsey.

With the acquisition of Franklin's branch network in 1974, EAB was transformed into one of the major consumer banking organizations on Long Island. But it wasn't until 1984 that EAB sharpened its regional focus and reestablished itself in the Franklin tradition as the bank for Long Islanders.

"We have focused everything we do for consumers and middle-market clients almost exclusively on Long Island," explains Dempsey. Indeed, of the bank's 90 branches, 60 are in Nassau-Suffolk and 8 are in Queens. A recent study showed that of EAB's Manhattan branch customers, 80 percent live on the island.

The bank's strategy for establishing its prominence is simple: Give customers the services they want and make it pleasant for them to do business with EAB. Dempsey says bankers who want to succeed must approach their business like any other retailer. "If there are two shoe stores in town, each selling the same product, you'll go to the one where the clerk says, 'Good morning. How can I help you?'" he explains.

"We don't plan any new, sophisticated services. Rather, we provide excellent basic services in a pleasant atmosphere, and provide our customers with an attractive rate of return on their money," he adds.

EAB has just completed a $14-million branch refurbishing program, has upgraded its computer systems to achieve maximum efficiency, and is undertaking an extensive employee-training program. The bank is also further enhancing its employee career path to develop more managers from within. Presently, about 50 percent of branch managers began working for EAB as tellers.

Automation has simplified teller transactions to give bank employees more time to interact with customers, according to Dempsey, who says EAB does not view automation as a way to reduce costs, but rather as an added

Some scenes from EAB advertisements (left and facing page): Matinecock is one of the many picturesque places on Long Island.

convenience to customers. "Nothing replaces the human element of our business," he notes.

The human element is especially important in servicing EAB's business clients. "When I talk to our lending officers, I always remind them that they are lending money to people. Companies are people. When you are dealing with the middle-market segment, you are dealing with the company's employees and suppliers, too. So, services have to be good all the way around," says Dempsey.

In refocusing the bank's efforts, Dempsey, a native Long Islander, says EAB recognized that—like any other geographic region—each of the island's small communities are distinct and have their own personality. "We're trying to make our branches operate like traditional local banks. Our branch managers are really more like presidents of small-town banks."

ABOVE: Pictured here is the Old Bethpage Restoration.

LEFT: Manhasset is another reason why Long Island has become such a desirable place to live.

BOTTOM RIGHT: Cold Spring Harbor.

It's on the local level, too, that EAB does most of its community service. Each branch has a budget for this purpose, and managers have flexibility in allocating it for projects ranging from little league teams and youth programs to services for the handicapped, to name only a few. On a corporate level EAB has an active community relations program that supports a wide range of activities designed to improve the quality of life in the community.

Perhaps Dempsey touches on what ultimately will be the key to the bank's success in establishing its regional presence when he says, "For our people, community service isn't something we even have to encourage. They're just interested in helping others."

191

LONG ISLAND

CITIBANK, N.A.

Customer service is nothing new at Citibank, N.A. It was the first commercial bank to offer personal loans and the first financial institution to popularize the concept of banking 24 hours a day through automated teller machines. These are just two of the innovative services that Citibank introduced and that have become industry standards.

"We believe that superior customer service not only is what our clients deserve but also that it will result in more business. Probably 30 percent to 35 percent of our business in the branches today is through customer referrals. Customers really talk to one another," explains John R. Buran, vice-president and director of Long Island Retail Banking.

"The main ingredient to service is being friendly. But you need to be competent, too," says Buran in discussing the bank's extensive employee training program. Buran, who oversees Citibank's 49 Long Island Retail Banking locations, notes that the bank does not have a two-tiered training system. Employees learn about personal and commercial banking products so they can help any customer.

Citibank, which employs 2,000 people in all its Long Island divisions, also invests time and money in continuing education. Branch personnel may enroll in Adelphi University's financial planning course. Other employees are being trained to complete the Series "F" and 63 stockbrokers exams, and numerous others have taken computer, marketing, and effective writing courses at Nassau Community College.

"When a customer comes in and asks a question about a current topic in finance, our people must be able to talk about it or at least know how to find the answers," says Buran, adding that Citibank employees will be ready to provide the new services bank deregulation is expected to introduce in the next few years.

The bank maintains an extensive network of automated teller machines throughout Long Island, not only at branches but also at retail stores and gasoline stations, to make banking convenient for its clients. These machines offer a complete menu of banking services, available 24 hours a day, and the customer can choose to communicate in English, Spanish, or Chinese. It also plans to install state-of-the-art Drive Up teller machines at various locations. Citibank recently introduced "CitiTouch," a free service that enables customers to get around-the-clock account information from any touch-tone telephone.

The modern interior and exterior of Citibank's Long Beach branch.

PROFESSIONS

soccer events in the region. It also sponsors cultural events around Long Island and offers a special seminar series for senior citizens.

Buran believes Citibank is at its best on a grass-roots level. When a fire destroyed a public school in Wyandanch, the local branch manager called the regional headquarters in Freeport to see if Citibank could help. Unused office equipment and supplies were soon dispatched from Citibank's warehouse. In yet another example, when Citibank updated its secretaries' workstations, the existing word-processing equipment was donated to a local nonprofit agency.

"We've gone out of our way to ensure that Citibank is involved in all those day-to-day activities that mean so much to the people of a local community," Buran concludes.

Direct Access, the computerized personal banking service, is steadily gaining users as people become more computer literate and the cost of hardware declines. Citibank also has introduced its Business Access personal computer banking program for commercial customers on a test basis.

Citibank is dedicated to the Long Island marketplace and since 1986 has opened seven new branches throughout Nassau and Suffolk counties. The unique needs of each marketplace are considered when each new branch is designed. For instance, the Executive Banking Center in Hauppauge's industrial park is specially staffed to provide special consumer banking services to local professionals and executives, and is equipped with a 120-person meeting facility.

However, if getting to the bank is still a problem, Citibank has solutions. A team of commercial lenders will go to customers' offices, if necessary, and at several branches special offices have been added to accommodate personal and business banking clients who need to meet with Citibank personnel after banking hours or on weekends.

Despite its international reputation Citibank enjoys a strong Long Island identity through its extensive community service. For example, Citigrants is a neighborhood-oriented program that emanates from the branches and awards grants of between $500 and $2,000 to nonprofit groups. Over the past five years nearly $200,000 has been given to some 270 agencies.

The bank also is the sponsor of the Brentwood Soccer Tournament, which for the past nine years has been one of the major intramural youth

Citibank's Huntington Village branch.

LONG ISLAND

FARRELL, FRITZ, CAEMMERER, CLEARY, BARNOSKY & ARMENTANO, P.C.

Several attorneys who have experience in zoning, real estate, and development activities review plans for a client's project in the Farrell, Fritz offices, which are located at EAB Plaza in Uniondale.

Litigation is one of the major parts of the firm's practice. In this photograph, an attorney is shown researching and writing a brief in the Farrell, Fritz library.

One of the senior partners of Farrell, Fritz, Caemmerer, Cleary, Barnosky & Armentano, P.C., describes his law firm, which is one of the largest full-service law firms on Long Island, as "a Long Island firm that is predominantly engaged in representing Long Island interests."

Its lawyers, which now number in excess of 40, were born or raised on Long Island, and have spent all or the larger part of their lives in the area.

They represent entities from virtually all of Long Island's different industries, from genetic engineering to professional hockey, from aerospace to hematology, and from oil to banking. Farrell, Fritz clients include hospitals, shopping centers, builders, publishers, insurance companies, and universities. The firm also regularly represents many Long Island governments and individuals.

Its diverse practice has enabled Farrell, Fritz to be intimately involved in the growth and expansion of Long Island. For example, the firm's lawyers regularly counsel parties in connection with the development, sale, and lease of commercial and residential properties, and have been involved in the purchase and sale of many major Long Island buildings. Its zoning attorneys assist clients in obtaining the necessary municipal approvals to build and expand these properties.

Farrell, Fritz is actively involved in the municipal finance field. It is the only Long Island law firm listed in *The Bond Buyer's Directory of Municipal Bond Dealers of the United States,* which is also known as "The Red Book." "Our work helps school districts and towns fund their day-to-day and long-term operations," a partner at the firm says.

Long Islanders starting out in business, as well as senior executives of large and established corporations, regularly turn to the corporate lawyers at Farrell, Fritz for assistance. These lawyers negotiate and draft complex merger and acquisition agreements for large and small businesses and professional practices. In addition, they negotiate and draft employment, partnership, and shareholders' agreements as well as other kinds of contracts that might be needed in a business situation, ranging from contracts to provide computer services to franchise agreements. They also help clients obtain venture capital or other financing.

Litigation is one of the largest parts of the firm's practice. Its lawyers litigate, on behalf of plaintiffs and defendants, over problems that include zoning, commercial, real estate, environmental, and products liability issues. Several attorneys concentrate on criminal law, with particular emphasis on white-collar crime. Farrell, Fritz represents clients in civil rights and constitutional law matters, and in probate and estate litigation. It does so at the trial court level and on the appellate level in all federal and state courts in New York.

The firm's wide-ranging litigation experience and large number of litigation lawyers means that "if a client is served with papers in the morning, we can be ready in the afternoon to defend that motion," a litigation partner says.

Long Islanders trying to deal with the complex estate tax laws often turn to the firm's trusts and estates lawyers for assistance.

These attorneys counsel clients on all aspects of estate planning and estate administration, including the drafting of wills and trusts, probate, conservatorships, guardianships, and accountings.

PROFESSIONS

Farrell, Fritz utilizes technologically advanced office equipment, including many on-site computers, to assist its attorneys in delivering legal services.

Several of the firm's lawyers prepare for a meeting with clients in one of the large conference rooms at Farrell, Fritz.

Nassau County Bar Association.

A Farrell, Fritz attorney is chairman of the board of trustees of Molloy College, another is the president of Winthrop-University Hospital, and a third is treasurer and trustee of the Church Charity Foundation, which owns and operates St. John's Episcopal Hospitals of Smithtown and Far Rockaway. In addition, lawyers at the firm are on the board of directors of the Long Island Philharmonic, the Friends of the Arts, the Nassau County Advisory Board of the Salvation Army, the Leukemia Society of America, the Family Services Association of Nassau County, Inc., and New Beginnings, an international adoption agency.

In addition to helping resolve the problems facing Long Island's businesses and individuals, Farrell, Fritz "often handles the legal aspects of many of the major problems and concerns that face Long Island itself," another partner explains.

One of the most important of those issues, of course, is the environment. Farrell, Fritz represents parties in many litigated (and nonlitigated) environmental actions, including three of the largest environmental cases currently pending in the federal courts in New York.

"We also are involved in other environmental problems," says a partner who concentrates on environmental law. Those range from representing individuals seeking a permit to build a dock to representing commercial entities in the permitting process in connection with the disposal of hazardous or infectious waste.

The lawyers at Farrell, Fritz take pride in both their professional and personal involvement in Long Island. Attorneys at the firm chair the Trusts and Estates Section of the New York State Bar Association, the Nassau County Bar Association Municipal Law Committee, and the Nassau County Bar Association Federal Courts Committee. One of the firm's lawyers is a New York town justice, and another is the New York State Assembly minority floor leader. Several have taught courses at local law schools and lecture frequently at bar association seminars, and one is an officer of the

The high quality of the firm's lawyers and support staff, supplemented by up-to-date computers and communications technology, will allow Farrell, Fritz to "address the issues that our clients will face in the upcoming years," according to a senior partner.

"Having been an integral part of Long Island in the past," he adds, "we fully expect to be an integral part of what happens here on Long Island in the future."

195

LONG ISLAND

MELTZER, LIPPE, GOLDSTEIN & WOLF, P.C.

It is not uncommon for clients of Meltzer, Lippe, Goldstein & Wolf, P.C., to ask the firm's attorneys to negotiate business deals on their behalf, not just to draw up the papers.

"One of our strong points is that we are very business oriented. When it is appropriate we act as an arm of the client. We are not just legal technicians. We put our legal decisions within a business framework," says Richard Lippe.

"We serve as a fountain of information and experience for our clients," notes Lewis Meltzer, adding, "Often we are asked to serve on clients' boards of directors and become involved in a policy-making role."

Established in Mineola in 1970, the firm today employs 20 attorneys and a support staff of 25. From its elegant headquarters building on Willis Avenue, the firm's attorneys provide clients with a broad range of sophisticated legal services. The building also houses many of the stunning modern artworks owned by the Contemporary Art Consortium—an art investment fund that Meltzer, Lippe, Goldstein & Wolf represents—which works are available for viewing by appointment.

While it represents at least five of Long Island's 10 largest companies, some of whom have revenues in excess of one billion dollars, the law firm also serves many medium-size and smaller businesses, with revenues of $5 million to $50 million. Several of the better known corporations that the firm represents on a regular basis are Esselte Business Systems, Inc., Computer Associates, Coinmach Industries Co., and Solgar Co., Inc.

"What we offer all our clients is the capability of a Wall Street law firm in a less formal atmosphere and with a much more hands-on approach. We do not get involved in too much delegation of duties," Sheldon Goldstein explains.

From left: Sheldon M. Goldstein, Richard A. Lippe, and Lewis S. Meltzer discuss the Gary Player signature golf course in Ocean City, Maryland.

David I. Schaffer (left) and Charles A. Bilich discuss a corporate merger.

Meltzer, Lippe, Goldstein & Wolf's ability to deliver such high-quality service rests on its legal staff's depth of experience. Nearly all the firm's attorneys have worked at major corporate law firms, primarily in New York City, and have been involved in cases of national significance. Many are considered leading authorities in their respective specialties, and lecture and publish extensively.

In its corporate representation, the firm has extensive experience in the securities, merger and acquisition, and franchise areas. These activities are guided by Chuck Bilich, who, prior to joining the firm, had substantial responsibility for the Chrysler reorganization, and David Schaffer, who, as general counsel to Avis Rent-a-Car supervised all ongoing legal work and had primary responsibility for developing and implementing the company's foreign franchise program. The firm also engages in a broad range of venture capital-related activities under the supervision of Richard Lippe and, in this connection, represents Poly Ventures, the largest venture capital fund

PROFESSIONS

Joseph Katz (left) and Gerald P. Wolf discuss a future seminar to be held by the firm.

on Long Island.

Real estate constitutes a major area of the firm's practice. Under the direction of Sheldon Goldstein, the firm represents clients engaged in real estate syndication, construction, development, and financing, and the firm also acts as an entrepreneur in these endeavors. Both Shelly Goldstein and Lew Meltzer are leading real estate development and syndication experts who also provide advice on residential and commercial conversion, shopping center and office leasing, and other real estate areas. The firm is presently engaged from both an entrepreneurial and professional standpoint in the construction of a golf course development in Ocean City, Maryland. When completed, the complex will consist of a Gary Player signature golf course, tennis club, marina, and 408 town houses.

The chairman for the past three years of a Practicing Law Institute Annual Seminar on Non-Qualified Deferred Compensation Plans is the firm's employee benefits partner, Gerry Wolf, a noted authority in the field who has an in-depth background in designing and implementing qualified pension, profit-sharing, employee stock option, and executive compensation plans, as well as in meeting the complex requirements of the Employee Retirement Income Security Act. Meltzer, Lippe, Goldstein & Wolf works on a continuing basis with the employee benefit matters of such companies as Computer Associates and Holmes Protection, Inc. Two of its attorneys, working with the Society of Personnel Administrators, have also helped establish a pension "hotline" to answer questions from benefits personnel located on Long Island.

Closely held corporations—of which there are many on Long Island—benefit from the firm's extensive corporate law experience. The owners of these corporations also can obtain expert personal financial planning with estate and tax advice, which is of particular importance to family-owned businesses. These services are coordinated by Joe Katz, who heads the firm's Estate Planning Department.

Labor and employment law is guided by Brian Conneely. One of the firm's areas of focus has been representing management in employment discrimination litigation. In two successfully concluded litigations, the firm had employment discrimination claims dismissed against a multinational corporation and a major hospital. The firm's labor law practice also includes such traditional areas as collective bargaining, union elections, unfair labor practice claims, and similar matters. With the recent increase in entrepreneurship, Meltzer, Lippe, Goldstein & Wolf has also been gaining a reputation as expert in litigation involving employees who establish companies that compete with former employers.

The firm maintains an active bankruptcy law practice under the supervision of John Westerman. It represents both debtors and creditors in reorganization and other proceedings.

In the municipal law area, Meltzer, Lippe, Goldstein & Wolf number among its clients the Village of Great Neck Plaza, for which it wrote one of the most innovative zoning codes in the region. A former Nassau Deputy County Attorney, Richard Lippe has acted as Village Attorney for more than 20 years.

The firm's litigation services are directed by Alan Mittman, who has

From left: John Westerman, Brian S. Conneely, and Alan L. Mittman at the conclusion of a meeting involving a Chapter 11 reorganization.

handled a number of significant antitrust matters. The firm's litigation activities are primarily of a corporate and commercial nature, and are litigated in both federal and state courts in New York and elsewhere in the country.

On a personal level, many of the firm's attorneys are involved in community activities as well as in professional organizations. Lewis Meltzer is president of the Bi-County Political Action Committee, which promotes the strategic relationship of the United States with the State of Israel, and Richard Lippe, as a trustee of the Pollock-Krasner Project, sponsored by the Stony Brook Foundation, is helping with the development of Jackson Pollock's East Hampton, Long Island, home into a research and study center.

With Long Island's economy growing by leaps and bounds, practicing law there is challenging and rewarding. "The Long Island business community is recognizing its own professionals. As Long Island continues to establish itself as an important economic region, we, as part of its professional community, are serving many companies and helping them achieve their full potential," Meltzer concludes.

LONG ISLAND

CUSHMAN & WAKEFIELD OF LONG ISLAND, INC.

Cushman & Wakefield of Long Island, Inc., served as the leasing agent when the Huntington Quadrangle, the precursor of Long Island's biggest office center, was created in the late 1960s. The 70-year-old diversified business real estate services firm has been in the forefront of local development ever since.

A decade later 900 underdeveloped acres of the former Mitchel Air Force Base in Uniondale began to draw interest. Again, Cushman & Wakefield played a pivotal role, bringing together a bank looking for a corporate headquarters and a developer with grandiose plans.

Spurred by Cushman & Wakefield, the DeMatteis Organization and European American Bank developed the 1.1-million-square-foot EAB Plaza, now the focal point of the Nassau-Suffolk region and the heart of a major commercial complex that is nearing completion.

Cushman & Wakefield of Long Island, which has been in the area for 25 years and is one of the most prestigious of the firm's 60 offices nationwide, offers the gamut of real estate services available anywhere. "We are not simply brokers who show space," explains Joseph A. Lagano, senior vice-president and manager of Cushman & Wakefield of Long Island, Inc.

"Showing space" is only one of the myriad of services the firm provides. Offering financial services, development consulting, management services, appraisal, brokerage, and market research are just a few of the reasons why Cushman & Wakefield has been involved in the leasing of approximately 50 percent of all commercial space in Nassau and Suffolk since the early 1980s.

"We are proud to have been involved in the orderly growth of Long Island," Lagano notes. "We've worked with developers and local government to ensure that things are done the way they should be."

Because Cushman & Wakefield is able to provide a wide range of services, a potential client located anywhere in the country who is interested in leasing, buying, or building a commercial facility on Long Island can approach Cushman & Wakefield with just an idea. The 43-member team will assess locations, financing options, zoning regulations, work force availability, and the countless other factors that must be weighed before making a final decision, large or small.

"We spend a lot of time and money in market research and support functions, and reinvest a substantial portion of our profits into the company to upgrade our services," states Lagano. "Serving our customers' needs—whether it's a large account or a smaller transaction—is our main concern."

Lagano believes that both small and large commercial development on Long Island is moving east. He believes that Cushman & Wakefield—with its years of experience and its emphasis on research—will play a significant part in the development of these major new commercial hubs and continue to provide services in the Long Island marketplace.

Flanked by Cushman & Wakefield brokers and managers, senior vice-president Joseph A. Lagano (center) stands in front of Long Island's largest and tallest privately owned office building—the 1.1-million-square-foot, twin tower EAB Plaza in Uniondale.

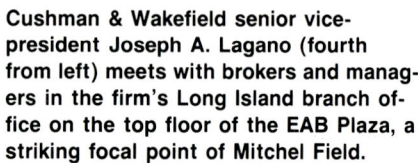

Cushman & Wakefield senior vice-president Joseph A. Lagano (fourth from left) meets with brokers and managers in the firm's Long Island branch office on the top floor of the EAB Plaza, a striking focal point of Mitchel Field.

Photo by R. Settles

XVI

Quality of Life

Medical and educational institutions, along with recreational activities, contribute to the quality of life and entertainment of Long Island area residents.

United Presbyterian Home at Syosset, Inc., 202

St. Joseph's College, 204

Healthplex, Inc., 206

C.W. Post Campus of Long Island University, 209

Board of Cooperative Educational Services, 210

Central General Hospital, 212

State University College at Old Westbury, 213

The State University of New York at Stony Brook, 214

Molloy College, 216

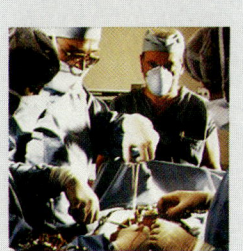

Southside Hospital, 218

Polytechnic University Long Island Campus, 220

New York Institute of Technology, 222

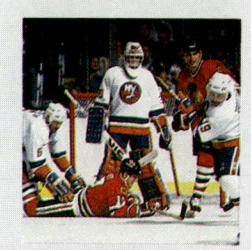

New York Islanders, 224

Photo by R. Settles

LONG ISLAND

UNITED PRESBYTERIAN HOME AT SYOSSET, INC.

The lush and carefully tended garden area that complements the neat, red-brick buildings within the complex contributes greatly to United Presbyterian's warm, welcoming aura.

Passersby might assume that the neat, redbrick buildings with their carefully tended grounds on Syosset-Woodbury Road in Woodbury are a typical suburban garden apartment complex. They would be partially correct. The buildings are homes, but to some 600 very special elderly residents, rather than to up-and-coming young executives and their families.

The United Presbyterian Residence in Woodbury, together with its sister facility, Flushing House in Queens, are the two nondenominational residences for the elderly operated by United Presbyterian Home at Syosset, Inc. The Woodbury facility provides 352 skilled nursing beds for individuals needing medical supervision, and 250 health-related facility beds for residents who require fewer medical services but prefer a communal atmosphere. Flushing House has 315 apartments, as well as communal dining and meeting facilities for residents.

These facilities have become a reality because of the hard work and dedication of churchwomen over the years. The Graham Home for the Aged was established in Brooklyn in 1848 to serve aged, economically deprived women. In 1916 a not-for-profit corporation was established to create a residence for widows in the Nassau-Brooklyn area. After operating a number of small facilities, United Presbyterian Home acquired the 11-acre Willock Estate in Woodbury in 1954 and set up a 23-bed nursing home facility in the mansion house. Sarah Lavinia Rasweiler, who was one of the women instrumental in obtaining the Woodbury site, is now in her nineties and enjoys the comforts of the facility she helped found.

By 1965 United Presbyterian Home had grown to accommodate 90 residents. The addition of a 150-bed health-related facility in 1973 and successive expansion thereafter brought the resident population to its current 600. Despite its growth United Presbyterian Home's 850 staff members strive to maintain the caring atmosphere of a smaller facility. "We have kept the same quality of care as we've grown larger," explains a spokesperson. "This place is a home in the true sense. We have some patients who go to visit their families and after a few days ask to be taken 'home' to UPR."

Health-related facility residents have a private room with bath and complete freedom to leave the grounds whenever they desire. Housekeeping, meals, and other services are provided, as well as a wide range of activities

Despite United Presbyterian's tremendous growth during the past 25 years, its current staff of 850 strives to preserve the caring atmosphere of a smaller, more intimate facility. Many of the residents in fact refer to United Presbyterian as "home," rather than "the home."

202

QUALITY OF LIFE

both on and off the premises.

Because of their need for medical supervision, nursing home patients are more carefully supervised, but nonetheless can participate in many recreation and education programs.

Many activities take full advantage of Long Island's richness and diversity. Fishing and boat trips are scheduled regularly, as are visits to historic and cultural sites such as the Bethpage Village Restoration. The endless list of parties, shopping trips, bingo games, musical programs, and arts and crafts classes for all residents would not be possible without the help of some 300 volunteers. "We have many long-term volunteers. Some people have been volunteers with us for as long as 15 years, and I don't know how we would get along without them," says the volunteer director.

United Presbyterian Home also operates two highly successful community outreach programs: United Lifeline and Long Term Home Health Care. The former program allows an individual to wear a radio signal device that, when activated, sends signals through the telephone to the central computer monitor. The message center then alerts a neighbor or another authorized person to investigate. A person who has fallen or become suddenly ill and cannot reach the telephone can get help in a matter of minutes by simply pressing their "help" button.

Physicians and geriatric professionals have come to realize that for many frail elderly, home care is the most beneficial treatment. United Presbyterian Home's Long Term Home Health Care Program provides typical nursing home services such as physical therapy, nutritional services, and home and personal care services in an individual's own home.

The home purchased the adjacent 22-acre Cass Canfield estate in 1977,

While United Presbyterian's residents are free to come and go as they wish, the home offers an array of indoor and outdoor activities such as fishing, boating, and shopping excursions. More than 300 volunteers assist the regular staff to make possible the musical and arts and crafts programs enjoyed by resident artists (above) and musicians.

Residents at United Presbyterian enjoy a healthy atmosphere of freedom and dignity. Here, a couple finds a quiet spot in the garden.

establishing a residence in the estate house to provide low-cost accommodations for families who desire to visit relatives residing at the home in order to supply emotional support for their loved ones. "We were finding that the cost of traveling to see members of the family was keeping people from visiting; we have families who travel from Colorado, California—everywhere. We get thank-you letters from people who are so appreciative of the chance to see their loved ones," says a staff member.

In 1987 United Presbyterian Home began a respite care program whereby it will take "health-related" individuals for short periods of time to allow their caretakers to have a vacation or some time away from the difficult task of caring for a family member at home. The home is establishing a hospice care facility that will permit families of terminally ill patients to remain together. A pediatric day-care center will serve its employees and provide both junior and senior members of the community with the opportunity to interact and enjoy one another.

LONG ISLAND

ST. JOSEPH'S COLLEGE

The noted economist E.F. Schumacher in his influential book, *Small is Beautiful: Economics as if People Mattered,* argues that small-scale production methods are the most beneficial for developing countries. The founders and administrators of St. Joseph College have taken his message to heart, and are applying small-scale, personal methods to educating men and women.

The college was founded in 1916 in the Clinton Hill section of Brooklyn, still the site of its main campus, serving some 1,000 students. An extension program was started in Brentwood in 1971, and eight years later, when enrollment outpaced the available space, the college purchased its present 25-acre lakeside campus in Patchogue. The Suffolk campus today is home to more than 1,600 students, an impressive increase from the 400 who passed through its doors in 1979.

Students have been attracted by the strong liberal arts and preprofessional programs as well as the affordable private-college tuition, traditionally the lowest in the New York metropolitan area. Meanwhile, the college has maintained its commitment to a high-quality personalized education.

Students are assigned an academic adviser who guides them through the duration of their studies. "Our faculty members' willingness to give time to students is one of their outstanding qualities. It is not unusual for instructors to spend many hours with students in both academic and extracurricular settings," explains Sister Jean Marie Amore, academic dean.

In addition to offering degrees in

TOP: St. Joseph's College's main campus, Brooklyn, New York.

ABOVE: St. Joseph's College's Suffolk campus, Patchogue, New York.

traditional areas of the arts and sciences, St. Joseph's is well known for its programs in child study, special education, and health-related fields. A pioneer in the study of child development, St. Joseph's opened a laboratory preschool at the main campus in 1934. Today the Dillon Child Study Center maintains that tradition and serves as

QUALITY OF LIFE

Dr. Carol Hayes, chairperson, biology department, with Gregory Branch, a premed student at St. Joseph's who participated in two NASA summer programs and was accepted to seven prestigious medical schools.

a modern, practical teacher training site.

The college's premed program is highly successful, sending approximately 85 percent of its graduates on to medical school. A certificate program in gerontology is offered, and the Suffolk campus' degree program in recreation is Long Island's only four-year major in this field. In this program, students are prepared for careers in therapeutic recreation—working with the elderly, the disabled, and other special populations—and in community recreation. Business administration and accounting have become popular areas of study in recent years, as have the certificate programs in leadership and human resources development, and data and information processing.

To meet the specific needs of adult students beginning or returning to college, St. Joseph's established the Division of General Studies, which serves an ever-growing population. A bachelor of science degree is offered in community health and health administration, nursing, human resources management, and general studies. Classes are held at a variety of locations in New York City and Long Island to facilitate attendance. In response to community interest, the college inaugurated a special program in which courses are offered free of charge to senior citizens on a noncredit basis.

Many Long Island students begin their postsecondary education at community colleges. To assist them in obtaining four-year degrees, St. Joseph's entered into a joint admissions agreement with Suffolk Community College that allows students to transfer into corresponding programs upon completion of their associate degrees.

To accommodate the growing number of students and to provide them with the best facilities possible, St. Joseph's has undertaken a building program. Ground was broken for a new library in the spring of 1988. In 1987 St. Joseph's installed a fully integrated computerized library system at the Suffolk campus, the first of its kind among Long Island colleges.

Plans are under way to raise funds for a new gym. Sports have become an important part of life on the Suffolk campus. St. Joseph's Golden Eagles compete in soccer and basketball, among other intercollegiate sports. They participate in the Division III level of the National Collegiate Athletic Association and in the National Association of Intercollegiate Athletics.

As St. Joseph's College continues to grow, it has every intention of maintaining its emphasis on personal attention for each student. As these dedicated educators know, well-prepared and self-assured men and women are the best hope for the future.

Lakeside tennis courts at the Suffolk campus in Patchogue.

205

LONG ISLAND

HEALTHPLEX, INC.

Dental health care coverage has rapidly emerged as the most sought-after employee benefit of the decade.

At the same time a critical lack of cost-containment efforts on the part of both traditional insurers and related providers has threatened to put dental plans out of the reach of many corporations, municipalities, unions, and other organizations.

When Drs. Martin Kane, Stephen Cuchel, and Bruce Safran, Long Island dentists, opened Healthplex with just three employees in a Valley Stream storefront in 1978, they were breaking new ground in the northeastern area of the country. The concept of delivering dental care similar to the way health care is provided by health maintenance organizations was well known in the western states, but not in the Northeast.

At this time Healthplex no longer administrates only prepaid dental services through affiliated dental companies. It has expanded over the years to offer administrative services to self-insured dental plans; it has joined with existing health insurers to manage dental packages; and it has established a subsidiary specializing in computer programs and supplies to help dentists operate their businesses. Through its Dual Choice program, members also can opt to retain the services of a non-affiliated dentist, although the patient's contribution may be high in this case.

"We can respond to the needs of any group purchaser of dental care, from the individual subscriber to major groups and companies," says Dr. Cuchel.

Indeed, Healthplex seems to have found its proper place in the dental care industry, which in the United States represented some $15 billion in 1987. The 60 employees at the Uniondale headquarters provide administrative services to three insurance service companies, with 300,000 subscribers and several thousand dentists in 18 states. "It took three years to get annual sales up to one million dollars. Six years later we're approaching $20 million," says Dr. Cuchel.

Due to the legal requirements of various states, Healthplex currently operates with three affiliates: Dentcare Delivery Systems, Inc., International HealthCare Services, Inc., and Garden State Dental Service Corporation. Participating dentists are carefully selected and monitored to ensure patients receive the highest-quality care.

Under Healthplex' comprehensive plan these providers accept a fixed monthly payment that covers 95 percent of regular dental services for each subscriber they treat. The patient pays copayments for services with lab charges, and routine preventive care is fully covered.

Participating dentists, who apply to the affiliates of Healthplex, are carefully screened. They must meet rigid re-

Headquartered in well-planned, modern facilities in Uniondale, New York, Healthplex, Inc., is an expanding publicly owned corporation that provides quality dental health care without spiraling costs to a rapidly growing number of corporations, municipalities, unions, and other organizations.

quirements regarding office cleanliness, sufficient and qualified staff, modern equipment, and, of course, professional ability. The firm also maintains an extensive listing of qualified dental specialists.

At the heart of Healthplex' success is an impressive two-gigabyte computer system equipped with highly specialized software especially designed for the dental care industry. This system allows the firm to provide admin-

QUALITY OF LIFE

istrative services, such as claims review and payment, cost management, and quality control.

In this regard, the firm employs dentists and dental hygienists to review complex claims to ensure that the work is necessary and part of a comprehensive treatment plan. The company also maintains a full printing shop on the premises to produce personalized claim forms and literature for all its customers.

With its strong technological background it was only natural for Healthplex to establish Healthplex Computer Group, Inc., to support the needs of dental office computer systems, as well as those of large insurers and health maintenance organizations. Software products include programs for front desk processing, patient billing, insur-

Healthplex executives carefully screen and continually monitor the company's expanding network of neighborhood professionals and full-service dental centers.

207

LONG ISLAND

ance billing, accounts receivable, appointment scheduling, practice management, word processing, and marketing.

Its depth of experience and proven track record have made Healthplex a logical partner for major insurance carriers, such as the United States Life Insurance Company. Healthplex administers the dental coverage portion of that company's health plan.

The firm's extensive client list includes businesses, municipalities, union locals, school districts, and professional associations, including such large organizations as the New York-New Jersey Port Authority and the New York City Uniformed Firefighters.

"For our first five or six years, we didn't have many Long Island clients. Now that's changing, and our local client base is expanding," explains Dr. Cuchel, noting that Healthplex now serves the Town of Hempstead, the Nassau and Suffolk Bar associations, the Long Island Chapter of the New York State Restaurant Association, and numerous school districts.

Dental care will only grow more sophisticated in the years to come, and Healthplex, Inc., believes it is well positioned to meet the industry's challenges. "All the different aspects of the dental profession are going to have to be integrated into one cohesive data base," says Dr. Cuchel. "A company such as ours is on the leading edge."

The company's pure dental system is one of the most advanced computer systems especially designed and programmed for dental health plan administration.

QUALITY OF LIFE

C.W. POST CAMPUS OF LONG ISLAND UNIVERSITY

An evening view of the Tilles Center for the Performing Arts at Long Island University's C.W. Post Campus in Brookville.

It is no secret that in the face of nearly full employment, Long Island's businesses are scrambling for workers. It's also a fact that many local students leave the area to attend college and don't return, making a difficult situation even worse.

Long Island University reasoned that something must be done to address this issue, and after much self-examination and a thorough study of students' needs and desires, it has unveiled a program offering alternating classroom study and professional work experience, a plan it hopes will benefit students and industry.

Known as the Long Island University Plan, the program, which will be phased in beginning in the fall of 1989, incorporates aspects of traditional cooperative education but enhances the concept by including an extensive counseling network for personal, academic, and career advisement. From the moment students enroll they will be helped to select personal and professional goals that match their interests and capabilities through an interest and goals assessment, a process unique among American colleges and universities.

Students who choose the plan will alternate semesters of study with semesters of career-related, paid jobs that not only will help them gain valuable work experience but also will help defray tuition costs. Potential employers also will be able to screen future workers through this arrangement.

In addition, the university recently announced an accelerated undergraduate degree track of 2.5 years, while continuing to offer a traditional four-year bachelor's degree program, as well as a five-year bachelor's/master's curriculum and a full range of master's programs.

The C.W. Post Campus in Brookville, one of the university's three residential campuses, was established on the estate of the late Marjorie Merriweather Post in 1954—a few years after the university began offering extension programs in Nassau County to meet the educational needs of World War II veterans. Today the C.W. Post Campus, with nearly 9,000 students and more than 400 undergraduate, graduate, and certificate programs, is the largest unit of the university.

In addition to classroom and other academic buildings on the 400-acre campus, C.W. Post offers many facilities of interest to students and nonstudents alike. The B. Davis Schwartz Memorial Library has more than 800,000 books and periodicals and is linked by computer to the university's 1.7-million-volume network. The library also houses the Center for Business Research, one of the finest research libraries for business, industry, and the professions in the Northeast; the Academic Computing Center; and numerous special collections.

The 2,200-seat Tilles Center is a major cultural resource for Long Island, presenting local performing groups such as the Long Island Philharmonic and the National Grand Opera, and major international attractions such as the Royal Philharmonic, violinist Itzhak Perlman, cellist Yo-Yo Ma, ballet star Rudolf Nureyev, and recitalists Leontyne Price and Kiri Te Kanawa.

A view of C.W. Post's Life Science Building/Pell Hall.

LONG ISLAND

BOARD OF COOPERATIVE EDUCATIONAL SERVICES

In this modern era of robotic assembly, automated teller machines, and cameras that talk, it's easy to assume that jobs in the skilled trades are fading fast. Nothing could be further from the truth, particularly on Long Island. Technology has given skilled craftspersons new tools to do their jobs better, and has opened new fields for individuals trained in electronics, health-related fields, and equipment maintenance and repair.

On Long Island the four Boards of Cooperative Educational Services (BOCES) offer a wide array of occupational education programs, and provide employers with hundreds of qualified workers annually. Training is available in auto mechanics, medical laboratory procedures, practical nursing, electronics, and printing and welding, to name only a few.

The New York State Legislature created BOCES in 1948 as an arm of the State Department of Education, initially to help local school districts educate and train the mentally and physically handicapped. The program was enlarged in the early 1960s to include occupational training for high school students and adults seeking to learn new skills.

Nassau and Suffolk counties are served by four Boards, one in Nassau (Nassau BOCES) and three distributed geographically in Suffolk (BOCES I, II, and III). Each is composed of member school districts that help finance and select the occupational courses to be offered based on the area's particular needs. For example, all four Boards offer training in marine and aviation mechanics and electronics to meet Long Island's high demand for workers in these particular industries.

The curriculum for each course is reviewed and monitored by a group of volunteers from a particular industry to ensure that training is relevant. Consultants keep BOCES informed of any changes occurring in the different industries.

High school and adult students are trained at regional vocational technical training centers maintained by each board. High school students attend regular classes for a half-day and receive occupational training during the other half. Adult students may participate in day, evening, or weekend sessions. Most courses take one year to complete, although licensing programs often require two years.

Approximately 25 percent of BOCES graduates go on to college, particularly those trained in health care fields and in communications programs such as advertising art, commercial photography, electronics, and computer science. Approximately 70 percent of BOCES graduates find em-

BOCES' electronics program is one of the best—and most popular.

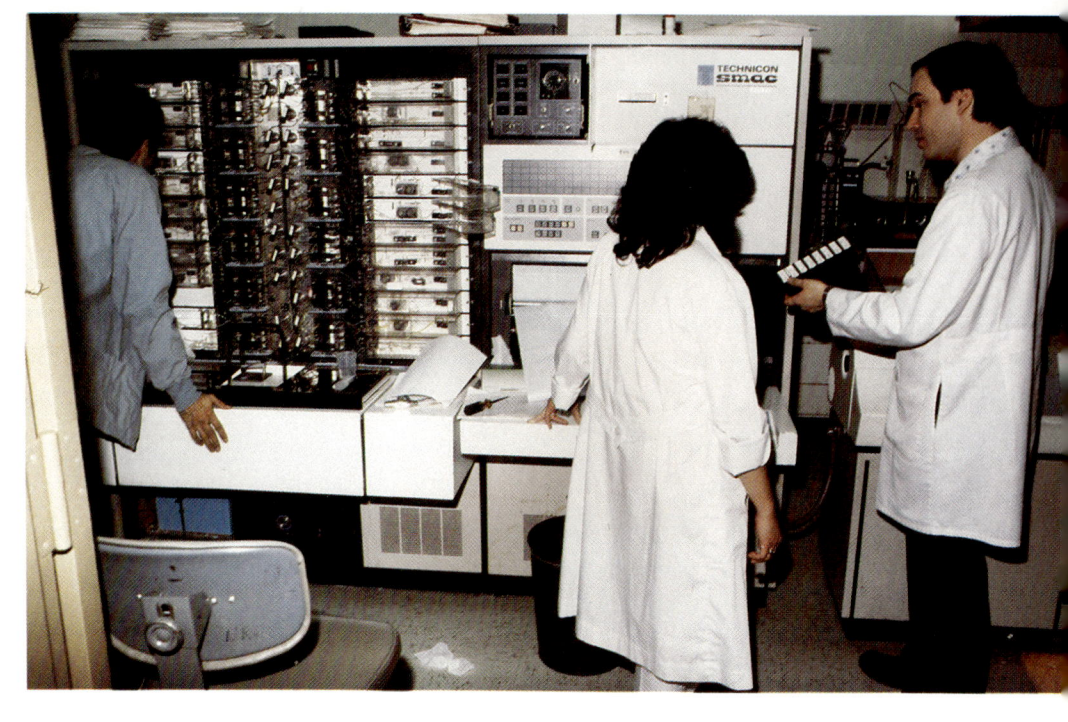

The health care program prepares students for careers in the medical field with state-of-the-art technology.

210

QUALITY OF LIFE

ployment after high school, many of them receiving multiple job offers.

Job placement is a priority at BOCES. Each board maintains a job bank and has personnel assigned to keeping in contact with area employers. These placement officers also work with organizations, such as Long Island Association, Inc., and the Long Island Forum for Technology, in placing graduates.

The need to educate workers in using new equipment and to assist foreign-born employees entering the area's work force prompted all the Boards to establish on-site corporate training programs. BOCES instructors teach technical skills and implement literacy programs, such as English as a Second Language and General Equivalency Diploma. Employers are assisting their employees in keeping up with

ABOVE: Computer programs at BOCES prepare students for careers in today's lucrative and growing computer field.

LEFT: Students test the equipment in one of BOCES' aviation classes.

technology. The on-site training programs have produced very good results.

The Boards also operate comprehensive career centers where individuals seeking to reenter the job market or move into new jobs can receive career planning, counseling, assessment training, and placement. Women returning to work and early retirees desiring new careers are among the most popular clients for the centers, which provide information not only about BOCES programs but also about other education options.

The job outlook for skilled craftspersons on Long Island is excellent. For example, in Suffolk alone, respondents to the County Department of Labor 1987-1988 Employer Survey identified some 14,500 openings for which qualified workers would not be available, a 68-percent increase over the previous survey. Demand occupations included auto mechanics, clerk typists, carpenters, and cooks—all trades taught at BOCES. A skilled craftsperson can do very well on Long Island.

LONG ISLAND

CENTRAL GENERAL HOSPITAL

From a 200-bed, 60-physician facility founded in 1961, Central General Hospital today boasts 300 beds and more than 400 medical staff who, combined, perform between 30 and 40 surgical procedures daily.

Central General Hospital in Plainview was established in 1961 with 200 beds by some 60 physicians who were then practicing in the suburban fringe of eastern Nassau County. The founders believed that the area lacked an easily accessible health care institution to meet their patients' needs.

Today the hospital boasts 300 beds and a medical staff of more than 400 engaged in all specialties. Approximately 13,000 acute care patients are served each year, and on any given day some 30 to 40 different surgical procedures are performed in the hospital's operating rooms. Central General's expanded emergency room handles approximately 30,000 patients annually.

The surrounding farms have given way to suburban sprawl during the years, and technology has brought rapid changes in medicine, but Central General has remained steadfast in its commitment to providing community health services. Detoxification services are offered to alcohol and substance abusers, and numerous self-help programs aim to assist the newly widowed or those suffering from diabetes, cancer, and other illnesses.

Twice a year the hospital hosts Cancer Detection Day, encouraging community residents to undergo various tests free of charge. Emergency Services Week and Senior Citizens' Health Awareness Week also are very popular. Central General's 900 employees, who also benefit from a number of employee health programs, participate in blood and food drives throughout the year. With the assistance of local service clubs, such as the Rotary and the Lions Club, the hospital donates medicines and equipment to health care facilities in developing countries.

The hospital maintains an active speakers bureau to promote health care professions. It operates a student internship program with the Plainview-Old Bethpage School District and the New York State Board of Cooperative Educational Services, and offers $1,000 scholarships to deserving graduates of Plainview and John F. Kennedy high schools who undertake studies in the health field.

To meet the needs of the area's growing business community, the hospital established Medscope. Under this plan Central General performs pre-hiring health screening and other procedures for participating companies, and also teaches CPR and emergency procedures to their employees.

"Like any hospital, we change to meet the needs of the community," explains administrator Robert Bornstein. "A special medical oncology unit now offers a program of services for the patient and family. We're also prepared for the new trend toward outpatient services and are expanding our facilities in this area."

The children's immunization program is one of Central General's many free community medical services, such as Senior Citizens' Health Awareness Week and Cancer Detection Day. The hospital also organizes food and blood drives, and promotes the health professions by selecting staff members to speak at local high schools and by offering a $1,000 college scholarship to qualified students who plan to undertake studies in the health services field. Courtesy, Marilyn Lehrfeld Photography

QUALITY OF LIFE

STATE UNIVERSITY COLLEGE AT OLD WESTBURY

Fall foliage beckons students at SUNY Old Westbury's Academic Village, an architecturally striking complex of four classroom buildings encircled by nine student residence halls.

Located on 605 acres along Route 107 on Long Island is the State University College at Old Westbury.

Situated on the former estate of agriculturist and sportsman F. Ambrose Clark, Old Westbury is very much a Long Island institution. Founded in 1965 as part of the State University of New York system, the college is Nassau County's only public four-year arts and science campus.

Classrooms, administrative offices, and the student dining hall overlook a skylit atrium in Old Westbury's Campus Center, which also houses the Maguire Theatre, Recital Hall, a triple-tier art gallery, dance and music studios, and the college library.

Most of Old Westbury's 3,600 students are from Long Island and the surrounding area, and about half transfer from local two-year colleges.

Approximately 40 percent of the college's students are of Hispanic-American, African-American, or Asian-American heritage. Forty-two percent are over the age of 25, and more than half are women, providing Old Westbury with an ethnic and cultural diversity that eludes many other educational institutions.

Degree programs are available in a wide range of liberal arts and science fields, but Old Westbury is well known for its programs in business and management, and in teacher education, particularly bilingual teacher education. Nearly one-third of Old Westbury's students are business majors, and it boasts the only state-accredited accounting degree among the region's SUNY schools.

Seventy percent of the college's 140 full-time faculty members have earned the highest degrees available in their fields. Old Westbury is particularly proud to have three of the 70 Distinguished Teaching Professors selected from among all state colleges by the SUNY chancellor.

State University campuses are noted for their architecturally daring buildings, and Old Westbury is no exception. The gleaming white, multi-tiered Campus Center houses dining and other student facilities, two theaters, an art gallery, and a 165,000-volume library and media center that also contains 290,000 bound and microfilm periodicals, audiovisual equipment, and language labs. The Natural Sciences Building houses state-of-the-art laboratories, research equipment, and classrooms.

The fully equipped Ambrose Clark Physical Education and Recreation Center, with its 3,000-seat Sports Hall, is the home court of Old Westbury's

Nestled in the center of SUNY Old Westbury's 605-acre wooded campus is its Academic Village.

men's basketball team—1987 Eastern Collegiate Athletic Conference metropolitan champions. An on-site International Child Creative Education Center serves the day-care needs of the college's students, faculty, and staff.

In the area of the sciences, Old Westbury is known for its successful programs to encourage science careers among Hispanic-American, African-American, and Asian-American students. The college offers, among others, two federally sponsored programs: the Minority Biomedical Research Support program and the Minority Access to Research Careers program.

Under these programs promising students are given stipends to work with professors as part of a research team. Students also attend scientific meetings, often to present their research results as well as to keep abreast of emerging trends. Fifteen students in the 1987 graduating class who participated in these programs have pursued postgraduate studies in science and health-related fields.

Teachers, managers, and research scientists will be much in demand in the twenty-first century, and on Long Island, the State University College at Old Westbury is doing its part to provide the region with well-educated men and women.

LONG ISLAND

THE STATE UNIVERSITY OF NEW YORK AT STONY BROOK

Like Long Island tself, which has experienced explosive growth over the past three decades, the State University of New York at Stony Brook (SUSB) in the same period of time has evolved from a small state teachers' college into a major research university of national and international stature.

Attracting more than $60 million annually in externally sponsored research funding, SUSB accounts for nearly 27 percent of all such moneys in the state university system. The Carnegie Foundation, which classifies higher education institutions in the United States, recently placed SUSB among its 70 Type I institutions, its highest ranking. The university was the only public institution among the six Type I universities selected in New York State.

SUSB plays a major role in Long Island's economy, not only because it provides industry with valuable and highly trained workers but also because, with some 1,412 faculty, 6,700 staff, and 1,500 research staff members, it is Suffolk County's third-largest employer.

Approximately 11,300 undergraduate and 5,400 graduate students study on the 1,100-acre campus. There are 103 buildings on campus, including a 480-bed teaching hospital and health sciences center that is one of the most modern facilities of its kind in the country, and a fine arts center containing a 1,100-seat concert hall, a recital hall, three theaters, and an art gallery.

SUSB's library, which is the only Library of Congress affiliate in Long Island, houses 1.6 million bound volumes and 2.5 million microforms, as well as the most complete collection of the papers of W.B. Yeats outside of the University of Dublin, and more than 2 million items comprising the public papers of the late U.S. Senator Jacob Javits.

By tradition SUSB is a leader in science research and education. The

Approximately 11,300 undergraduates and 5,400 graduate students study on the 1,100-acre campus.

Health Sciences Center (HSC), Suffolk's only tertiary care facility, is home to the schools of medicine, nursing, allied health professionals, dentistry, and social welfare. A nursing home for the area's veterans is now under construction near the campus and also will serve as a teaching facility.

HSC not only is a regional center for highly specialized health care services such as organ transplantation, joint replacement, and the treatment of burns, but it is also the site of innovative and timely research. For example, SUSB is the major AIDS research center in the downstate area, and has established a center for the study of Alzheimer's disease, as well as a program to study Lyme disease—a regional tick-borne infection.

SUSB also was selected by New York State as the site for two important economic development initiatives: the Center for Advanced Technology in Medical Biotechnology, offering state incentives to foster industry-university cooperation in research and development, and the High Tech Incubator, a facility designed to nurture emerging enterprises by providing low-cost space, shared overhead services, and management advisory services.

The Marine Sciences Research Center, one of SUSB's best-known research facilities, concentrates on addressing coastal zone problems such as fighting brown tide and managing the disposal of solid waste—major issues facing Long Island. The university's proximity to Brookhaven National Laboratory, Cold Spring Harbor Laboratory, and the federal animal-research facility on Plum Island provide researchers and students with access to the most sophisticated data and techniques available.

This outstanding reputation in the sciences should not obscure SUSB's accomplishments in the humanities and social sciences. Its English, history, sociology, psychology, and economics departments are ranked among the top 20 in the nation. Its graduate music department is highly regarded. "Music is an extremely good department in a state that has many fine music departments and conservatories," says president John Marburger, adding, "We know we're good, too, because we compete successfully with them for students and faculty."

A critical component of the success SUSB has achieved in a relatively short time is its faculty, which boasts numerous award winners, including a Nobel laureate, a Pulitzer Prize winner, two MacArthur Fellowship recipients, and several Sloane and Guggenheim Foundation fellows. "We have people on the faculty who are making an impact in their own fields," explains Marburger, adding, "We try to capture this brilliance to create a strong educational program."

As Long Island's civic and business leaders rise to meet the challenges presented by the area's rapid expansion, the collective "brain power" offered by a major institution such as SUSB will prove invaluable.

"We have provided expertise to Nassau and Suffolk counties on many occasions. We view ourselves as a major partner in the effort to develop Long Island in a way that is compatible with its beauty and uniqueness," says Marburger.

"Stony Brook is not unusual for a large public research institution," he says. "But, we are unusual for Long Island and the New York metropolitan area, and we're proud of being unusual."

There are 103 buildings on campus, including a 480-bed teaching hospital and health sciences center that is one of the most modern facilities of its kind in the country, and a fine arts center containing a 1,100-seat concert hall, a recital hall, three theaters, and an art gallery.

215

LONG ISLAND

MOLLOY COLLEGE

Molloy College was founded in the tradition of the Dominican Order, stressing the Dominican's liberal arts heritage. Photo by Gene Luttenberg

The Dominican Order from its origin in the thirteenth century has dedicated itself to the preaching and teaching of truth—especially on the university level. While many U.S. colleges moved away from the liberal arts to career-oriented curricula in the 1970s, Molloy College never wandered from its stated mission of providing men and women with a well-rounded education, believing in the importance of the humanities.

From its humble beginnings in 1955 with 45 students, Molloy today boasts 1,300 students and 6,000 alumni, many of whom hold executive positions in business, education, and health care, among other fields.

On its picturesque 25-acre campus in Rockville Centre, the college offers 35 degrees in diversified disciplines, and has instituted a graduate program in nursing—traditionally a strong discipline at the school. Of the Molloy nursing students who take the state certification examination annually, some 90 percent pass on the first attempt. All graduates must meet a foreign language requirement and must choose courses from the arts and the sciences.

"One source of pride for us is that we never abandoned our Dominican liberal arts heritage. That is something that makes us unique—that and the personal attention that every department can give each student because of

Starting with 45 students in 1955, Molloy College today boasts 1,300 students and 6,000 alumni. Photo by Gene Luttenberg

Sister Patricia Morris, vice-president/academic affairs, O.P., Ph.D, at a graduation ceremony. Photo by Gene Luttenberg

our size. Nobody is lost in the shuffle," says vice-president/academic affairs Sister Patricia A. Morris, O.P.

Molloy is the only college in New York State to award a major in cardiorespiratory sciences, and it was the first New York college to grant a baccalaureate degree in gerontology. Senior citizens can audit many classes for a modest fee, and alumni enjoy lifetime auditing privileges.

A fully equipped, modern cable-

Right: Molloy College provides its students with a well-rounded education, offering 35 degrees in diversified disciplines.

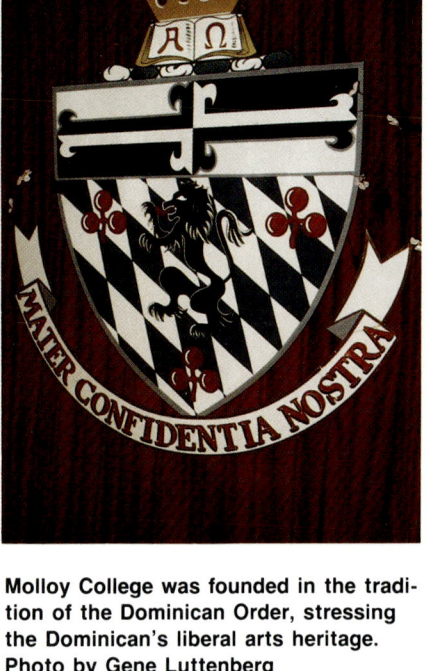

television studio where students produce several government affairs broadcasts, including the daily program, "Eye on Molloy," is maintained on campus. The school also serves as "home" for Long Island's only equity theater group, Long Island Stage, and

216

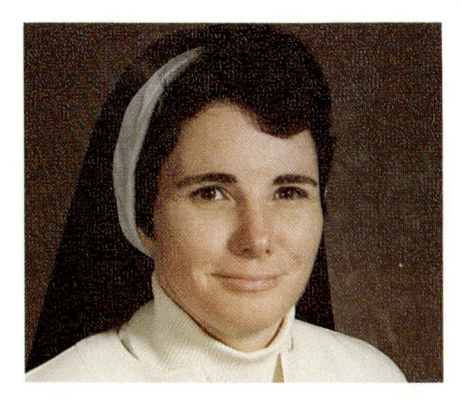

QUALITY OF LIFE

Sister Janet Fitzgerald, president of Molloy College, O.P., Ph.D.

maintains a 100,000-volume library.

Courses and schedules are geared to fit the life-styles of its students, many of whom are working people or individuals returning to college. However, the fact that it is a commuter school does not detract from campus life or student involvement.

For example, Molloy's women's athletic program is thriving and successful, boasting three Academic All-America athletes. Molloy's equestrian team has won numerous regional competitions in Division III of the National Collegiate Athletic Association, the most recent being the Reserve Champions in February 1988. The women's softball team finished third among New York's Division II schools in 1987, and the tennis team was 1985 Metropolitan Collegiate Tennis Conference champion. Club teams exist in various sports, including basketball and soccer.

Other extracurricular activities include an active dramatic society and the College Glee Club, which was awarded a gold medal in the 1988 Classic Intercollegiate Women's Glee Club Association. In all, more than 20 clubs and honor societies are in existence.

Under the guidance of Sister Janet A. Fitzgerald, O.P., Ph.D, its president, and former ITT executive vice-president and ITT Telecommunications Corporation president John W. Guilfoyle, who chairs the board of trustees, Molloy is looking toward expanding its graduate programs and providing greater opportunities for students.

The administration is seeking funds to expand the scope of the recently created Academic Resource Center, which provides assistance for students with academic difficulties. Molloy College is enlarging this program to include all students who want to improve reading and writing skills, and for student teachers who want to use it as a laboratory. Eventually the college would like to open the center to area high school students needing college preparatory assistance.

While Molloy hopes to offer more specialized majors to give students greater choice and flexibility, it will not waver from its liberal arts orientation. As its mission statement states, "Molloy College believes that a liberal education aims at the total fulfillment and realization of the person's ultimate goal."

Below: Molloy College is located on a picturesque 25-acre campus in Rockville Centre.

Molloy's women's athletic program is thriving and successful. The equestrian team has won numerous regional competitions in Division III of the National Collegiate Athletic Association, the most recent (pictured here) being Reserve Champions in February 1988.

217

SOUTHSIDE HOSPITAL

The woman lifts a bag from the supermarket shelf and into her shopping cart. The physical therapist is there to make sure that she lifts it correctly—so as to relieve any stress on her back.

Is health care now available in shopping malls? No, this "supermarket" is located in Southside Hospital's Health Institute, where patients recovering from serious injuries receive special rehabilitation treatment and learn how to resume the routines of daily life in a manner that will prevent a recurrence of their physical problem. Other components of the rehabilitation facility, called Easy Street, include an office and a factory setting to help patients learn how to avoid reinjury on the job.

This unique rehabilitation program is a prime example of Southside's focus on preventive medicine. The 489-bed facility on Montauk Highway in Bay Shore is Suffolk County's largest community hospital. Founded in 1913, Southside sees its mission as making it easier for area residents to stay healthy, and its myriad of programs proves that it takes its work seriously.

To complement its Easy Street and physical medicine programs, Southside is building a new 24-bed inpatient Physical Rehabilitation Unit, thus providing one of the most comprehensive physical rehabilitation programs in America—both inpatient and outpatient.

The Health Institute also is the home of Southside's Back School, arthritis management program, prenatal fitness programs, and the TMJ (temporomandibular joint) clinic for the treatment and relief of head, neck, and fa-

LEFT: Easy Street, part of Southside Health Institute, is the first outpatient industrial rehabilitation center of its kind on the East Coast.

BELOW: Southside Hospital has been selected by the Hospital Trustees of New York State to serve as a "model community hospital for quality assurance."

QUALITY OF LIFE

cial pain. It also serves as the headquarters for the Optifast Program at Southside, as well as a meeting place for clubs and support groups for victims of stroke, multiple sclerosis, and other afflictions.

Southside services thousands of patients through family health centers in Brentwood and Bay Shore, which are major training facilities for the Family Practice Residency program operated in conjunction with the State University of New York at Stony Brook Medical School. Approximately 50 percent of the program's graduates remain on Long Island to practice family medicine.

Recently doubled in size, an ambulatory surgery program has been extremely well received by patients who appreciate receiving treatment and being discharged on the same day. The hospital's extensive home health care program, which aims to help patients avoid institutionalization, has been cited by the Joint Committee on the Accreditation of Hospitals and the New York State Health Department as a model program.

Home health care personnel, who make more than 20,000 visits annually, provide a wide range of services to individuals who face a long recuperative

As a leader in acute care, Southside utilizes advanced laser and ultrascopic modalities in its seven surgical suites.

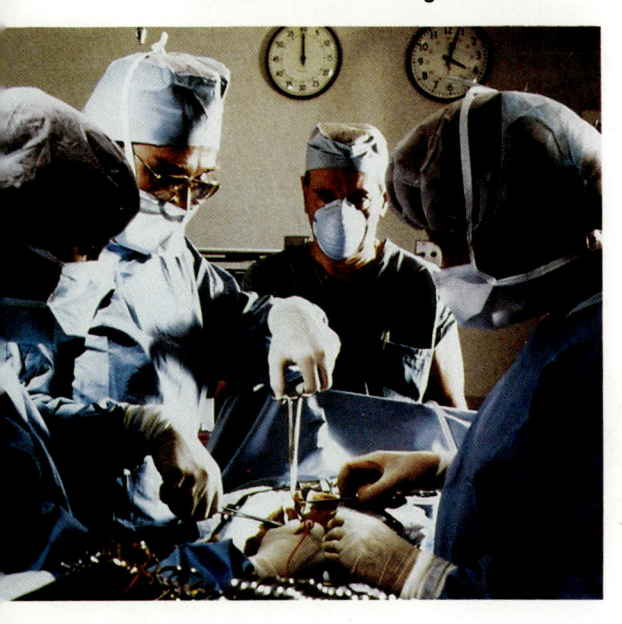

period or who are recovering from a serious injury and require physical therapy, as well as to senior citizens whose medical conditions affect their ability to live alone or to terminally ill patients who desire to be cared for at home.

In keeping with its efforts to help patients improve their health with the least amount of surgical or other intervention, Southside has invested in the most sophisticated computerized diagnostic equipment available. The Radiology Department contains CAT scan, ultrasound, and cardiac catheterization equipment, as well as a computerized radiographic/tomographic unit for the production of highly detailed radiographs.

Southside also has a digital subtraction angiography unit that rotates around the patient taking X rays that are transformed into computerized information. The unit "subtracts" all overlying opacities, such as bone matter, producing an unobstructed image of the precise arteries under examination. This tool is a key nonsurgical procedure for the treatment of hardening of the arteries.

The hospital's interest in new technology extends to its administrative departments. In 1987 Southside introduced Long Island's first rapid-admit card for its patients. Called Southside

Complete maternity services range from prenatal exams and exercises to a specially designed delivery room and a call-a-nurse-for-advice phone service for new patients.

Health Card, this plastic, wallet-size card magnetically holds medical and other basic data to help speed the admission process.

However, Southside's most valuable asset is its people. The hospital employs 1,800 individuals who each make important contributions to the effective delivery of quality health care in its service area. Many employees are "oldtimers," having been affiliated with the institution for as many as 30 years.

As a nonprofit community hospital, Southside depends on the generosity of the area's residents. Its nearly 400 volunteers donate more than 70,000 hours annually to projects ranging from reading stories to hospitalized children to organizing major fund-raising events. The Advisory Council, composed of some 100 area business executives who volunteer their time and experience, advises the hospital board on numerous matters, primarily financial subjects.

Southside Hospital is comprised of Long Islanders working to help Long Islanders.

LONG ISLAND

POLYTECHNIC UNIVERSITY
LONG ISLAND CAMPUS

Polytechnic University, the Long Island campus. Photo by Bob Klein

An airplane that can fly from New York to Tokyo in 2.5 hours or a space station manned with U.S. scientists studying the worlds beyond the earth's galaxy are not yet part of the modern world. However, in the research laboratories of Polytechnic University's Long Island Campus, faculty and students are developing the technology that will make these dreams reality.

Polytechnic's thriving research programs include a wide range of government and industry-supported research projects conducted in some of the most modern facilities available, including New York State's Center for Advanced Technology in Telecommunications, the Institute of Imaging Sciences, the Weber Research Institute, the Aerodynamics Research Laboratory, and the Center for Digital Systems. With this strong tradition in relevant and applications-oriented research, it's no wonder that one out of every five working engineers on Long Island and more than 100 founders or chief executive officers of Long Island technology firms are Polytechnic alumni.

Polytechnic University, founded in 1854 as the Polytechnic Institute of Brooklyn, is the second-oldest independent technological university in the United States. In 1973 it merged with the New York University School of Engineering and Science to become the Polytechnic Institute of New York. Its name was changed to Polytechnic University in 1985 to reflect more accurately its breadth of programs and research.

The university historically has had strong ties with industry, by providing professional staff and by offering evening programs, often developed with local corporations, to allow working engineers and scientists an opportunity to pursue further study. Polytechnic came to Long Island initially at the request of several large corporations that were sending their engineers to the Brooklyn campus for courses.

In the early 1960s Republic Aviation Corporation offered the university 25 acres at Republic Airport in Farmingdale to establish a campus. Polytechnic accepted and moved the

220

QUALITY OF LIFE

aerodynamic research laboratory that had been in Freeport since the 1950s to the new site on the then-emerging Route 110 corridor. At first only graduate courses were offered, but in 1974 Polytechnic instituted Long Island's first undergraduate degrees in aerospace, civil, mechanical, and electrical engineering.

Today the Long Island Campus has some 1,400 students, approximately half of them undergraduates. Degrees are offered in engineering, arts and science, and management. Most students come from the Long Island area, with nearly 80 percent of them ranked among the top 20 percent of their high school classes. Approximately 93 percent of students are offered career-path jobs by graduation, with many of them going on to work for local companies.

Nearly half of Polytechnic's Long Island students major in electrical engineering. The university enjoys a distinguished reputation in this area, and is ranked among the top 10 electrical engineering departments in the nation and first in the New York metropolitan area.

A large part of Polytechnic's success is due to its outstanding faculty. Three of the 13 winners of the Institute of Electrical and Electronic Engineers Microwave Career Awards have been Long Island Campus professors. The Long Island faculty includes three members of the National Academy of Engineering, as well as numerous individuals known for pioneering work in their respective fields. Dr. Ernst Weber, for whom the prestigious Weber Research Institute on the Long Island Campus is named, received the National Medal of Science from then-president Ronald Reagan in 1987.

The campus also is home to the

Polytechnic students at work in the Computer Science Laboratory.

Long Island Forum for Technology, an organization Polytechnic created to stimulate economic growth through industry and academic partnership. PolyVentures, a private venture capital fund, was launched in 1987 to invest in promising technology developed at Polytechnic.

College should be a social as well as an educational experience, and Polytechnic's small Long Island Campus gives students the opportunity to know each other and their teachers.

"It's not unusual to see a student and a professor hunched over a table in the cafeteria discussing a homework problem at lunchtime," says Dr. James Conti, Long Island Campus director. "It's a very intimate place. Our students benefit from unique access to world-class professors and facilities."

Individual attention and academic excellence are the keys to Polytechnic University's success.

221

LONG ISLAND

NEW YORK INSTITUTE OF TECHNOLOGY

The history of New York Institute of Technology points with particular interest to its mission-oriented beliefs. Although substantial information is contained in its many publications, this synopsis is intended to pinpoint and highlight certain outstanding specifics.

Fully accredited, NYIT is a personalized, independent college where career education has been the mainstay since its inception in 1955. Thirty-four years later more than 15,000 students attended campuses in mid-Manhattan near Lincoln Center, and on Long Island in Old Westbury and Central Islip. An alumni roster of more than 35,000 are engaged in all phases of business, industry, and the professions, or are enrolled in postgraduate institutions worldwide.

An open-access college, New York Institute of Technology has been able to provide education and training for men and women of all ages and from all walks of life who may not otherwise have been able to obtain higher-education advantages. Low, affordable tuition rates and fees have been available to all NYIT students over the years and until the current time. A Cooperative Education Program is of great value in that students earn while they learn.

The college offers a variety of curricula, ranging from associate through baccalaureate and master's degrees in many disciplines and to the doctorate in osteopathic medicine through its medical school, New York College of Osteopathic Medicine. Located in Old Westbury, the medical college is the only one of its kind in New York State and the only medical school in Nassau County. Its beginnings were made possible through the efforts of former governor and vice-president Nelson A. Rockefeller, former secretary of state Henry Kissinger, and the Rockefeller Foundation.

Career-oriented programs include accounting, engineering, architecture (four- and five-year programs), business administration, computer science, hotel administration, general studies, communication arts, behavioral sciences, technological management, life sciences, fine arts, design graphics, physics, political science, osteopathic medicine (combined BS/DO seven-year program), preprofessional, interior design, labor management, technical writing, teacher/occupation education, advertising, culinary arts, and telecommunications management, among others.

Overview of the Central Islip Campus—a sprawling property that once was a state hospital.

With origins that date back to a predecessor school founded in 1910, New York Institute of Technology has a continuous history of providing quality education in specialized areas. Grants of equipment and property by the Schure family led to the founding of the present college at its original location in Brooklyn. In 1955 New York Institute of Technology was chartered by the State of New York as a two-year college granting the associate in applied science degree. Three years later a Manhattan facility was purchased to house an expanded program.

The college continued this growth and expansion pattern by purchasing portions of the former Cornelius Vanderbilt Whitney estate in Old Westbury. The additional purchase of other estate properties—that once were part of the famed North Shore Gold

QUALITY OF LIFE

The Student Activity Center, Old Westbury, which provides the backdrop for all student activities and adjoins the gym and fieldhouse/locker rooms.

Coast—now comprise the Dorothy Schure Old Westbury Campus, a scenic sprawling and contiguous 750 acres. Included is a 100-acre estate and mansion that once belonged to the late Winston Guest and that is now known as the NYIT deSeversky Conference Center. The center serves both the academic and the business community.

The college's most recent acquisition is the Central Islip Campus in Suffolk County—a recycled former state hospital property—where NYIT students began classes in the fall of 1984. This campus contains dormitories, the first on-campus accommodations as such for NYIT students. The Central Islip Campus will include a high-technology park, among other exciting plans for that facility.

New York Institute of Technology bears the imprimatur of such national and regional accrediting agencies as Middle States Association of Colleges and Schools; Engineering Accreditation Commission of the Accreditation Board for Engineering and Technology, Inc., for day programs in electrical and mechanical engineering, Old Westbury Campus, and electrical engineering, Metropolitan Center; Technology Accreditation Commission of the Accreditation Board for Engineering and Technology, Inc., for electromechanical computer technology, Old Westbury Campus and Metropolitan Center, and aeronautical technology, aeronautical operations technology option; National Architectural Accrediting Board for the Bachelor of Architecture; Foundation for Interior Design Education Research for interior design programs; and American Osteopathic Association for New York College of Osteopathic Medicine.

The college is capable of offering—through its distant learning arm, the American Open University—computer teleconferencing programs that lead to degrees in various disciplines. AOU/NYIT computer networks are available to students nationwide for communication with faculty and each other.

New York Institute of Technology is especially renowned for its outstanding research efforts and accomplishments in the fields of computer graphics, lasers and holography, robotics, biomechanics, medical electronics, ultrasonics, telecommunications, and high-definition television. The college's Computer Graphics Laboratory in Old Westbury has received worldwide recognition; it contains some of the foremost technical equipment possible in addition to a cadre of senior scientists who have been recipients of such honors as Emmy awards, numerous Best in Computer Animation citations, and much more.

NYIT has been successful over the years in bringing to the communities where it has settled a sense of permanence, an economic contribution, and an overall long-term social contribution. The college enjoys a prestigious reputation for certain aspects of technology amid sister institutions known and admired for their expertise.

Truly steeped in the knowledge business, New York Institute of Technology is a multifaceted institution. A steady progression of achievements make up its history. Much has come to pass—all adding up to the major milestones recorded for an institution still young in years.

Students in a lab work with their faculty member. NYIT labs are high tech and cover the entire spectrum—from culinary arts to engineering.

LONG ISLAND

NEW YORK ISLANDERS

If there is any one entity that is instantly associated with Long Island by people across the United States and beyond its borders, it's the New York Islanders hockey team. In its 16 years of existence, the four-time Stanley Cup winner has made it clear, at least in the minds of sports fans worldwide, that Long Island is not New York City. It's Long Island.

"Our first goal is to play the best-possible hockey that we can. Our fans deserve nothing less," explains president and general manager William A. Torrey. "But we understand our role as representatives for Long Island, and that's why it's doubly important for us to maintain the highest-quality program possible," he adds.

As unofficial ambassadors, the Islanders excel. They also play an important role in the region's economy: Some 700,000 fans attend games at the Nassau Coliseum during the season. Not only do fans purchase more than $10 million in tickets annually, which generates approximately one million dollars in sales tax for Nassau County, but also they pay for parking and buy food and souvenirs—generating even more dollars for government and private industry. A 1984 Nassau County audit estimated the Islanders' annual economic impact at more than $50 million.

In addition, the 30-year lease that the Islanders signed with Nassau County for use of the coliseum was a major factor in the rapid and successful development of the entire Mitchel Field hotel and office space complex surrounding the arena.

While team members are familiar figures at Long Island charity events, serving as honorary chairmen or guest speakers, the franchise itself is very active in community affairs. Islanders tickets are a familiar item at local charity auctions and raffles. The Islanders organization works closely with major local corporations to sponsor the attendance of school children at Islanders games. It also is a major promoter of youth hockey programs and of the Boy Scouts.

In the topsy-turvy world of sports, the New York Islanders organization is known for its calm, long-range management style. "We've developed this business with consistency. Our style of management has given us the stability to succeed, and we are looking forward to many more good years," concludes Joseph H. Dreyer, vice-president/administration.

Some 700,000 fans attend games at the Nassau Coliseum during the season. The sales from tickets, more than $10 million, generate approximately one million dollars in sales tax for Nassau County. Photo by Bruce Bennett

In existence for 16 years, the New York Islanders are four-time Stanley Cup winners. Photo by Bruce Bennett

224

Photo by R. Settles

INDEX

PROFILE INDEX

Allstate Insurance Company, 172-173
Altana Inc., 158-159
AT&T, 146
Bank of New York, The, 184-185
Board of Cooperative Educational Services, 210-211
Central General Hospital, 212
Chase Manhattan Bank, N.A., Long Island Region, 188-189
Citibank, N.A., 192-193
Cushman & Wakefield of Long Island, Inc., 198
Dale Carnegie & Associates, Inc., 170-171
EAB, 190-191
Fairfield Properties, 174
Farrell, Fritz, Caemmerer, Cleary, Barnosky & Armento, P.C., 194-195
Florence Building Materials, 168-169
Grumman Corporation, 160-162
Halbro Control Industries, Inc., 167
Healthplex, Inc., 206-208
Henderson and Bodwell, 178-179
Law Offices of Andrew D. Presberg, The, 182
Long Island Association, Inc., 166
Long Island Lighting Company, The, 142-145
Long Island Rail Road, The, 147
Lumex, Inc., 150-151
Marine Midland Bank, N.A., 183
Meltzer, Lippe, Goldstein & Wolf, P.C., 196-197
Molloy College, 216-217
National Westminster Bank USA, 186-187
New York Institute of Technology, 222-223
New York Islanders, 224
Pall Corporation, 156-157
Polytechnic University
Long Island Campus, 220-221
Post Campus of Long Island University, C.W., 209
Quantronix Corporation, 154-155
St. Joseph's College, 204-205
Sedco, A Raytheon Company, 152-153
Southside Hospital, 218-219
State University College at Old Westbury, 213
State University of New York at Stony Brook, The, 214-215
TSI, 180-181
United Presbyterian Home at Syosset, Inc., 202-203

GENERAL INDEX

Italicized numbers indicate illustrations

A
Abraham & Straus, 58
Accounting, 62
Adelphi University, 72
Advertising, 63
Aerospace, 68-70
African-American Museum, 34
Agriculture, *31*, 31-32, 46-47
American Revolution, 32-33
Anton Community Newspaper Chain, 103
Around Long Island Regatta, 115
Associated Universities, Inc., 71
Aviation, 21, *27*, 28, 35-36, *36*, 68-70, 96

B
Baittinger, Anne, 70
Banking, 61-62
Battle of Long Island, 32
Beaches, 111-115
Bell, Steve, 74
Belmont Park Race Track, 120
Berlin, Irving, 37
Bicycling, 120
Bierworth, John C., 70, 125
"Big Duck, The," 82, 83, *83*
Big E Farm, 79
Black history, 33-34; Slavery, 31, *32*
Block, Adriaen, 28
Block Island, 28
Boating, 44, 115, *116*
Boegner, Peggy Phipps, 51, 128
Bookman, Theodora "Teddy," 124, 131
Bossy, Mike, 119
Bouris, Greg, 118, 119, 121
Brady, Courtney, 124
Brookhaven Airport, 97
Brookhaven National Laboratory, 66, 70-71
Brookhaven Service Center (IRS), 60
Brooklyn Bridge, 92, 93
Bryan, C. Russell, 72
Buses, 96

C
Cablevision Systems Corporation, *104*, 105
Cabot, John, 28
Camp Siegfried, 37
Camp Upton, 37, 70
Carroll, John J. "Jack," 67, 70, 75
Cathedral of the Incarnation, 34
Cattle, 80
Caumsett State Park, *123*, 124
Center Moriches Chamber of Commerce, 83
Chanry Communications Ltd., 103
Chauvin, Marvin, 107
Clams, 85
Coalition of Leadership Organized to Upgrade Transportation (CLOUT), 97
Cold Spring Harbor Laboratory, *70*, *71*, 72
Cold Spring Harbor Whaling Museum, 33
Colleges, 72-74
Coney Island, *38*
Conlon, Skip, 66
Construction, 74-75
Corrigan, "Wrong Way," 36
Cradle of Aviation Museum, 129
Cullen, Michael, 58

D
Deep Hollow Ranch, 21
Defense industry, *65*, *66*, 67, *68*, *69*
Depression, Great, 28
Dolan, Charles F., 21, 104-105, 107
Ducks, 78, 82-83

E
EAB Plaza, 60, *61*
East End, *20*, 44, 46-47, 48
East Hampton, *4-5*
East Hampton Airport, 97
East Meadow, 90, *91*
Eglevsky Ballet, 124
Electronics industry, 67-68
European-American Bank (EAB), 62
Execution Rocks Lighthouse, *42*
Exporting, 75

F
Fairchild Republic, 68
Farmland Preservation Act, 87
Fein, Norman, 100
Ferries, 92, 96
Fey, George, 18
Fine Arts Museum of Long Island (F.A.M.L.I.), 131
Fire Island, 18, 47, 114-115, *115*
Fire Island Lighthouse, *13*, 18, 20, *21*, 22, 114, 125
Fire Island National Seashore, 114-115
Fisher, Carl, 48
Fishing, *84*, 86-87, *116*, 117
Fitzgerald, F. Scott, 36
Five Towns, The, 48
Fleishman, Paul, 107
Flower, Heather, 31
Floyd, William, 32, *32*
Foreign Trade Zone, 75
Fox hunting, *34*
Friends of the Arts, 124

G
Garden City, 34
Garden City Hotel, 56, *57*
Gardiner Elizabeth, 30
Gardiner, Lion, 20, 30, 31
Gardiner, Robert David Lion, 20, 44
Gardiner's Island, 20, 44
Garvies Point Museum, 29
Glen Cove, *24*, 36
"Gold Coast, The," 43, 44, 127-129; *See also* North Shore
Golfing, 117, *120*
Gordon, Irv, 90
Gosman's Dock, *54*
Government, 48, 60
Grapes, 81-82
Gravesend, 31
Great Neck, 20
Great South Bay, 18, 22
Greenport, *35*
Griffen, John, 103

Grumman Corporation, 36, *65*, 66, 68, *68*, *69*, 69-70
Grumman, Leroy, 36, 68
Guggenheim, Harry, 102
Guild Hall, 129
Gurney's Inn, 56

H
Hale, Nathan, 33
Hammon, Jupiter, 34
Hamptons, 18, 44, *46*, 47
Hargrave, Alex, 78, 79, 81-82, *82*
Hargrave Vineyard, 78, 81-82
Health Care, 58-60
Heckscher Museum, 131
Heckscher State Park, 112
Hempstead, 32
Hempstead Plains, 35
Hempstead Post Office, *27*, 28
High technology, 66-74
Hither Hills State Park, *133*, 134
H.J. Heinz Company, 74
Hofstra University, *73*, 73-74
"Home Sweet Home," 50, 51
Horse racing, 21, 120
Horses, 83
Hospitals, 58-60
Hotels, 56
Hudson, Henry, 28
Hurricane Gloria, 24, 39

I
Ice Age, 42
IMIS, 95
Indians, 28-30, *29*, *30*, 33, 79
Insurance, 62
Internal Revenue Service (IRS), 60
Ittelson, Al, 104, 105

J
Johnson, Robert M., 101, 102, 103, 107, 135, 137
Jones Beach State Park, 110, *111*, 112-115, *113*, *114*, 115
Jones Beach Water Tower, 110
Jones, Garland, 25
Jones Inlet, *18*

K
Kahn, Otto, 20
Kenigsberg, Kenneth, 63
Kessler, Gerald S., 129, 131
Kidd, William, 31
King Kullen, 21, 58
Kirdahy, Donna, 127, 131
Kirdahy, Mikki, 127
Kirdahy-Scalia, Jesse, 127
Klein, John V.N., 87
Koppelman, Lee, 20, 25, 90, 112, 135, 136
Ku Klux Klan, 37
Kulka, Jack, 75

L
Lake Ronkonkoma, 111
Lakes, 23
Lalia, Rhonda, 19
Langhans, Rufus, 39

Larocca, Jim, 21, 135
Lattimer, Lewis, 34
Laurel Hollow, 20
Legal Services, 62
Lenti, Bob, 112, 113-114
Lenz Vineyards, 82
Leuthardt, Ron, 81, 82, 87
Levittown, 19, 34, 38
Levitt, Willliam J., 38
Lindbergh, Charles A., 28, 36, *36*
Lohr, Heather, 19
Lohr, Sheila, 19
Long Island; Dutch Settlement of, 31; English Settlement of, 30-31; Ethnicity, 49, 50; Geography of, 21-23, 42-44; Islands local to, 23; Naming of, 48-49; Population, 38-39, 51
Long Island Advertising Club, 63
Long Island Association (LIA), 97, 135-136
Long Island Board of Realtors, 58
Long Islander, The (newspaper), 103
Long Island Expressway (LIE), 18-19, 90-91, *90*, 94, 95, 97
Long Island Fair, *126*
Long Island Farm Bureau, 81
Long Island Forum for Technology, Inc. (LIFT), 67
Long Island Herald (newspaper), 103
Long Island Housing Partnership, 136
Long Island Lighting Company (LILCO), 60, *60*, 61
Long Island Philharmonic, 131
Long Island Power Authority, 137
Long Island Press (newspaper), 102
Long Island Project 2000, 135
Long Island Rail Road (LIRR), 35, 91, *92*, 92-93, 95
Long Island Sound, 19, 22
Long Island Stage, 129
Long Island Star (newspaper), 103
Long Island Tourism and Convention Commission, 55
Long Island University, *73*, 74
Lowe, Ed, 91, 96
Lurrie, Esther, 19
Lurrie, Sol, 19

M
MacArthur Airport, 18, 19, 96, 97
McIver, Bruce, 93, 95, 97
Macy's, 58
Magazines, 104
Manhasset, 20
Manhasset Bay Yacht Club, *116*
Manufacturing, 74
Marcuse, Bill, 71, 75
Marro, Anthony, 100
Melville, *100*
Merchant Marine Academy, 74
Merolla, C.R. "Rick," 63
Metropolitan Suburban Bus Authority, 96
Metropolitan Transit Authority (MTA), 93
Micklos, David, 72
Mill Neck, 20
Montauk, 48
Montauk Manor, 48
Montauk Point Coast Guard Station, *59*

Montauk Point Lighthouse, 48, 125
Moody, Deborah, 31
Moses, Robert, 93, 94, 112-113, 114
Mounty, Joel, 56
Museums, 126
Muttontown, 20

N
Nassau, 48
Nassau Community College, 72
Nassau County, 19, 21, 38, 39, 57
Nassau County Bar Association, 62
Nassau County Medical Center, *99*
Nassau Symphony Orchestra, 131
Nassau Veterans Memorial Coliseum, 121
Nellen, Bob, 112, 113-114
New Jersey Nets (basketball team), 119
Newsday (newspaper), 100-103, *101*
Newsday/Long Island Marathon, 102
Newspapers, 100-104
"News 12 Long Island," 100, 101, 104-105
New York Islanders (hockey team), 118-119, *120*
New York Jets (football team), 119
New York Mets (baseball team), 119, *119*
New York Newsday (newspaper), 103
New York Technical College, 72
New York Telephone Company, 60, 61
Northern State Parkway, 90
North Fork, 42, *43*, 46, 47
North Shore, 19 *19*, 43, 44, *50*, 51

O
"Ode to the Expressway," 96
Old Bethpage Village Restoration, 32, 126, *126*, 127
Old Westbury Gardens, *45*, 127
Orient Beach State Park, *10-11*
Orient Point, 42, *43*
Oyster Bay, 32, *84*
Oyster Festival, 127
Oysters, 80, 85

P
Pally, Mitchell, 97
Parks, 110, *111*
Parrish Art Museum, 131
Patterson, Alicia, 102
Payne, John Howard, 50, 51
Pennysaver, 103
Performing Arts, 129-131
Pharoah, Stephen, *28*
Pindar Vineyard, 82
Pine barrens, 18
Plum Island Animal Disease Laboratory, 72
Police, *53*, 54
Poosepatuck (Indian) Reservation, 30
Port Jefferson, *59*
Potatos, 78, 79, 80-81, *81*
Potvin, Denis, 119
Printing, 74
Pro Bono Project, 62-63
Prohibition, 36-37
Public Relations, 63
Public utilities, 60-61
Publishing, 74
Purcell, Francis T., 105

229

Q
Quimby, Harriet, 36

R
Radio, *106*, 107
Real Estate, 58
Record Newspapers, 103
Recreation, 110-121
Religion, 51
Republic Airport, 97
Republic Aviation Corporation, 36
Research, 70-71
Restaurants, 54, 55-56
Retail, 57-58
Rivers, 23
Robert Moses State Park, 112, 114
Rockefeller, Nelson, 93
Roosevelt Field, 58
Roosevelt, Theodore, 21, 28, *34*, 128
Roslyn, 20
Ryder, Douglas, 63
Ryder, Jeffrey, 63

S
Sagamore Hill, *128*
Sag Harbor, 33
Sag Harbor Whaling Museum, 33
Sailing, *17, 22*
Sanok, Bill, 78
Scallops, 80, 85-86
Schneider, Howard, 100-101, 103, 134
Shea Stadium, 119
Shelter Island, *46*, 47
Sheridan, John, 110, 121
Shinnecock (Indian) Reservation, 30
Shipbuilding, 74
Shopping Malls, 58
Shoreham Nuclear Power Plant, 39, 60, 137
Simpson, Eleanor, 127
Smith, Alfred E., 112
Smith, Billy, 118, 119
Smith, Michael F., 39
Smith, Richard, 31
Smithtown, 31
Society for the Preservation of Long Island Antiquities, 125
Sod, 85
Soos, George, 67
Southampton, 46, *47*
South Fork, 44, 46, 48
South Shore, 18, *18*, 42, 44
Sperry, Lawrence, 21
Stagecoach, 92
State University of New York (SUNY), 72
Stewart, Alexander Turney, 34-35
Stony Brook, 57
Stony Brook University, 73
Strong, Nancy, 33
Suburbia, 34-35
Suffolk Community College, 72
Suffolk County, 19, 21, 39, 57
Suffolk County Airport, 97
Suffolk Life (newspaper), 103
Suffolk Marine Museum, *129*
"Sunck Squa" (Montauk Indian), 30, *31*
Sunrise Highway, 94, *94*
Supermarkets, 58

T
Tackapausha (Massapequa Indian chief), 29
Taxis, 96
Television, 104-107, *106*
Throgs Neck Bridge, 23
Tilles Center for the Performing Arts 124, 129, *130*
Toedtman, James, 103
Tourism, 55
Transportation, 56, 90-97
Trolleys, 93
Trottier, Brian, 119, 121
TSS-Seedmans, 58
Turnpikes, 92

U
Unisys Corporation, 68
Universities, 72-74
U.S. Open Golf Tournament, 117

V
Vanderbilt Motor Parkway, 93, 120
Vanderbilt Museum and Planetarium, 128
Vanderbilt, William K. Jr. ("Willie K"), 93, 120, 129
Verrazano, Giovanni, 28
Volunteer Lawyers Project, 62-63

W
WALK-AM/FM (radio station), 107
Walton, Joe, 119
Wampum, 29
Washington, George, 32, 43
WBAB-FM (radio station), 107
WBLI-FM (radio station), 107
Weather, 23-24
Webb Institute of Naval Architecture, 72
Wells Farm, *77*
Wells, Vernon F. Jr., 78, 79, 80-81, 87
Werner, Alfred E., 96, 97
Wetlands, 22
WGSM-AM (radio station), 107
Whaling, 33
Whitestone Bridge, 23
Whitman, Walt, 18, 21, 103
WHLI-AM (radio station), 107
Wiandanbone (Montauk Indian), 30, *31*
Wichterman, Katherine, 131
Wickham Farm, 78, *79*
WLIG-TV (television station), 101, 105, 107
WLIW-TV (television station), 101, 105, 107
World War II, 37, 68; German spies, 37
Wright, Norm, 18, 25
Wyandanch (Montauk Indian chief), 20, 29, 30, 31, *31*

DOES NOT CIRCULATE

Life
Skills Training
Promoting Health and Personal Development

Level Three: Grades 5/6
Student Guide

Gilbert J. Botvin, Ph.D.

Professor of Public Health and Psychiatry
Director of the Institute for Prevention Research
Cornell University Medical College

Princeton Health Press
1-800-293-4969
www.lifeskillstraining.com

Copyright © Gilbert J. Botvin, 1998-1999. All Rights Reserved. No part of this manual may be reproduced in any form or by any means, electronic or mechanical, including photocopying, recording, or by any information storage or retrieval systems, without permission in writing.

Table of Contents

Introduction	4
Self-Esteem	5
Goal-Setting	5
Worksheet 1 — Short-Term Goals	6
Worksheet 2 — Long-Term Goals	7
Worksheet 3 — Self-Esteem Journal Topic	8
Decision-Making	9
What is Decision-Making?	9
The 3-Step Method to Decision-Making	9
Worksheet 4 — What Decision Would You Make?	10
Worksheet 5 — Decision-Making Journal Topic	11
Smoking Information	12
Smoking and Society	12
Immediate and Long-Term Effects of Smoking	13
Worksheet 6 — New Smoking Laws	14
Worksheet 7 — Smoking Information Journal Topic	15
Advertising	16
How Advertising Affects You	16
Tricky Techniques	16
Worksheet 8 — Places Where Products Are Advertised	17
Worksheet 9 — Creating a Healthy Product	18
Worksheet 10 — Advertising Journal Topic	19

Dealing With Stress — 20

- What Is Stress Anyway? — 20
- Worksheet 11 — Brainstorming: Stress Through the Ages — 21
- Worksheet 12 — Time-Wasters Inventory — 22
- Worksheet 13 — Time-Management Calendar — 23
- Study Skills — 24
- Test-Taking Techniques — 25
- Worksheet 14 — Stress Journal Page — 26

Communication Skills — 27

- Listening is Part of Communication — 27
- Worksheet 15 — Passive Listening — 28
- Worksheet 16 — Active Listening — 29
- Worksheet 17 — Communication Journal Topic — 30

Social Skills — 31

- Conflict Resolution — 31
- Worksheet 18 — Conflict Styles — 33
- Worksheet 19 — How Does This Scenario End? — 34
- Worksheet 20 — Social Skills Journal Topic — 36

Assertiveness — 37

- Standing Up For Your Rights — 37
- Worksheet 21 — Which is Which? — 38
- Worksheet 22 — How Do You React? — 39
- Worksheet 23 — Assertiveness Journal Page — 40

My Life Skills Training Dictionary — 41

Introduction

This is the **Student Guide** you will be using to complete the *Life Skills Training* program. You, your classmates and your teacher will be studying about many things this year. Some of the things you will be learning include:

- How to set realistic goals for yourself

- An easy way to help you make the best decisions

- Important information about the new smoking laws

- Creating your own advertisement

- Decreasing school stress through better study habits and test-taking skills

- The difference between passive and active listening

- How to resolve conflicts and increase win-win situations for yourself

- How to stand up for your rights

You will get to play games, make great projects and act things out in front of the class. You will also get to create your own dictionary. Most importantly, you will be learning skills that will make you a stronger person and help you stay healthy for the rest of your life.

So good luck with completing the activities in your **Student Guide**. Have fun and remember, you can always ask your teacher or your parents if you have any questions.

Self-Esteem

Goal-Setting

Goal-setting helps you review successes in your life and think about what you would like to accomplish in the future. Set realistic goals for yourself. For example, if you have a goal to become fluent in a second language or become the next NBA star, it may take years to do so. Don't become discouraged if it doesn't happen overnight. That is really a long-term goal. Setting short-term goals, like learning the words to your favorite song, or saving enough money to buy a new pair of sneakers, will help you reach your long-term goals. Those goals are more realistic, and you will feel good about yourself when you accomplish them.

If you are thinking about taking risks, think about how those risks will affect your future. Risky behaviors can seriously jeopardize the goals you have for the future. Hopefully, this will help you think twice if you ever get in a risky situation.

What are my Goals?

Self-Esteem

Worksheet 1
Short-Term Goals

Directions: Think about some short-term goals you would like to achieve. Write them in the spaces provided. Then think of what you have to do to achieve those goals and write that down as well. Finally, set a goal date for yourself and get to work making it all happen!

Goal	How Can You Achieve This Goal?	Goal Date	Did I Achieve the Goal?
1. To be on the honor roll all year.	To do my homework	June 2008	
2. To not fill test. I have a t...	To study everyday	June 2008	
3. To be foruces, ...	To stop talking	June 2008	
4.			
5.			

Worksheet 2
Long-Term Goals

Directions: Look at the timeline below. Write your current age in the space provided. Now think about what some of your long-term goals are and the age you want to achieve them. Write the ages on the timeline and use the corresponding lines and spaces to write your goals. Feel free to add extra lines if you have more goals than spaces provided.

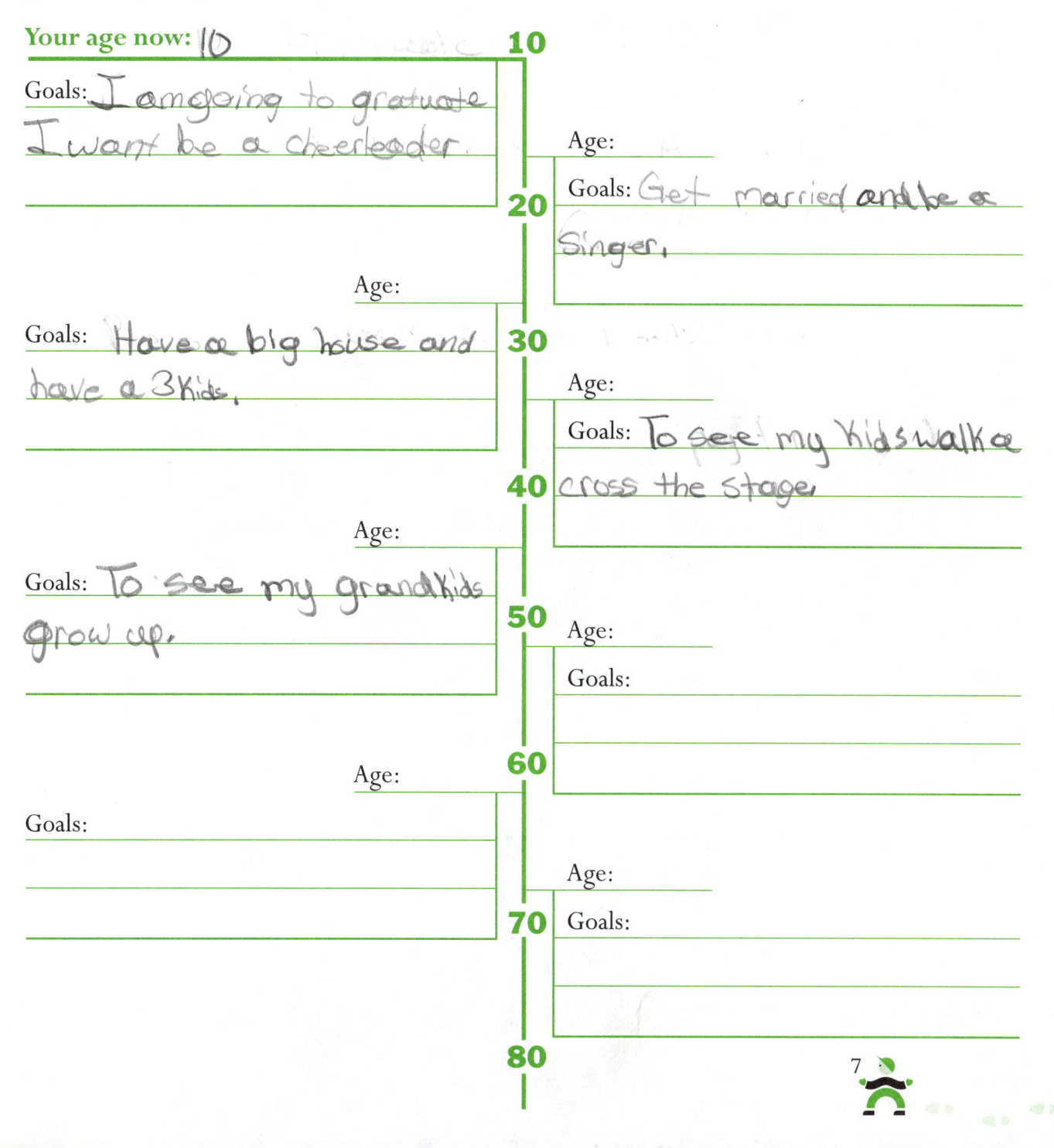

Your age now: 10

10

Goals: I am going to gratuate. I want be a cheerleader.

20

Age:
Goals: Get married and be a singer.

30

Age:
Goals: Have a big house and have a 3 kids.

40

Age:
Goals: To see my kids walk a cross the stage.

50

Age:
Goals: To see my grandkids grow up.

60

Age:
Goals:

70

Age:
Goals:

80

Self-Esteem

Worksheet 3
Journal Topic

You have been unhappy with the way your town has been run for a long time. There are not enough things for you and your friends to do after school. You decide to run for mayor. At least this way, you can get something done that affects not just adults, but young people as well. The newspapers want to know what your campaign platform will be. What will some of your short-term and long-term goals be as mayor of your town?

If I was Mayor I would fix the sidewalks. I clean up the trash that is on the ground. I will fix the roads. I will fix the school playgrounds. I will help homeless child.

Decision-Making

What Is Decision-Making?

We are involved in making decisions everyday. Sometimes we make snap decisions without really thinking them through. That's all right sometimes, but if you do this too often, you run the risk of being disappointed that you made the wrong choice. Other decisions require more time and conscious effort to determine whether we are being influenced, or whether it's something we really want for ourselves. As people get older it is likely that they face more difficult and challenging problems to make decisions about. Practicing decision-making skills can help prepare you for a time when a serious decision must be made. Using the **Stop-Think-Go!** model can help you slow down and make the best decision.

Step 1: **Stop** — Ask yourself what the decision or problem is.

Step 2: **Think** — Ask yourself what your choices or options are. Also think about the possible outcomes of each choice.

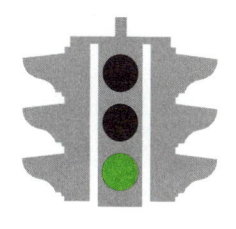

Step 3: **Go!** — Do what is best for you!

Decision-Making

Worksheet 4
What Decision Would You Make?

Directions: Read the decision-making scenario that was given to you by your teacher. Use the **Stop-Think-Go!** steps that were discussed in class to reach a decision about the problem you have been given. Record your answers below.

Describe the situation. _____

_____

_____

Stop and identify the problem. _____

_____

_____

Think about the choices and possible outcomes.

Choices	Outcomes
1.	1.
2.	2.
3.	3.
4.	4.

Go! Do what is best for you. _____

_____

What is your group's decision? _____

_____

_____

Worksheet 5
Journal Topic

You just moved and are new to the school. You are having a hard time making friends, everyone already seems to have friends. Someone is nice to you in gym class, and you see that person with a bunch of other kids after school. They are smoking cigarettes. You go up to talk to them and one of the kids asks you if you want one. Use the space below to brainstorm about different decisions you might make and their outcomes. Then describe the decision you think is the best one to make.

Smoking Information

Smoking and Society

People are beginning to get the message about tobacco. Since the first Surgeon General's report on tobacco in 1964, there have been many other reports that have helped to educate people of all ages about the serious health consequences of smoking. Since then, more than 40 million people have quit smoking and fewer people are taking up the habit, especially kids. That's the good news. However, there are still too many people who smoke in this country. Because of this, the federal and many state and local governments have been creating laws that limit the use of tobacco in public places and decrease the amount of advertising a company can use to sell their products. Do you know what the laws are in your town and state?

Immediate and Long-Term Effects of Smoking

Immediate Effects

- Eyes—Causes the eyes to become red.
- Mouth—Deadens taste buds, causes bad breath and mouth infections.
- Throat—Causes bad coughs.
- Nose—Decreases the ability to smell.
- Skin—Causes wrinkles on the face to appear more quickly.
- Teeth and Fingers—Stains teeth and fingers a brownish-yellow color.
- Heart—Speeds up the heart rate.
- Lungs—Begins to turn lungs black from tar.

Long-Term Effects

- Lungs—Causes chronic bronchitis, emphysema or lung cancer
- Heart—Causes heart disease.
- Brain—Causes a stroke.
- Mouth—Causes mouth cancer.

Smoking Information

Worksheet 6
New Smoking Laws

Directions: Use the space below to write five laws that you would make to decrease or limit tobacco use in this country.

Law 1: _____

_____

_____

_____

Law 2: _____

_____

_____

_____

Law 3: _____

_____

_____

_____

Law 4: _____

_____

_____

_____

Law 5: _____

_____

_____

_____

Worksheet 7
Journal Topic

You are on a national committee related to tobacco legislation. After many years, your committee finally got permission to vote on whether or not tobacco should be completely outlawed. On the day of the vote, you were ill and the other members of the committee voted without you. They tied, half of the people on the committee voted to outlaw tobacco, and half of the people voted to keep selling tobacco. When you returned, they told you that yours would be the deciding vote. Use the space below to explain which way you will vote and why.

Advertising

How Advertising Affects You

Advertising is a very powerful source of influence in our lives. Many of our daily decisions are shaped by the advertisements that we see and hear all the time. Many of our choices as consumers are a result of gentle, and not so gentle, pressure from advertisers that tell us to choose their products over others. If we look at advertising closely, we can learn about the many techniques that are used to persuade us to purchase things that we may or may not need.

Advertising is all around us, twenty-four hours a day. We see and hear so much of it that we may think we are immune to it, but we are not. Be critical when you see or hear an ad. Learn to be cautious when exposed to advertising, because the real objective of advertising is to make money for the company selling the product. Young people are especially vulnerable to advertising because they are often targeted for products. Don't believe everything you see and hear in advertising. When a product claims to be better than the rest, ask how and why. Think for yourself.

Tricky Techniques

- **Bandwagon** — Everyone smokes, so you should too.

- **Image Appeal** — You will be more glamorous or macho if you smoke.

- **Maturity** — If you smoke cigarettes you will appear older.

- **Have a Great Time** — Smoking cigarettes is fun and enjoyable.

- **Popularity** — You will have more friends if you smoke.

- **Free Stuff** — If you smoke our brand you can mail away for free stuff.

- **Health Appeal** — Our brand is healthier than all the others.

- **Scientific Evidence** — Says our brand is better than all the rest.

Worksheet 8
Places Where Products Are Advertised

Directions: Make a list of places where you've seen advertisements for various products. Use the left column to list where you saw the ad and the right column to list the type of product being advertised.

Where you saw it advertised.	What was it?
1.	1.
2.	2.
3.	3.
4.	4.
5.	5.
6.	6.
7.	7.
8.	8.
9.	9.
10.	10.

Advertising

Worksheet 9
Creating a Healthy Product

Directions: Now it's your turn to become the advertiser. Use your "smarts" about advertising techniques to create an advertisement for a healthy product. You may choose a product that already exists or create a fictitious product. Use the spaces below to write about your product and target audiences.

Company: _____

Product: _____

_____

Target market: _____

_____

What places could you advertise that would appeal to your target audience?

_____

_____

What will your advertisement say and look like? Describe below. (If you would like, draw a picture of your advertisement.) _____

_____

_____

Worksheet 10
Journal Topic

The U.S. Congress passes a law stating that companies have to tell the truth about their products in all advertisements. Think about some advertisements that you believe are misleading. Use the space below to describe what those advertisements would really look like after the new law goes into effect.

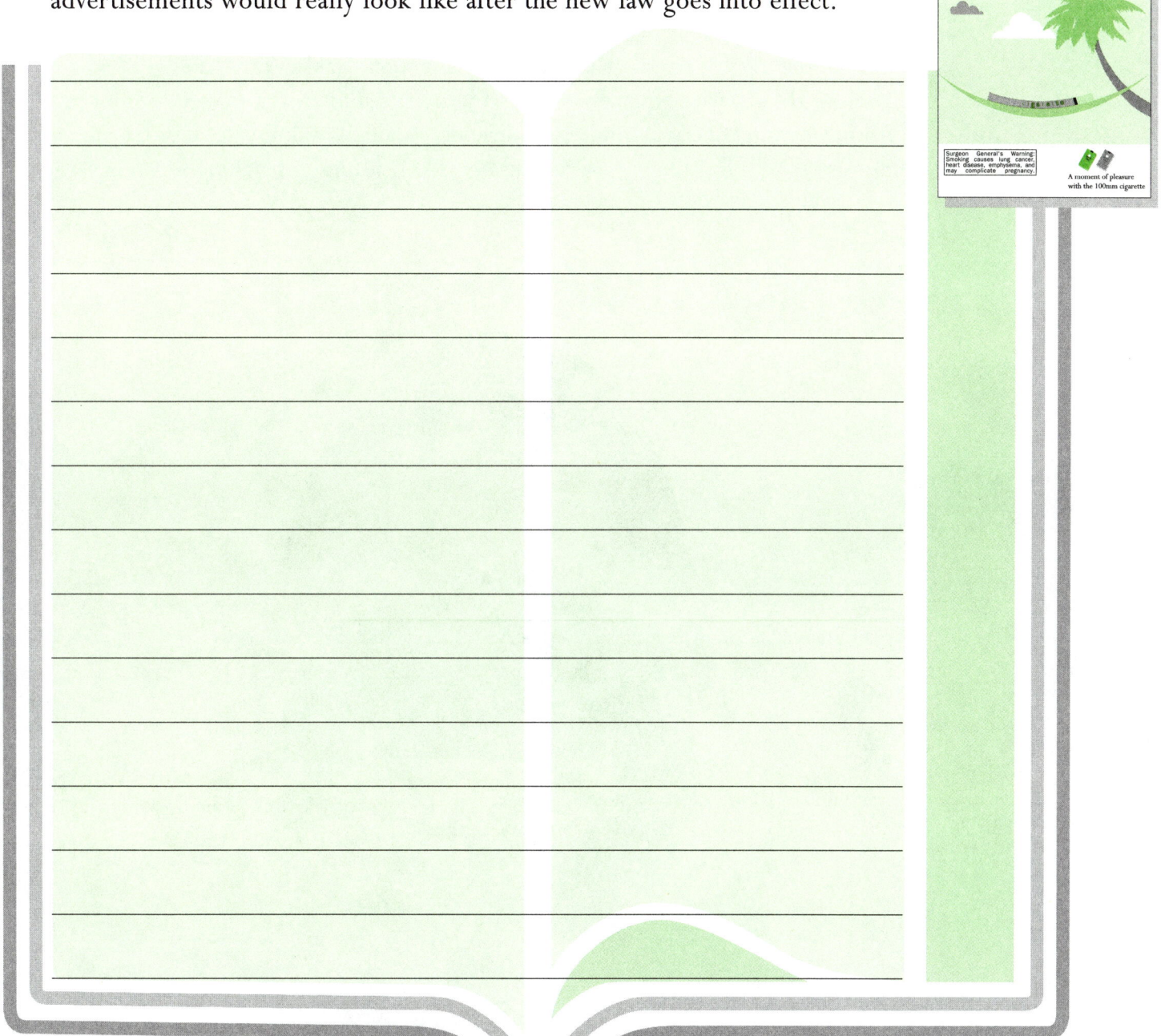

Dealing With Stress

What Is Stress Anyway?

We all feel nervous at times. That feeling of being nervous or tense is called stress. It is important to learn what kinds of situations cause us stress. Knowing what causes us stress is the first step in learning how to cope with it. Since we are going to be facing stress for our whole lives, one of the best ways to cope with it is to prevent it from occurring in the first place.

One of the biggest stressors for students is school—taking tests, doing homework, or writing papers. One of the ways a student can prevent school from becoming overwhelming is to develop good study skills. Another way to prevent school from being overwhelming is by learning test-taking techniques.

Worksheet 11
Brainstorming: Stress Through the Ages

Directions: Use the space below to list causes of stress for your assigned age group.

1. Kids want to fight
2. Moving to a new house,
3. Kids teasing you
4. To much homework
5.

Dealing With Stress

Worksheet 12
Time-Wasters Inventory

Direction: Read the list below and check any of the items that are time wasters for you. Then go back and rank the three biggest time wasters in your life. Finally, use the space provided to indicate how you can modify your behavior to stop wasting so much time.

_____ Talking on the phone

_____ Watching television

_____ Playing video games

_____ Too many activities

_____ Forgetfulness

_____ Hanging out with friends

_____ Messy room and locker

_____ Listening to music

_____ Fighting with siblings

_____ Playing on the computer/internet

_____ Shopping

_____ Napping

_____ Gossiping

Top three time wasters

1. _____

2. _____

3. _____

What can you do to stop wasting so much time?

_____

_____

_____

_____

Worksheet 13
Time Management Calendar

Directions: Look at the calendar below. Think about your schedule for the next five days. Use the spaces provided to help you manage your time. The steps to time management are listed below.

1. List all the tasks for a particular day or week.
2. Estimate the time needed to complete each task.
3. Plan for delays, setbacks and problems.
4. Implement a daily schedule that included planned tasks.
5. Evaluate your time management plan for effectiveness.

Week of _____

Day of the Week	Task	Completed ✓

Dealing With Stress

Study Skills

Studying is a habit like any other habit. If you develop good study habits when you are young, you will get better grades with less effort as you grow older. Listed below are some good study habits that you can practice.

1. Assemble necessary books and materials. You want everything you need at your fingertips so you don't have to keep getting up to find things.

2. Eliminate all distractions. Close your door and turn the television and radio off. You want to be able to focus on the task at hand.

3. Study one subject at a time. Decide which subject needs the most time; the course that is the is hardest, or the class that has a test coming up.

4. Make notes about important facts. Writing things down can help you remember them.

5. Repeat important points to yourself several times or make note cards that you can carry around and review.

Test-Taking Techniques

Studying for and taking tests is one of the biggest stressors for students, whether they are in elementary school, middle school, high school or college. Unfortunately, you probably couldn't count the number of tests you will have to take before you graduate. The best thing you can do is learn how to cope with them in the least stressful way. Read the tips below to help decrease your stress when you are taking tests.

1. *Plan ahead.* Figure out before hand how much time you will need to study for the exam. Make sure you leave enough time to complete homework for other classes. Pack any supplies you need and remember to include extra pencils, erasers and pens.

2. *Get a normal night's sleep the night before the test.* Staying up late to study at the last minute is sure to cause stress. In addition, you'll be so tired when you have to actually take the exam that you won't be able to concentrate.

3. *Eat a good breakfast or lunch before the test.* Some people skip meals when they get stressed out. Not eating, however, will just make you tired. You won't have enough energy to think straight when answering questions on the test.

4. *Do not talk about the test with the other students once you get there.* If you need to, sit in a corner by yourself. Stress is contagious. If other students are stressed out, they make you feel more anxious than you need to be.

5. *Take a deep, relaxing breath.* During stressful situations, breathing becomes short and rapid. Deep breathing not only helps to keep your brain supplied with oxygen, it will also help you relax before the exam.

6. *Read the entire test through before starting.* Then go back and prioritize the questions according to their importance to you and their point value.

Dealing With Stress

Worksheet 14
Journal Topic

There is a big problem in your school district. All the high school students have developed strange symptoms. Some kids are drooling. Other kids' eyeballs have rolled backward in their heads. Other kids can't stop chewing on their fingernails or pulling out their hair. The high school principal brings in a team of doctors to help treat the kids, and they find out that all these things are happening to them because of stress! The doctors say that the only way this problem can be stopped is to teach students how to prevent stress in their lives. Because you are such a calm, cool and collected kid, you are asked to be on the advisory committee on how to prevent stress in the lives of students. Use the space below to write the advice you would give the committee.

Communication Skills

Listening Is Part of Communication

Active and passive listening are two ways of listening to someone when they want to talk. Sometimes a person just needs to talk to get something off their chest. They are not necessarily looking for advice, they just want someone to listen to them. This is a good time to be a passive listener. Active listening really demonstrates that a person is paying attention to whomever is communicating with them. This technique allows the listener to provide feedback to whomever they are talking with. No one likes to be interrupted or ignored when they have something to say. By practicing active and passive listening you will become a better communicator.

Passive-Listening Techniques

Passive listening is showing a person that you are interested in what they are saying without actually speaking to them. Below are some passive listening techniques:

- Not talking, but using short verbal responses like, "hmmm", "really" or "uh-huh."

- Making eye contact when the person speaks.

- Nodding or shaking your head in response to something that was said.

- Leaning forward toward the person you are taking to.

- Using facial expressions to demonstrate your feelings about what they are saying.

Active-Listening Techniques

Active listening is using verbal responses to show acceptance, understanding, respect, sympathy and encouragement. Below are some active listening techniques:

- Encouraging the person to express their feelings — "I guess you must have felt…."

- Encouraging the person to tell you more information — "Tell me about…."

- Restate the person's ideas into your own words — "So you are saying…."

- Use verbal responses like "really" and "I see" to show you are paying attention.

- Make comments about what is being said, but don't give advice unless it is asked for.

Communication Skills

Worksheet 15
Passive Listening

Directions: Passive listening is showing a person that you are interested in what they are saying without actually speaking to them. With your partner, practice passive listening by telling each other about your favorite holiday. First one partner will speak while the other passively listens, and then you will switch. When both partners have had a chance to speak and listen, answer the questions below.

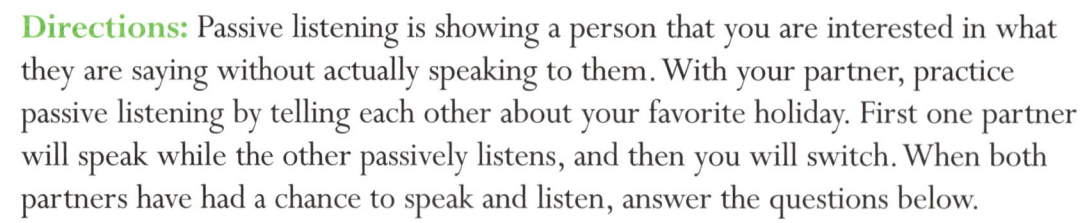

1. When you were the listener, did you find it difficult to not to talk back? Why or why not?

2. Did you have to concentrate on listening passively or was it easy for you?

3. Have you ever spoken to someone who didn't care about what you had to say, but just wanted to talk themselves? How did that feel?

4. Did you like speaking when your partner was the passive listener? Why or why not?

5. Did it seem like your partner was interested in what you had to say? How did that feel?

Worksheet 16
Active Listening

Directions: Active listening is using verbal responses to show acceptance, understanding, respect, sympathy and encouragement. With your partner, practice active listening by telling each other about your favorite memory. First one partner will speak while the other actively listens, and then you will switch. When both partners have had a chance to speak and listen, answer the questions below.

1. When you were the listener, did you find it difficult to actively participate? Why or why not?

_____

_____

2. Did you have to concentrate on listening actively or was it easy for you?

_____

_____

3. Have you ever spoken to someone who constantly interrupted you? How did that feel?

_____

_____

4. Did you like speaking when your partner was the active listener? Why or why not?

_____

_____

5. Did it seem like your partner was interested in what you had to say? How did that feel?

_____

_____

Communication Skills

Worksheet 17
Journal Topic

Your friend got you tickets to a TV talk show for your birthday. You are sitting in the audience for a little while when you start to get an awful headache. The guests are all arguing and yelling at one another and no one is hearing what anyone else has to say. The talk show host pleads with the crowd and asks if anyone thinks they could get control of the panel. You get up to the microphone and explain to the panel about active and passive listening. Use the space below to write what you might say to the guests.

Social Skills

Conflict Resolution

When people disagree with each other they can behave in three different ways. Sometimes when people disagree they get in a fight. That is called *confrontation*. Other times when people are mad they pretend that nothing is wrong and keep all their feelings inside. That is called *avoidance*. Another option in a disagreement is to make a compromise. That is called *problem-solving*.

In most circumstances, problem-solving is the best way to resolve conflicts. However, if a situation is unsafe, avoidance may be the best conflict resolution technique. If a person's basic rights are being violated, confrontation may be necessary.

Social Skills

Conflict Styles

There are three main conflict styles that a person can use to respond to any given conflict:

- Confrontation: Attacking the person you disagree with by yelling at them or physically pushing or hitting them.

- Avoidance: Not dealing with the disagreement by pretending that it does not exist or changing what you do so you do not see the person that you are disagreeing with.

- Problem-Solving: Working together with the person you are disagreeing with to make a compromise.

Different conflict styles lead to different conflict outcomes.

- A win-win situation is when both sides' need are met.

- A win-lose situation is when only one side's needs are met.

- A lose-lose situation is when no one's needs are met.

A lose-lose situation is usually caused by confrontation. A win-lose situation can be caused by avoidance or confrontation. Problem solving usually leads to a win-win situation. The more you practice problem solving, the easier it will become.

Worksheet 18
Conflict Styles

Directions: Read the behaviors below. Decide if you think a behavior is an example of confrontation, avoidance or problem-solving. Next to each behavior below write:

"**C**" if you think it is an example of confrontation
"**A**" if you think it is an example of avoidance
"**P**" if you think it is an example of problem solving

_____ criticizing	_____ yelling	_____ stating needs
_____ postponing	_____ insulting	_____ threatening
_____ interrupting	_____ restating	_____ blaming
_____ stereotyping	_____ being sarcastic	_____ asking questions
_____ stating wants	_____ being defensive	_____ changing the subject
_____ stating feelings	_____ apologizing	_____ walking away
_____ listening	_____ denying	_____ ignoring
_____ giving reasons	_____ informing	_____ judging

1. How many conflicts have you had in the past week?
_____

2. On the above list, circle the behaviors you used to deal with these conflicts.
_____

3. Which of these behaviors did you use the most? Why?
_____

4. Which conflict style did you tend to use most often?
_____

5. Which conflict style is the best in most circumstances?
_____

6. Is there ever a circumstance when a person might want to use avoidance? When?
_____

7. Is there ever a circumstance when a person might want to use confrontation? When?
_____

Social Skills

Worksheet 19
How Does This Scenario End?

Directions: Read the situations below. With your partner, write how each person could have dealt with the conflict by confronting, avoiding or problem-solving about the situation. Also write what would happen, or the outcome, of using each conflict-style technique. Finally, write the best way to deal with each situation.

1. Maxine hears that her best friend is spreading rumors about her.

Confrontation: _____

What outcome would the confrontation lead to? Why? _____
_____
_____

Avoidance: _____

What outcome would the avoidance lead to? Why? _____
_____
_____

Problem-Solving: _____

What outcome would the problem solving lead to? Why? _____
_____
_____

What is the best thing for Maxine to do in this situation? _____
_____
_____

2. Paul is at the mall waiting for the bus to take him home. A group of boys from another school start throwing rocks at him.

Confrontation: _____

What outcome would the confrontation lead to? Why? _____
_____
_____
_____

Avoidance: _____

What outcome would the avoidance lead to? Why? _____

_____

_____

Problem-Solving: _____

What outcome would the problem solving lead to? Why? _____

_____

_____

What is the best thing for Paul to do in this situation? _____

_____

_____

3. Antonio's little brother keeps taking his stuff out of his room. Antonio has told him many times not to, but his brother won't stop.

Confrontation: _____

What outcome would the confrontation lead to? Why? _____

_____

_____

Avoidance: _____

What outcome would the avoidance lead to? Why? _____

_____

_____

Problem-Solving: _____

What outcome would the problem-solving lead to? Why? _____

_____

_____

What is the best thing for Antonio to do in this situation? _____

_____

_____

_____

Social Skills

Worksheet 20
Journal Topic

All the national athletic associations (football, basketball, baseball and hockey) are sick of having their players fight during games. Not only is it poor sportsmanship, but there are too many players paying fines and sitting out of games because of punishments given to them for fighting. The leaders of these athletic associations decide to hire some young people to help teach these athletes what the game is really supposed to be about. They start a commission to look for some kids who can teach the athletes how to problem-solve instead of fight with each other. Use the space below to write a letter to the commission stating why you would be a good person to help teach the athletes how to problem-solve.

Assertiveness

Standing Up for Your Rights

There are three basic types of behavior; passive, aggressive and assertive. Assertiveness means being able to stand up for yourself calmly and firmly. Sometimes, when people are in a new situation, it is difficult for them to think of how to act and what to say. If they think something is not a good idea they may not say so because they're afraid people will laugh at them or won't want to be their friend. Students who are taught how to be assertive are less likely to participate in behaviors where they feel uncomfortable.

By practicing assertive skills, you may begin to feel comfortable with them. When faced with a real situation, you may be more likely call on the behavior you practiced in class and feel capable of reacting in the appropriate way.

Assertiveness

Worksheet 21
Which Is Which?

Directions: Read the statements below and their responses. Decide if the response is an example of a passive, assertive or an aggressive response. Circle the term that best describes the response.

1. Statement: Let's go smoke a cigarette. I stole them out of my mom's purse!
   Response: I'm not sure if that's a good idea..but, ok, I guess no one will catch us.
   passive   aggressive   assertive

2. Statement: Let's cut lunch today and go to the deli.
   Response: I'm not taking a chance like that. I don't want to get detention.
   passive   aggressive   assertive

3. Statement: Can you help me study for the exam? I don't really understand what we have been doing in class.
   Response: Why should I help you? Its your own fault that you weren't paying attention. It's not my problem if you fail the test!
   passive   aggressive   assertive

4. Statement: Can I borrow your new sweater?
   Response: Well…I didn't get to wear it yet, but..I guess it's o.k.
   passive   aggressive   assertive

5. Statement: Do you want to sleep over tonight?
   Response: Well…I have a lot of homework, but, alright, I guess I can do it later.
   passive   aggressive   assertive

6. Statement: Let me see your homework. I need to copy it, I forgot mine at home.
   Response: No way dummy! Do your own work!
   passive   aggressive   assertive

7. Statement: I'm going to the movies with my friend but I don't have any money. Can I borrow it from you?
   Response: I'm not able to lend you the money. Sorry I can't help.
   passive   aggressive   assertive

8. Statement: Let's go to Shelly's this weekend and hang out. Her parents aren't going to be home.
   Response: I don't want to go to Shelly's, I'd rather go to the mall.
   passive   aggressive   assertive

9. Statement: Can I be on your baseball team?
   Response: You can't play baseball! Why don't you leave us alone!
   passive   aggressive   assertive

Worksheet 22
How Do You React?

Directions: For each scenario, write one example of how a passive person might react, how an aggressive person might react and how an assertive person might react.

1. You left your diary in the library. When you go back to get it, you see a friend reading it.

   passive _____

   aggressive _____

   assertive _____

You are at a friend's house and you would like something to eat.

   passive _____

   aggressive _____

   assertive _____

2. You have been waiting in a long line at lunch and someone tries to push ahead of you.

   passive _____

   aggressive _____

   assertive _____

3. Your parents buy you a birthday present that you really dislike.

   passive _____

   aggressive _____

   assertive _____

4. Your friend wants to go to a movie that you have no interest in seeing.

   passive _____

   aggressive _____

   assertive _____

Assertiveness

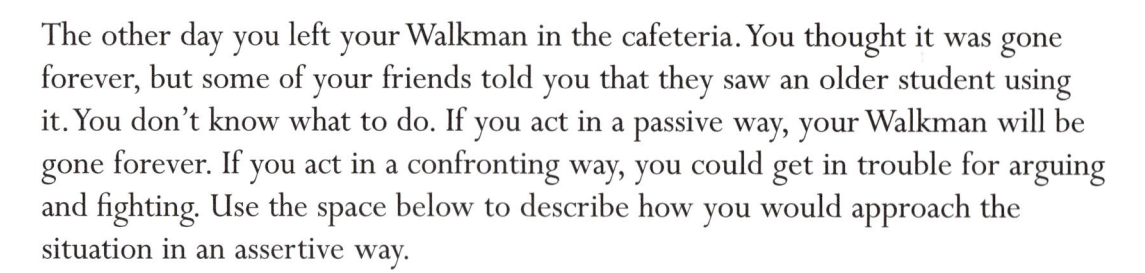

Worksheet 23
Journal Page

The other day you left your Walkman in the cafeteria. You thought it was gone forever, but some of your friends told you that they saw an older student using it. You don't know what to do. If you act in a passive way, your Walkman will be gone forever. If you act in a confronting way, you could get in trouble for arguing and fighting. Use the space below to describe how you would approach the situation in an assertive way.

My Life Skills Training Dictionary

My Life Skills Training Dictionary

Active listening:

Aggressive behavior:

Assertive behavior:

Advoidance:

Communication: _____

_____

_____

_____

Conflict resolution: _____

_____

_____

_____

Confrontation: _____

_____

_____

_____

Consumer: _____

_____

_____

_____

My Life Skills Training Dictionary

Distress:

Eustress:

Goal:

Long-term goal:

Passive behavior: _____

_____

_____

_____

Passive listening: _____

_____

_____

_____

Problem solving: _____

_____

_____

_____

Risk behavior: _____

_____

_____

_____

My Life Skills Training Dictionary

Short-term goal:

Stress:

Stressor:

Target marketing:

Notes